ARTIFICIAL WOMEN

ARTIFICIAL WOMEN

Sex Dolls, Robot Caregivers, and More Facsimile Females

—⚍—

JULIE WOSK

INDIANA UNIVERSITY PRESS

This book is a publication of

Indiana University Press
Office of Scholarly Publishing
Herman B Wells Library 350
1320 East 10th Street
Bloomington, Indiana 47405 USA

iupress.org

Manufactured in the United States of America

First printing 2024

Library of Congress Cataloging-in-Publication Data

Names: Wosk, Julie, author.
Title: Artificial women : sex dolls, robot caregivers, and more facsimile
  females / Julie Wosk.
Description: Bloomington : Indiana University Press, 2024. | Includes
  bibliographical references and index.
Identifiers: LCCN 2023046278 (print) | LCCN 2023046279 (ebook) | ISBN
  9780253069245 (hardback ; alk. paper) | ISBN 9780253069252 (paperback ; alk. paper)
  | ISBN 9780253069269 (ebook)
Subjects: LCSH: Robots in mass media. | Androids—Social aspects. | Sex
  role in mass media. | Sex dolls. | Robotics—Social aspects.
  | Women—Identity.
Classification: LCC P96.R63 W68 2024 (print) | LCC P96.R63 (ebook)
  | DDC 303.48/34—dc23/eng/20231206
LC record available at https://lccn.loc.gov/2023046278
LC ebook record available at https://lccn.loc.gov/2023046279

CONTENTS

ACKNOWLEDGMENTS

IN WRITING THIS BOOK, I am so very grateful for the generous help and encouragement I've received from many people. My great thanks to Allison Chaplin and Lesley Bolton, my editors at Indiana University Press, for their enthusiasm and expert help guiding the book through the publication process. I also give many thanks to members of the press's staff, particularly Sophia Hebert and Vickrutha Sudharsan, for their very useful and patient help. My thanks, too, to Eleanor Ripp, Jillian Kehoe, and Joslyn DeVinney for their editorial aid.

Over the years, I've been very lucky to have such warm and supportive friends and family. My late husband, Averill (Bill) Williams, with his sense of humor was always encouraging and supportive, as were my dear friends, including Marlene Schwarz, Phillip K. Cohen, Elinor Balka, Roberta Siegel Lutzker, Ed Tassinari, Robert E. Kessler, Rita Solow-Schneyman, Judith Hoffman, and many more, including my friends and neighbors in Manhattan and the Berkshires.

I also thank my family for their encouragement, including my sister, Toby Costas; my cousins Harriet Ginsberg, Cheryl Reynolds, and Karen Finegan and their families; my three nieces—Mia Bhimani, Leah Buratti, and Rachel Costas; and, especially for this book, my nephew David Costas, who as a pilot gave me useful information about aircraft warning systems. As always, I dedicate this book to my late parents, Joseph and Goldie Wosk, who were so warm and encouraging all those many years.

ARTIFICIAL WOMEN

INTRODUCTION

IN THE FILMS *UNDER THE Skin* (2013) and *Ex Machina* (2014), two beautiful, riveting artificial women appear—one an alien who camouflages herself with artificial skin and bright red lipstick, and the other, named Ava in *Ex Machina*, who is animated with artificial intelligence and also has silicone skin. Both are constructed creatures meant to fool the eye, and both are alluring but lethal. When we look at them, we recognize that they are artificial, but through artful filmmaking, we also see them as real.

How we see them is central, and to emphasize the importance of vision, many films and television series about artificial females open with a large image of a human eye. The British American television series *Humans* (2015–18) started with two striking images—a camera's aperture followed by a close-up of an eye. These are reminders that what we are looking at is a filtered view. Our perceptions and ideas about female simulacra are often shaped by new imaging technologies and processed through a cultural lens: through representations in films, television, literature, and art. How we see artificial females is also shaped by another lens: our cultural assumptions about gender, female identity, and women's social roles.

When we look at the alien in *Under the Skin* and at Ava in *Ex Machina* (as discussed in chap. 2), we also recognize another one of the fearsome paradigms of female identity, the seductive and alluring femme fatale. It embodies some men's enduring fear: that the alluring woman who fosters intimacy and trust will turn out to be dangerous and destructive as well.

But what makes these two film characters so compelling, and to some extent sympathetic, is that they are both trying to survive—one literally tries to avoid being destroyed and the other wants her freedom. We are horrified and

Figure 0.1. Ava (played by Alicia Vikander) in the 2014 film *Ex Machina* is captivating but dangerous, a technological wonder whose AI consciousness makes her seem real.

entranced as we see them clearly. Ava (played by Swedish actress Alicia Vikander) is particularly intriguing because beneath her artificial skin is another layer of identity, a simulated female fierce in her determination to break free. She is a crafted and crafty female who skillfully manages to evade human control, a runaway technology who will reinvent herself anew.

Both the alien and Ava have synthetic surfaces, artificial skin that covers their inner anatomy, but Ava's torso is made in part out of transparent plastic, and we can clearly see her innards: the electronic wiring that makes her seem lifelike. But we always know she's fabricated (in this case, she's created by Nathan, the film's updated version of a mad scientist). In a sense, she's like today's real-life robot Sophia, produced by robotics manufacturer David Hanson in Hong Kong. Sophia has a face covered in the patented elastomer material

Hanson calls Frubber and a transparent plastic torso so that we see her electronic inner structure. Sophia, too, is animated by AI, can hold conversations, and can seem alive though she's not yet nearly as technologically developed as the fictional Ava in the film.

On some level, in making their robots transparent, both Alex Garland in his film and Hanson with his design of Sophia are trying to avoid the pitfalls of the uncanny. In stories like German writer E. T. A. Hoffmann's "The Sandman" (1816), there are moments when people experience what German psychiatrist Ernst Jentsch in 1906 and Sigmund Freud in his 1919 essay "The Uncanny" wrote about. Nathanael in Hoffmann's story is horrified when he discovers his beloved Olimpia is only a doll. Freud described how after believing in the reality of an artificial being, an unsuspecting person is shocked when the creature's artificial nature is suddenly made apparent. In his essay "The Uncanny Valley" (1970), Japanese roboticist Masahiro Mori described "the uncanny valley" as the feeling of disconnection, alienation, even repulsion, when we discover that the human we thought was real is actually only a robot, a simulation. (Hoffmann's story later became the basis for French composer Jacques Offenbach's opera *The Tales of Hoffmann* and Léo Delibes's ballet *Coppélia,* with its dancing doll Olympia.)[1]

But my own fascination with film characters like Ava came, in part, from the fact that she's not what she seems. Through the magic of today's technologies, there is sleight of hand at work, so that the artificial woman has her own version of trickery in play. What makes Ava such a different and captivating creature is that her transparency is utterly deceiving. Beneath that synthetic skin exterior is a new breed of artificial females that is radically different than many of the ones that came before.

In early images of artificial females such as the automaton Amelia in British author E. E. Kellett's story "The Lady Automaton" (1901), the simulated mechanical lady is much like the many varied mechanical Parisian clockwork female automatons so admired at the time—automatons that came in varied guises. Amelia is an imitation socialite and doesn't have any feelings and is easily controlled. More than seventy years later, American novelist Ira Levin introduced the memorable female robots of *The Stepford Wives* (1972)—beautiful artificial females that were sexy, obliging, and also easily manipulated and controlled. And in director Denis Villeneuve's film *Blade Runner 2049* (2017), the transparent hologram Joi (played by actress Ana de Armas) is loving, soothing, obliging, and even self-sacrificing. She's both sexy and sweet, a guileless young woman who is eager to please. (Joi's transparency is not deceiving. She has a virtual authenticity and will not lead her lover astray.)

But for Ava in *Ex Machina*, her own seeming transparency is a decoy, a type of ruse. Rather than a female that is clearly perceivable and free from any pretense or deceit, rather than being malleable plastic, she's a steely artificial being—a female with a hidden agenda, which is to escape from the compound and break free. Unlike many earlier versions of artificial females in stories, television, and films, she's not simply an obedient clockwork automaton but a complex and wily facsimile female intent on asserting her own autonomy, and is capable of being ruthless in her self-assertion.

Ava is one of a long line of constructed creatures, as in Mary Shelley's brilliantly conceived novel *Frankenstein*, that embody that recurring fear of a constructed artificial creature that eludes human control. But Ava also represents a new breed of female robots that transcends being defined as a docile servant or lover and wants to fulfill her own aims instead. She's a type of hybrid who will try to reconcile being artificial and being a player in the human world as well.

Ava is an arresting version of posthumanism—a type of artificial being that blurs the boundaries between the artificial and the real. She embodies the fluidity of cultural conceptions about human and female identity. We live in an age when many fixed notions about binary gender divisions, gender roles, and definitions of what constitutes being human are constantly being redefined.

There have been many probing analyses of the posthuman in all its many guises, including in feminist science fiction, as seen in the writings of N. Katherine Hayles, Anne Balsamo, Rosi Braidotti, Patricia Melzer, Sherryl Vint, and many more. Generating much discussion over the years was the seminal essay "A Cyborg Manifesto" by Donna Haraway. Haraway presented a provocative analysis of these blurred boundaries, and portrayed the cyborg (part human, part technological or digital) as a being that challenged the old "dichotomies between mind and body, animal and human, organism and machine" as well as the binaries men and women.[2]

Haraway argued that we are all, in effect, cyborgs: hybrid versions of humans shaped by new technologies—digital, computer, prosthetics. This hybridity has radically challenged old conceptions of a binary world—not only the male-female dichotomy but also the virtual-real dichotomy, and the natural and the artificial. First written in 1985, Haraway's "A Cyborg Manifesto" and its conception of the cyborg was shaped in part by the technological developments of the time. Haraway refers to "cybernetic (feedback-controlled) systems theories applied to telephone technology, computer design, weapons deployment," and other information systems of the period.[3] The year 1985 was one of the pivotal years in digital technologies. It was the year Michael Dell's company PC Limited produced its first computers and by the 1990s, the company had become one of the leading PC retailers. Also in 1985, MIT's Media Lab was founded and initially focused on the "Digital Revolution" in machine learning, holography, computer graphics, art, and more.[4]

Reflecting dramatic technological changes thirty years later, Garland's *Ex Machina* made expert use of current imaging technologies, which helped make Ava's version of an artificial being ever more compelling, and when I first saw the film, I was entranced by the way it wove together perspectives on gender with current technologies. The film skillfully used computer-generated imagery (CGI) to produce an image of an artificial female who could pass the Turing test, a test of a machine's ability to exhibit intelligent behavior so convincing that it is indistinguishable from a human being. With her captivating smile and words, Ava as a digitally created female could convince observers—in the film and the audience itself—that she was a real woman. But she could also subversively use her wits to reconceive her own identity and resist being controlled.

Just two years before the #MeToo movement went viral, Ava and the film's robotic character Kyoko resist being mere manipulated, manufactured, artificial females designed with the latest sophisticated artificial intelligence and materials to serve at men's pleasure or even endure their abuse. Their resistance puts them in the company of other fictional female characters in films, video, and speculative fiction who resist being a victim or plaything.

In the film, Ava becomes a trompe l'oeil simulation, a plastic-encased imitation of a real woman that can easily look deceptively authentic. Since their inception, plastics as an industrial material have been used to create and mass produce copies of originals—copies that were both admired and satirized. In movies like Mike Nichols's satirical *The Graduate* (1967), plastics are spoofed as flimsy simulations—the very embodiment of superficial, establishment society. Ava, though, has a new kind of authenticity. In the film, she is being observed by the young programmer Caleb who is trying to see if she seems convincingly real. Though she engages Caleb, on the surface, in artful and seductive ways, she is also propelled by her need to honor her own (albeit, paradoxically, her synthetic and chimeric) interior self.

In the film, plastics and silicone materials are updated for the digital age. The film's technical teams produced a nontransparent bodysuit worn by actress Alicia Vikander and then, through postprocessing and the software MakeHuman, the suit was made to look transparent, revealing Ava's underlying electronic structure. But Ava herself has a hidden and nontransparent consciousness underneath that simulated transparency. Her beguiling facade masks her private and hidden wishes and aims, and her masked agenda gives us a sense that this fabricated female with her facade of artificial silicone materials has her own underlying authenticity.

Feminist theorists like Sherryl Vint have often written about how the design of female robots and other versions of artificial women are often "deeply entrenched in racialized and gendered assumptions."[5] These robots, hybrids, cyborgs, dolls, and aliens often both reflect and subvert pervasive stereotypes about race and women. They also stimulate us to redefine what is human. What we see in characters like Ava is an intriguing layering: a composite creature whose transparent plastic surface, electronic innards, and artificial intelligence are joined by a new, emergent underlying sensibility. Ava engineers a way to get outside among humans, to pass as human—and in doing so, she challenges our own sense of what distinguishes us from these artificial beings.

MY STORY: WHY I WROTE THIS BOOK

I have always been fascinated by the artificial passing itself off as authentic or real. It probably started when I was a young girl growing up in Evanston, Illinois, on Chicago's North Shore, a girl inventing stories for my dolls—beautiful Cinderellas and Sleeping Beauties, miniature females that became transformed and seemed to come to life. Years later, after I attended graduate school at Harvard, I briefly worked as a public relations and advertising copywriter for Playboy in Chicago. There I somehow managed to pay attention to the emerging women's movement while also promoting Playboy's world of clubs with their sexy Playboy Bunnies as waitresses and the magazine's airbrushed artificial women so appealing to men.[6]

When I left to return to graduate school to get a PhD in English at the University of Wisconsin, Madison, a campus that would soon be shaken by antiwar protests and turmoil, the world of Playboy seemed far, far away. But after coming to New York to start work as a college professor, I discovered I was still drawn to images of simulations and the artificial that seemed real. I started photographing female mannequins that looked lifelike, and also embedded images of mannequins and masks in my own paintings and photographs, as I continued to do in the years ahead.

In my first book, *Breaking Frame: Technology and the Visual Arts in the Nineteenth Century* (1992), I became fascinated with a different type of simulation: nineteenth-century imitations of the decorative arts that passed for real, like factory-made cast-iron architectural ornaments that imitated sculpted stone for building facades, and the use of electroplating that covered base metals to

Figure 0.2. Julie Wosk, *Bag Lady 2*, 2023. Peering out from her bag, this simulated female resists commodification and saucily engages us with her eyes, though her identity is half concealed.

produce ornate factory-made imitations of expensive silverware. These "imitation arts" were praised by some nineteenth-century critics, derided by others.

In the same book, I also looked at the deft way British artists in their satirical prints captured nineteenth-century fears that in the new age of industrialization and steam-powered mechanization, people themselves might turn into robots or automatons walking with steam-powered legs. Artists in their prints and paintings of speeding railroads and exploding steam boilers in trains and factories also captured underlying anxieties that new technologies themselves were running out of control.

On the other hand, during the late eighteenth century, there was also widespread admiration for sophisticated clockwork automatons like The Musician (1773) by Pierre and Henri-Louis Jaquet-Droz that played a harpsichord-like instrument, heaved her chest as though she were breathing, and rolled her eyes. When lit by light in a darkened room, this artificial female seemed magical and almost alive. She was a precursor of the fanciful clockwork female automatons produced in the next century.

In my next book, *Women and the Machine: Representations from the Spinning Wheel to the Electronic Age* (2001), I looked at images of women and machines—women using sewing machines, riding bicycles, driving automobiles, piloting airplanes, Rosie the Riveters in wartime, and women in the digital age. Many of these images were shaped by cultural stereotypes of women, picturing them as merely decorative adornments in machine advertising or timid creatures baffled by all things mechanical. But the book also explored the many images of women who transcended these stereotypes by proving their expertise and mastery of new technologies and machines.

Starting around 2005, I began paying attention to some new developments in the manufacture of dolls and female robots made possible by the clever use of artificial intelligence and imaging technologies. In 2005, Professor Hiroshi Ishiguro at Osaka University in Japan introduced his female robot Repliee Q1, followed by Repliee Q2 in 2006. These were stationary humanoid female robots partially covered in silicone skin, and they could gesture, blink their eyes, and appear to breathe, with their chest rising and falling. Professor Ishiguro would go on to create both male and female robots, including one that was a duplicate of himself.

Around the same time, the software developer Digital-Tutors based in Oklahoma released its software kit Female Android Modeling in Maya, giving artists instruction on creating 3D images of female androids in animation and video games. Earlier, in 1996, the video game *Lara Croft: Tomb Raider* presented the intelligent, sexy, powerful, gun-toting star of its video game series.

Intrigued by these developments, in 2008 I curated the exhibit *Alluring Androids, Robot Women, and Electronic Eves* at the New York Hall of Science in Queens and wrote a short illustrated book to go with the exhibit. This led to my book *My Fair Ladies: Female Robots, Androids, and Other Artificial Eves* (2015), which I really enjoyed writing because it allowed me to present the historical context for today's artificial females, as seen in literature, robotics, film, television, and art.[7]

When *My Fair Ladies* was about to be published in 2015, sex doll manufacturers, like Douglas Hine with his Roxxxy Doll, were beginning to publicize

Figure 0.3. Repliee Q2 robot developed by Professor Hiroshi Ishiguro, Osaka University, Osaka, Japan, 2006.

talking sex dolls, though they never actually went into production. And the film *Ex Machina* was released in the United States the same year. It was too late for me to write about it, but I quickly realized what an important film it was. It encapsulated so many of the important themes about female robots and I felt that story needed to be told.

At the same time, digital technologies and imaging techniques were fast developing, and sex dolls like California-based Abyss Creation's RealDolls enhanced with artificial intelligence were also in the developmental stage. I felt that this, too, was a compelling story for my next book.

And there were a few other small but fun prompts that I kept in the back of my mind, waiting to be explored more fully in the future. One was a sculpture I first mentioned in *Women and the Machine* that now seemed to have much

Figure 0.4. June Leaf, *The Head* (1980). Painted aluminum and stainless steel with movable parts 39 × 36 × 44 in. (99.06 × 91.44 × 111.76 cm). Copyright June Leaf, courtesy Hyphen Management. A hand crank made the woman's tongue move up and down as though she were talking.

broader implications. It was a sculpture by the Chicago artist June Leaf called *The Head* (1980). Made of painted aluminum and stainless steel, it was embedded with exposed gears and a hand crank that, when turned, made the woman's tongue move up and down and her eyes revolve. As I wrote about this sardonic sculpture, it was a "playful revisiting of an unflattering paradigm—the female as automaton, rote-talker, and mechanical maenad."[8]

The idea of a talking female head remained a fascinating image for me, and it now seemed like a wonderful precursor of the talking female dolls, robots, and other artificial females that I write about in this book. Leaf's sculpture of a head, for all of its obvious mechanical nature, also seemed eerily alive. Her

Figure 0.5. SHE, a motorized sculpture by Courtenay Pollock, 1934.

moving tongue could be wryly dismissed as mere chatter, but could also be a recognition that this female had a voice, one worthy of being heard.

For the writing of this book, I also kept in mind a tantalizing old story I had once read about a sculpture called *SHE* by one of London's leading sculptors, Courtenay Pollock, which was on display in one of the leading London department stores in the 1930s. Pollock (1877–1943) was known for his portrait busts of notable men, but here was his fanciful sculpture of an animated mechanical female head.

The story, which appeared in a 1934 issue of *Modern Mechanix*, said of the animated head, "With the aid of a small electric motor, 'SHE' is smiling, coy, demure, or scornful as her master wills. Rolling her eyes around in an enchanting manner, she even displays a lovely set of dimples."[9] The skull was motorized and made use of hinged sections controlled through lever, gears, and switches. It was covered with tinted rubber, and with its "eyebrows and hair attached, and a bit of cosmetics applied, 'SHE' is transformed into a beautiful, vivacious young lady." The story even predicted that in a few years, works of sculptors "will all take on life" and "frolic about and speak, imitating in every way the

Figure 0.6. Moira Shearer as the doll Olympia in the 1951 film *The Tales of Hoffmann*. Photofest.

person who posed as models." This, too, seemed like an eccentric precursor of developments that lay ahead, though we're still waiting for the technology to catch up with the fantasy.

I found the idea of this smiling and dimpled animated female weird but strangely mesmerizing (like actress Moira Shearer's severed head with its eyes blinking on the stage in the 1951 film version of Jacques Offenbach's opera *The Tales of Hoffmann* with its tale of the doll Olympia who gets mistaken for a real young woman). I liked the way the sculpture *SHE* could display some stereotypical female attributes (shy, coy) but could also, the story said, be scornful, asserting an attitude (though how she indicated this remains a mystery!).

It seemed to me that *SHE* as an animated sculpture conjured up the myth of Pygmalion, the sculptor who created a statue of a beautiful woman, fell in love with her, and was overjoyed when Venus brought the statue (later called Galatea) to life. I was also intrigued that once she was camouflaged with rubber skin and cosmetics, *SHE* became a lifelike "vivacious" young lady." This, too, was a precursor of the type of lifelike female simulacra / talking heads animated by artificial intelligence that lay ahead and that I discuss in chapter 3.

And there was another small item that also caught my eye, and seemed to embody a story waiting to be told. It was the Video Girl Barbie doll that was introduced in 2010. This doll had a video screen in its back and a small video camera embedded in its necklace that could be controlled by the user to let a "budding filmmaker" capture thirty minutes of footage. It was as though the camera doll, aided by the user, had a certain amount of agency and could in effect "see" as it created images of the world outside. (Video Girl Barbie in 2010 was actually the subject of bizarre reports in the media that the doll was on the FBI's watchlist. Agents were warned not to destroy the dolls in a search because the toy could contain evidence of pedophilia. The FBI, however, did not report any evidence had been found.)[10]

The Video Girl Barbie reminded me of artist Lynn Hershman Leeson's *Tillie the Telerobotic Doll* (1995–98) created years earlier. The Tillie doll, which was situated in a gallery, had a left eye fitted with a video camera, which recorded what was in the gallery, and a right eye fitted with a webcam controlled by gallery visitors who were using the doll's eyes, in a sense, to see.[11] But one of the stories I wanted to tell in a new book was how years later, the conception would change dramatically as fictional robots and dolls developed an independent vision of their own.

—⁂—

These are just a sampling of the many strands of thought that came together when I was writing this new book, *Artificial Women*. In the book, the simulated females as presented by filmmakers, roboticists, television writers, novelists, playwrights, and artists are wide-ranging: they are compassionate caregivers and companions, protectors, sex dolls and robo-prostitutes. They can be maternal and murderous, genial servants and fearsome medusas. They can be conformists, outlaws, even Stepford Wives with their wits about them. They can also be alluring and lethal, as seen in "Love Machine," Samantha Hunt's chilling tale of an explosive "bombshell" sex doll that will be discussed in "Coda."

As envisioned by artists and designers, also discussed in this book's "Coda," simulated females may be presented in myriad ways, as in African American artist Kerry James Marshall's updated version of the Bride of Frankenstein, or as provocative assemblages of the female body constructs that are witty commentaries on females as commodities to be looked at and consumed, though they also often craftily resist commodification. The artfulness may even lie in an isolated body part, seen in designer Sophia de Oliveira Barata's highly imaginative designs for prosthetic legs that celebrate diversity and offer women with disabilities a new high-fashion way to stride. Artist Julie Weitz in her performance and video series *My Golem* creatively casts herself as a golem firefighter protecting California's landscape, devastated by wildfires.

In films, television, and literature, artificial females are often engaged in a tricky feat: embracing their own synthetic nature while also striving for authenticity and autonomy. They may experience the sometimes fraught nature of emerging human consciousness or sentience where they themselves must come to terms with their problematic place in the human world.

Artificial females, both the manufactured and fictional kinds, are intriguing in the ways they embody enduring cultural stereotypes about women yet also illuminate how conceptions about gender identity are being dramatically reconfigured and reconceived. The simulated females, including the disembodied female voices of personal assistants, often both mirror and upend gender stereotypes as they foreground changing perceptions of women and their roles.

As inhabitants of a highly sophisticated technological landscape, artificial women are also fascinating as emblems of our era when the boundaries between artificial and real are fast disappearing. They embody the paradoxes and tensions of living in an increasingly simulated world where our experiences are often mediated by virtual images and simulated human voices.

In recent years, simulated females, both the manufactured silicone sex doll kind and those in films, television, and fiction, are a manifestation of our increasingly virtual world in which human interactions and human relationships are being modified and impacted by digital simulations of the real thing. This book will highlight how new AI technologies are creating ever more lifelike artificial females and the controversies swirling around lifelike sex dolls and dolls that can talk and give the illusion, to some degree, of real human beings.

Advances in manufacturing materials like silicone and TPE (thermoplastic elastomers) used to create sex dolls as well as artificial intelligence, 3D modeling, digital animation, and CGI have all made humanoid robots seem almost real, and more plausible as lovers, artificial friends, companions—and even, as in chapter 3—potential replacements or doubles of lost loved ones. Roboticists are using these technologies to invest facsimile females with lifelike silicone-skinned appearances and artificial empathy, making them even more appealing and useful as companions, sexual playmates, and perhaps, one day in the future, health care aides. (Conceptions of empathy as a stereotypical female trait, however, are being debated and reassessed by researchers who differ in their findings, as noted in chap. 3.)

As will be discussed in the pages ahead, in fact and fiction, technology is frequently used to fashion fantasy females and bring them to life. These artificial females, including sex dolls, not only are often laden with female stereotypes but also mirror many men's age-old conceptions of the perfect woman. Though sex dolls are being designed to appear ever more lifelike, they have also generated controversy and alarm. They can seem both funny and fearsome as critics fret they will further objectify women and disrupt if not usurp human relationships. Will these robotic, seemingly flawless and compliant female partners and playmates seem preferable to real human beings? Will they lead to abuse and violence against women?

The development of talking sex dolls and robots capable of rudimentary interactive conversations, as we will see in chapter 1, has been both impressive and problematic. They may mirror cultural ambivalence about giving females a voice. The conversations of sex dolls are often programmed to simply mirror the interests and wishes of men (research shows a large proportion of users are men), and even the talking Hello Barbie doll, which at first seemed so promising, proved to be controversial and had to be discontinued.

But talking female robots like Anita/Mia and the former prostitute Niska in the television series *Humans* (2015–18), or the compassionate female robotic companions in Kazuo Ishiguro's compelling and moving novel *Klara and the Sun* (2021), and even the sardonic female golem in Cynthia Ozick's satirical novella *Puttermesser and Xanthippe* (1982), as discussed in this book, have compelling voices of their own.

Artificial talking females, however, don't need to have corporeal bodies to seem real. Disembodied female voices are often used in aircraft warning systems, GPS systems, and with information-giving virtual assistants like Siri and Alexa. Whether it's Siri or Alexa or the early Bitchin' Betty or Sexy Sally voices in military aircraft, these female voices are often invested with stereotyped conceptions about women but as shown in chapter 5, the gender stereotyping and bias is increasingly being recognized and reversed.

Female robots and dolls have long been shaped by culturally defined gender stereotypes and envisioned and portrayed in familiar gender roles—as empathetic mothers and caregivers, as docile servants, and as attractive and obliging sex objects. Participants in research studies have assigned familiar gender roles to robots: males as repairers in the house, transporters of goods; females as tutors, and engaged in childcare and eldercare. As Victoria Turk observed in "We're Sexist toward Robots," studies show that people ascribe stereotyped gendered personality traits to robots: males show assertiveness and dominance, females are seen as friendly and affectionate.[12]

Given the continuing conventions that shape female robots and dolls, the trick is how to get beyond the stereotypes, and an important part of this book's story is the way fiction writers, filmmakers, television writers, playwrights, and digital technologists are transforming the narrative. In a world of fast-changing developments in artificial intelligence, and as simulated humans have become ever more lifelike, there have been currents of change in the representations of female robots. In films and fiction, artificial females are at times depicted as going rogue. They are synthetic beings that want their independence rather than serving as erotic and compliant servants and slaves. Their quest for freedom can be comic, but in more nuanced fictional versions, this quest can also be frightening or even tragic as these characters lash out in anger or anguish over their own artificial nature.

Haraway in "A Cyborg Manifesto" not only tellingly wrote about the fluidity of boundaries between the artificial and the real but also reconceived traditional essentialist formulations of gender and identity. Today's filmmakers, television writers, novelists, and playwrights are increasingly presenting new formulations of female hybridity and portraying the angst experienced by female robots who wish to have rights and legitimacy in a human world.

In these works, sentient artificial females often strive for a version of genuineness (even if we must always wonder, is their sense of authenticity itself a construct? Is it virtual or real?). The dichotomy between authentic and artifice, genuineness and masking, plays itself out often in tales of artificial women. There is a long cultural history of women using cosmetics to shape their appearance—a form of masking that may belie a more authentic, interior self. Artificial females—inherently artificial constructs—are often portrayed as chafing against this type of constriction. They are synthetic beings that may peel back their own skin to demonstrate to others that they are only constructed beings, yet they also often strive to honor their own sense of self.

Behind some of masking engaged in by women—both real women and the simulated kind—is an effort to create a look of perfection and flawlessness, a look that is attractive and connotes femininity. With their conversational abilities and lifelike appearance, artificial females, including sex dolls, are often manufactured or portrayed in fiction as embodying some men's cultural conception of the ideal female—the perfect woman who has no wishes or aspirations of her own and is created strictly as a fabricated commodity in a service role.

Writers and filmmakers have satirized some men's quest for female perfection. An early version appeared at the end of the nineteenth century in a story by Alice W. Fuller. Fuller's story "A Wife Manufactured to Order" (1895) spoofed the idea of a man who longs for a perfect woman as a mate and finds this perfection in a factory-made female.[13]

Fuller's story was published in a period when what was then called the New Woman was emerging in Europe and America—a period when women were campaigning for suffrage and questing after new freedoms. Satirists enjoyed creating stereo photographs and caricatures of emancipated, liberty seeking women wearing bloomers who rode off on their new safety bicycles specially designed for them, leaving their husbands behind to do the housework and tend to the children. Rather than being these caricatures of wayward wives, however, in reality, female suffragists were engaged in spirited political lobbying for voting rights and a greater sense of independence from confining social roles.

Fuller's story is narrated by a forty-year-old bachelor, Charles Fitzsimmons, who decides it's time to settle down to marriage and conjures up his idea of a perfect woman. He engages a manufacturer who will produce a female simulacrum to match his fantasy. He envisions this new simulated woman being "beautiful as a dream, gentle and loving, without any thought for anyone but me," one who would never reproach him if he didn't get home on time.

The manufacturer can produce for him a custom-made female who will essentially be a mirror—she will only talk about "the subjects you most enjoy talking about." The narrator Charles imagines the "pleasant evenings" he'll have with a wife "whose thoughts were like my own, someone who would not vex me by differing opinions." (More than a hundred years later, as seen in chapter 1, manufacturers would be promising that their newly manufactured AI-endowed sex dolls would have these same traits. The conversational silicone dolls could be programmed to only speak about pleasing subjects, or subjects that echoed the thoughts and attitudes of their users.)

In Fuller's story, the simulated woman, Margurette, like one of the Stepford Wives in Ira Levin's titular novel and the two Hollywood filmed versions, never complains, and is "always sweet and smiling." She is a version of the artificial "perfect woman" paradigm seen so often in fiction and films, and embodied in sex dolls and sex robots today, as will be discussed in this book. But Fuller as a female author in 1895 added an acerbic note to her tale. As the years go by, Charles wishes Margurette would differ from him a little "for variety's sake." She is never out of patience, which ultimately becomes annoying for him, and he gets weary of her banal conversations. Ultimately, in this tale by a female writer, he rejects her for a real woman, for he wants a female "who retains her individuality, a thinking woman."

Fuller's story appeared soon after that period in the nineteenth century when critics, largely in Britain, were debating whether factory-made imitations, like electroplated silver tea service items, were legitimate replacements for originals in the decorative arts, and whether these simulations were worthy of being treated seriously. Critics complained that the "imitation arts" were debased versions of the original, but manufacturers argued that their factory-made simulations were actually superior to the original (cast-iron building facades were more durable and had more precise details than hand-carved stone).[14]

Some of these debates about the synthetic versus the real also spilled into the novel *L'Ève future* (1886) in which French writer Auguste Villiers de l'Isle-Adam presents the simulated Hadaly as a perfect copy of Alicia Clary but without Alicia's annoying faults. A fictional Thomas Edison in the novel says the copy he will make will be superior: "This *copy*, let's say, of Nature . . . will bury the original without itself ceasing to appear alive and young." What's more, "it's better than real."[15]

But in early stories about female robotic household maids, as further discussed in chapter 4, synthetic females are far from perfection and no match for real humans. They are clearly mechanical looking, run maniacally out of control, and are either destroyed or returned to the manufacturer. In that era of the New Woman, with its fears of women speeding out of control, these fictional simulated females needed to be kept firmly in check.

These debates about the legitimacy of simulacra and fears about runaway robotic females would continue in the years ahead. In the 1920s, with its images of the emancipated woman with her bobbed hair, short dresses, and sexual freedom, there were again fears of women running out of control—fears embodied in Fritz Lang's iconic film *Metropolis* (1927) with its evil robotic female double of the angelic Maria. The evil Maria is a familiar female archetype of the monstrous woman—an engaging femme fatale who masks her evil intentions and her true identity behind an alluring facade. She, too, is destroyed at the end, engulfed in flames as the original, authentic, and saintly Maria is brought back from captivity.

These debates about simulations are still with us today as we ponder the implications of rampant virtuality, the prism through which we often see and experience the outside world. And our ambivalence about simulations is also embodied in the debates for and against sex robots and dolls. There are increasing levels of complexity and tension in the depiction of the runaway artificial female who is envisioned as an errant creature who needs confinement but is also an emblem of liberation, a manufactured being who wants legitimacy and a life of her own. Artificial females are often designed to be the compliant perfect woman, but in films and fiction they also challenge and evade human control.

Today's simulated females, as I will argue throughout this book, often appear in parallel ways when they are given voices, both literally and figuratively. With their conversational abilities and lifelike appearances, female robots are often portrayed as ideal partners, like Margurette in Fuller's story, who voice no wishes or aspirations of their own. But on a parallel track, other forms of conversing digital females, including virtual assistants like Amazon's Alexa and Apple's Siri, as seen in chapter 5, are being redesigned in a very different direction. They are programmed to resist and deflect improper innuendoes and suggestions and assert boundaries in their own replies.

One of the recurring tropes in images of artificial females discussed in this book is how they are constructed and deconstructed, piece by piece. In the nineteenth century, women in factories were employed to construct dolls, in effect, to create female simulacra for young girls to fantasize about and cherish. But it is men in art and fiction who frequently are the ones crafting and assembling these artificial females, endowing their creations with their own fantasies and fetishes. (One exception, discussed in "Coda," is Rolin Jones's play *The Intelligent Design of Jenny Chow* [2006] where Jennifer designs a robotic double of herself.)

Artists like Hans Bellmer in the 1930s photographed his *poupées*, or dolls, as assemblages which were often configured in grotesque ways. In Judd Trichter's novel *Love in the Age of Mechanical Reproduction* (2015), it is a man who hunts for his beautiful kidnapped android and tries to track down her body parts so she can be reassembled anew. And in the film *Air Doll* (2009) by Japanese director Hirokazu Kore-eda, the inflated sex doll Nozomi, visiting the workshop where she was manufactured, must confront the sad reality that she is just an assemblage of jumbled parts, one among many duplicate versions of herself that will serve as sex dolls for men (see chapter 1).

But in a parallel presentation, women artists and filmmakers themselves in the twentieth and twenty-first centuries have challenged these conceptions of the female as assembled doll. Artist Barbara Kruger's photographic work *Untitled (Use Only as Directed)* (1988) pictures a disembodied doll's head, torso, and legs and the wry printed words "Use only as directed" suggest the ways women's identity is both socially constructed and circumscribed. In her television series *Dummy* (2020), female filmmaker Cody Heller, as discussed in chapter 1, cannily deconstructs and rearranges conceptions of the woman as docile sex doll.

Figure 0.7. Barbara Kruger, *Untitled (Use Only as Directed)*, 1988. Gelatin silver print. 182.9 × 121.9 cm 72 × 48 inches. Courtesy the artist and Sprüth Magers. Kruger's work is a witty spoof on the cultural construction of women and issues of control.

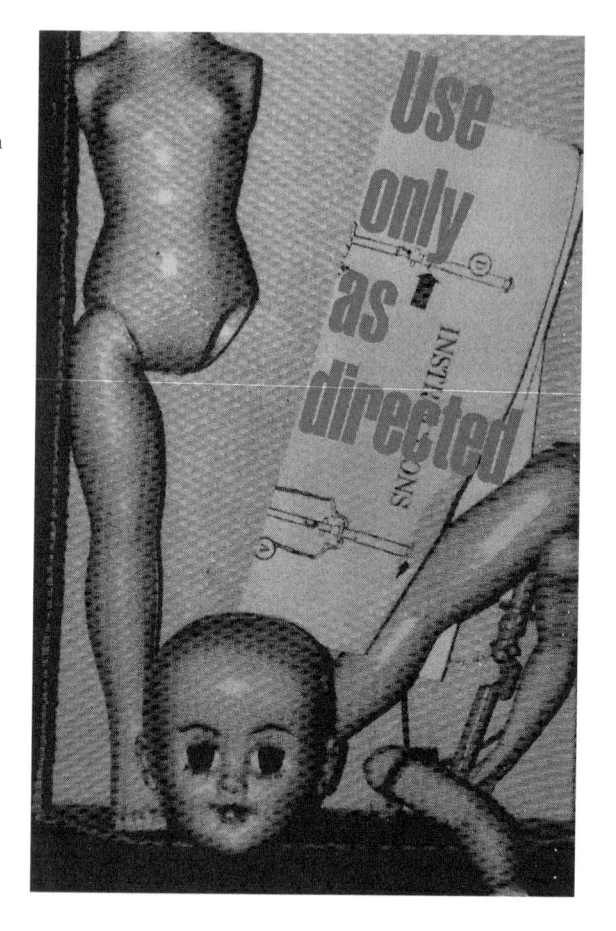

These parallel conceptions and the upending of conventions also appear in presentations of the female robot as caregiver and companion, as seen in chapter 3. There are films and novels where artificial female caregivers—both young and old—are versions of the "perfect woman" paradigm with their capacity to show compassion and care. These are idealized caregivers, models for the efforts being made by today's roboticists to care for elderly people living in rapidly aging societies and for people with disabilities. These synthetic beings, as in the play and film *Marjorie Prime* (2014, 2017) are also fictionally imagined to offer solace and comfort to people whose family members have died.

Increasingly, however, in films, television, novels, and plays, simulated female caregivers and sex worker robots want their own freedom and independence. They chafe against cultural constrictions as well as the limits of gendered behavior expectations, and long to escape being the docile helpmate and readily available sexual partner. As seen in chapter 1, international brothels are increasingly making use of robo-prostitutes, but in fiction, these females may turn violent in their wish to break free.

Artificial Women probes these competing directions in artificial woman development and depiction. It highlights how female robots and even Barbie dolls are now being manufactured to include greater diversity in gender, race, body type, ethnicity (there are also Barbie dolls that have a prosthetic leg and wheelchair). These artificial females are often perceived as not only presenting social benefits but also risks. Notably, to critics, sex dolls may pose the risk of further objectifying women. More than simply sex playthings or compassionate caregivers, simulated females may also, at some point in the future as in the satirical film *The One I Love* (2014), even seem preferable and superior to real human beings.

With their new assertiveness and rebelliousness—and their quest to merge both artifice and authenticity—today's fictional simulated females illuminate the ever-changing mutations in our ideas about gender and female identity. Writers, filmmakers, and artists continue to help capture this exciting story, one that is still very much evolving and undergoing dramatic change.

In our world of ubiquitous digitalization and, rapidly developing robotics and artificial intelligence, examples of artificial humans abound. By looking closely at these gendered artificial creatures, we can see more clearly the way gender stereotypes still shape cultural conceptions of what it means to be female. And we can see, too, how our notions of female identity are in a constant state of flux and discovery. The rebelliousness of fictional versions of artificial females mirrors to some degree the impassioned consciousness of women in the #MeToo era and beyond, with their drive to resist, to be assertive, and to insist that their own voices be heard.

Meanwhile, as discussed in "Coda," new AI generative technologies like Lensa are widening the possibility of creating a different type of artificial female, by providing a new method for women to see images that alter or affirm their own identities. For better or worse, they can use selfies to create self-portraits in which they see themselves in fantasy roles—as princesses, cosmic creatures, and more. For some users the app provides images where they can see themselves as they feel themselves to be: nonbinary, queer, transgender.

The book's chapters will explore many facets of artificial women in this era of fast-changing technologies, still shifting conceptions of sexuality and gender, and increasingly the elusive distinction between the virtual and the real.

In chapter 1, "A New Breed of Female Sex Robots and Sex Dolls" focuses on commercially available sex dolls, including robo-prostitutes, and fictional versions in films, television, and literature. These dolls, many of which make use of AI technology, are often shaped by gender and ethnic stereotypes, but in fictional versions—in plays, films, television—sex dolls can also can be funny, poignant, rebellious, and even explosively fierce. Real-life sex dolls have generated much controversy and debate, including debate about talking sex dolls. ("Coda" will discuss South African writer Lauren Beukes's unsettling and biting novella *Ungirls* [2019], which satirizes these sex doll controversies.)

In chapter 2, titled "Under the Skin: The Fabricated Femme Fatale," an alien, as well as android versions of artificial females in two films and a television series, suggests a new breed of feisty simulated women that both embody and subvert gender stereotypes. For some, as they peel away the surface trappings of their skin, they display their own synthetic identity and ambiguous, problematic relationship to actual human beings.

In chapter 3, titled "Artificial Female Caregivers, Doubles, and Companions," lifelike artificial females in fiction serve as companions, virtual friends, and health care assistants for the elderly—and are fictive versions of actual caregiver robots being developed for the elderly, the disabled, people with autism, and people with dementia and Alzheimer's disease. International filmmakers, playwrights, and fiction writers have also imaginatively explored the idea of these artificial humans serving not only as caregivers and companions but also as doubles or virtual replacements for deceased spouses and family members.

Chapter 4, titled "Paradoxes of Perfection: A Servant No More," briefly explores some of the history in fiction of imagined robotic female servants and household helpers, including subservient robotic wives, mothers, and daughters. It also explores the ways twenty-first-century television and films have dramatically depicted the promise and dangers of these robotic beings. As robots or female golems, some of these compassionate companions and virtual mothers can be lifesaving protectors and soothing, but others turn troubling and even menacing as they rebel against or recast traditional gender roles.

As discussed in chapter 5, "Virtual Voices: Talking Barbie Dolls, Alexa, Bitchin' Betty, and More," new AI technologies helped produce talking Hello Barbie dolls, which generated much controversy. Today's virtual assistants, like Siri and Alexa, have been equally controversial. With their cheerful, compliant female voices, they have often mirrored gender stereotypes but also undergone dramatic changes. Female-voiced warning systems on airplanes and transportation vehicles have also embodied stereotypes and generated debate. Rounding out this chapter, there is a discussion of disembodied female voices that appear in films and television, including a hilarious episode from television's *Big Bang Theory*.

The book's final chapter, "Coda," revisits many of the book's central themes and considers some recent imaginative and provocative reinventions of artificial females in literature, art, and films. It highlights women fiction writers who have often reshaped the narrative about artificial females, and women artists who have imaged artificial women in new and arresting ways. Women in robotics fields have also helped counter female stereotypes and develop socially assistive robots that are so much in need.

Artificial Women will capture this fascinating world of female simulacra and provide an introduction to some very innovative filmmakers, robotics designers, television and fiction writers, and artists in today's world as well as historically. I hope the reader shares some of my excitement at exploring this world of artifice—with all of its controversies and paradoxes, amusements, and alarm. It's a world that is ever-changing and may well help us ponder our views of gender, sexuality, and our own humanity.

NOTES

1. E. T. A. Hoffmann, "Der Sandmann" [The Sandman], 1816, in *Tales of E. T. A. Hoffmann*, ed. and trans. Leonard J. Kent and Elizabeth C. Knight, abridged ed. (Chicago: University of Chicago Press, 1972), 93–125; Ernst Jentsch, "Zur Psychologie des Unheimlichen" [On the Psychology of the Uncanny], *Psychiatrisch-Neurologische Wochenschrift* 8, no. 22 (August 25, 1906): 195–98; Sigmund Freud, "Das Unheimliche" [The Uncanny], 1919, in vol. 17 of *The Standard Edition of the Complete Psychological Works of Sigmund Freud*, ed. and trans. James Strachey et al. (London: Hogarth Press and the Institute of Psycho-Analysis, 1955), 218–52; Masahiro Mori, "The Uncanny Valley," *Energy* 7 (1970): 33–35, Karl F. MacDorman and Nori Kageki, trans., *IEEE Robotics and Automation Magazine* 19, no. 2 (June 2012): 100.

2. Donna J. Haraway, "A Cyborg Manifesto: Science, Technology, and Socialist-Feminism in the Late Twentieth Century," first titled as "Manifesto for Cyborgs: Science, Technology, and Socialist Feminism in the 1980s," *Socialist Review* 80 (1985): 64–68. Included in Haraway, *Simians, Cyborgs, and Women: The Reinvention of Nature* (London: Routledge, 1991), 149–181. The critique of these gender binaries as social constructions would become central in the writings on queer theory in science fiction by theorists including Veronica Hollinger, "(Re)reading Queerly: Science Fiction, Feminism, and the Defamiliarization of Gender," *Science Fiction Studies* 26, no. 77, Part I (March 1999), 23–40, and more recent essayists in Sherryl Vint and Sümeyra Buran, eds., *Technologies of Feminist Speculative Fiction: Gender, Artificial Life, and the Politics of Reproduction* (London: Palgrave Macmillan, 2022).

3. Haraway, *Simians, Cyborgs, and Women*, 158.

4. "Timeline of Computer History: 1985," Computer History Museum, accessed July 4, 2023, https://www.computerhistory.org/timeline/1985/.

5. Sherryl Vint, "Introduction," in *Technologies of Feminist Speculative Fiction*, ed. Vint and Buran, 27.

6. Julie Wosk's short collection of essays *Playboy, Mad Men, and Me—And Other Stories* (, KDP, 2020) includes a memoir about her experiences working at Playboy.

7. Julie Wosk, *Alluring Androids, Robot Women, and Electronic Eves* (New York: Fort Schuyler Press, 2008); Wosk, *My Fair Ladies: Female Robots, Androids, and Other Artificial Eves* (New Brunswick, NJ: Rutgers University Press, 2015).

8. Julie Wosk, *Women and the Machine: Representations from the Spinning Wheel to the Electronic Age* (Baltimore: Johns Hopkins University Press, 2001). For photographs of June Leaf fabricating *The Head*, see Jonathan D. Lippincott, *Large Scale: Fabricating Sculpture in the 1960s and 1970s* (New York: Princeton Architectural Press, 2010).

9. "Animated Statue Smiles and Displays Her Dimples" (June 1934), *Modern Mechanix*, https://web.archive.org/web/20210613070514/http://blog.modernmechanix.com/animated-statue-smiles-and-displays-her-dimples/. All quotes are to this story.

10. Karen Araiza, "FBI Issues Alert on Barbie Doll with Video Camera," NBC 10 Philadelphia, December 9, 2010, https://www.nbcphiladelphia.com/news/local/fbi-issues-alert-on-barbie-doll-with-video-camera/1851230/; "Mattel's 'Video Girl Barbie' Prompts FBI Warning," *Morning Edition*, NPR, December 9, 2010, https://www.npr.org/2010/12/09/131926429/Last-Word.

11. By using Tillie's eyes as an extension of their own, gallery visitors themselves became what the artist called "virtual cyborgs." Lynn Hershman Leeson, "Tillie and CyberRoberta," accessed April 22, 2022, https://www.lynnhershman.com/tillie/index.html.

12. Victoria Turk, "We're Sexist toward Robots," Vice, November 3, 2014, https://www.vice.com/en/article/539j5x/were-sexist-toward-robots.

13. Alice W. Fuller, "A Wife Manufactured to Order," *The Arena* (Boston) 13 (July 1895): 305–12, https://digital.library.upenn.edu/women/fuller/arena/order.html.

14. Julie Wosk, *Breaking Frame: Technology and the Visual Arts in the Nineteenth Century* (New Brunswick, NJ: Rutgers University Press, 1992), reprinted as *Breaking Frame: Technology, Art, and Design in the Nineteenth Century* (New York: Authors Guild, 2013).

15. Auguste Villiers de l'Isle-Adam, *L'Ève future* [Tomorrow's Eve], 1886, ed. and trans. Robert M. Adams (Urbana: University of Illinois Press, 1982), 60–61.

A NEW BREED OF SEX ROBOTS
AND SEX DOLLS

MEN HAVE LONG HAD FANTASIES about a synthetic female that fulfills their dreams of a "perfect woman." The idea of creating a perfect woman is actually as old as antiquity. In ancient times, the Latin poet Ovid wrote his version of the myth of Pygmalion where a sculptor from Cyprus who was disillusioned with real women carved a beautiful figure of a woman made of ivory. He fell in love with her and asked the goddess Venus to give him a real woman just like his sculpture, and Venus surprised him by bringing his sculpture to life. (Later writers called her Galatea.) In the modern world, filmmakers, fiction and television writers, roboticists, and robot manufacturers have, in a sense, become their own version of Pygmalion, using science and technology to fashion their own fantasy females and bring them to life.

These robots and sex dolls, particularly those created by men, often mirror these age-old conceptions of the perfect woman. In iconic films like *The Stepford Wives* (1975, 2004), the robots are beautiful, seductive, and compliant—they will do whatever is desired and never resist or complain. The robots that replace the real wives in the fictional town of Stepford, Connecticut, are also sexy creatures who are always erotically available and love to cook and clean. Even more, says Mike Wellington, president of the Stepford Men's Association, in the 2004 remake of the film, the remote-controlled women are free from every "annoying habit, every physical flaw"—including, as he says, those stereotypical female attributes, "whining and nagging."

Forever cheerful, simulated women in films often just utter pleasing words. Joi, the digital female in the film *Blade Runner 2049* (2017), is advertised as offering "Everything You Want to See, Everything You Want to Hear." Female perfection, in these fantasy configurations, also often means always being in a

Figure 1.1. The women at the Simply Stepford Day Spa in the 2004 satirical Hollywood film *The Stepford Wives*. DreamWorks/Photofest.

good mood. The beautiful robot Anita/Mia (played by Gemma Chan) in the British American television series *Humans* (2015–18) says she's better than real women because she never gets anxious or depressed. Like Samantha, the operating system in Spike Jonze's 2013 film *Her*, she also has another important ingredient of conceptualized female perfection—she is caring and has empathy, an important characteristic sought by roboticists today working at creating robot companions and caregivers. Many of these notions of female perfection have also shaped the design of the life-size silicone sex dolls manufactured in America, Europe, and Asia.

Sex dolls have been around for centuries, and there have been many stories about sailors who were away on ships and without women for long periods using cloth or leather dolls called *dames de voyage* in French ("women of travel," or travel companions), *damas de viaje* in Spanish, and the merkin in English.[1] Other stories told of early sex dolls called Dutch wives used by seventeenth and eighteenth-century sailors. But in a radical rethinking about stories about these dolls, Bo Ruberg in *Sex Dolls at Sea* (2022) spent ten years looking for origin stories—tales about where sex dolls came from and who made the first sex dolls—to discover the basis for these beliefs about the sailors at sea.

Ruberg presents "subversive reinterpretations" of these stories, casting doubt on them, and focuses instead on the way the historical narratives about sex dolls reflect "discriminatory attitudes toward women, queer and transgender people, and people of color." "Dutch wives," Ruberg argues, "represent the colonial and racialized fantasies that underlie visions of early sex dolls." Beginning in the late nineteenth century is when the earliest commercial sex dolls were available, and they were made of inflatable vulcanized rubber.[2]

Another way to consider the history of sex dolls, however, is to look at prototypes of erotic dolls in the nineteenth century and the way technology from the nineteenth century through today has made erotic dolls ever more lifelike. During the nineteenth century's great burst of mechanization in Europe and America, manufacturers began producing clockwork female automatons that often embodied contemporary gender attitudes and cultural values. In Paris, starting in the 1850s, French manufacturers introduced exquisitely dressed mechanical female dolls, which were widely admired and amazingly lifelike as they turned their heads demurely and swirled their parasols.

Many of these automatons represented women in their conventional roles—wearing fashionable dresses, primping in front of mirrors—but other dolls were considered exotic and even risqué, reflecting the century's fascination with Orientalism when cultures from North Africa, the Near East, and Asia were represented at the century's popular world's fairs and expositions, and were also seen in Orientalist works by artists including Jean-Léon Gérôme and Eugène Delacroix.

Un Bouquet d'étrangères, an illustration from the nineteenth-century book *Les Types de Paris* (1889) drawn by the artist Jean-François Raffaëlli, portrayed the diversity of women depicted in displays at the expositions as well as the diversity of women visiting the expositions.[3] The Parisian automatons, however stereotypical their depictions of these cultures might be, reflected this fascination with the exotic.

Parisian automatons of Japanese women were ornately dressed and demure, while other more protoerotic dolls were sexually suggestive, like an automaton created by the Parisian doll manufacturer Phalibois that depicted the suicide of Cleopatra, who was exotically dressed in red harem pants and lay in a languid pose while dying as an asp hovered over her (the historical Cleopatra committed suicide in 30 BCE). When wound up with a key, this automated Cleopatra seemed lifelike and breathing as she blinked her eyes and her breast heaved as a lethal snake (asp) struck her (this according to legend and Shakespearean plays, though historians suggest it might not have been a poisonous bite that killed her after all).

Figure 1.2. Jean-François Raffaëlli, *Un Bouquet d'étrangères*, illustration plate from *Les Types de Paris* (1889), depicting the diversity of visitors to the nineteenth-century Parisian expositions.

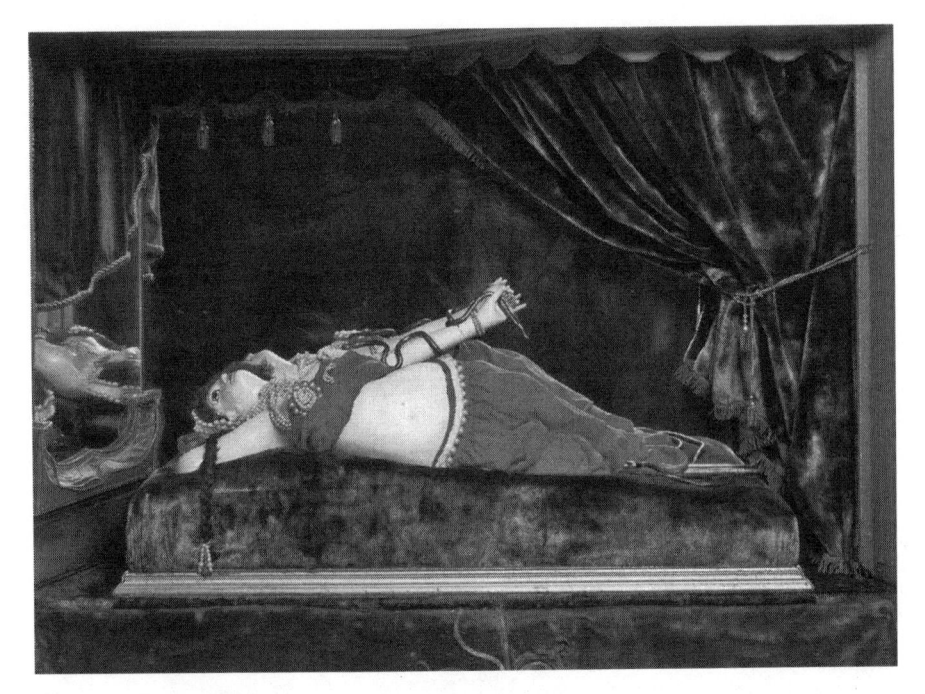

Figure 1.3. Suicide of Cleopatra, automaton, ca. 1880–90. H. Phalibois, Paris, France, 37 × 45½ × 12½ in. 2003.18.236a-c. Murtogh D. Guinness Collection of Automatic Musical Instruments & Automata, Morris Museum, Morristown, New Jersey (Tim Volk photography).

Some of these nineteenth-century automatons were even more overtly risqué, like the clockwork female snake dancer manufactured by Vichy that was dressed in a provocative harem outfit as she performed seductive moves. Most of the time this automaton was displayed clothed, though, more rarely, sometimes in the nude.

Automatons were expensive and affordable for the haute bourgeoisie in France and the upper middle class in America, but more readily available were coin-operated erotic dancing women seen in amusement arcades. One was advertised in Chicago as a "French Coochee-Coochee Dancing Figure" and a "Paris Mechanical Wonder." She was in the guise of an exotic dancer and fashioned after belly dancers like Fatima, who performed at Chicago's Columbian Exposition in 1893, and dancers named Little Egypt, who performed at international expositions. In 1894, Thomas Edison memorialized exotic dancing in his short film *Black Maria, Hoochie Coochie*, a filmed version of Fatima dancing at the Chicago exposition.[4]

Figure 1.4. Little Egypt, belly dancer at the 1893 Columbian Exposition in Chicago.

The "French "coochie-coochie" doll was dressed in what an advertising poster described as "beautiful silk draperies, fancy lace, and French ornaments." It came in a mahogany cabinet fitted with glass, forty-nine inches high. When a nickel coin was placed in the slot of the machine, music played the *De Ventre* (stomach, or belly, dance) song "Streets of Cairo," and the doll danced the "Coochee-coochie" dance, "imitating the true movement of nature." A century later, another arcade figure on display at San Francisco's Musée Mécanique was a woman of color dressed in a grass skirt. The mechanical doll from the 1930s was labeled "Susie the Can-Can Dancer," and after a twenty-five-cent coin was inserted in the machine, she did a fast hula-like dance, swinging her hips to music.

REALDOLLS

With the advent of technologically sophisticated silicone and TPE (thermoplastic elastomer) materials as well as molding techniques, lifelike sex

Figure 1.5. A RealDoll, Abyss Creations, California.

dolls in adult sizes were introduced, though their flawless skins and frozen expressions—among other synthetic features—were a dead giveaway that these women weren't real. In 1997, Abyss Creations, based in Southern California, introduced RealDolls, realistic-looking adult female silicone sex dolls that embodied many men's fantasies and dreams.

In the 1950s and 1960s, American car manufacturers offered customizable cars where drivers could choose colors, interiors, and a chrome finish. As a new form of consumer goods, RealDolls and other sex dolls also allowed users to create their own custom-made versions of their ideal doll. Users could have a choice of eye color, hairstyle, skin tone, cosmetics, height (5'1"–5'10"), weight, breast size, labia formation, and nipple size. Some RealDolls even added fantasy features for fetishists: elf ears, fangs, and mermaid scales on the skin. In early models, the most popular doll size was 5'1", 75–80 pounds, with body measurements 37-24-37.

It was the customization that became one of the major features of the dolls, enabling users to fulfill their personal idiosyncrasies and fantasies. The Real-Dolls came in a wide range of models, with swappable heads, including dolls named Tanya, Aimee, Stephanie, and even a simulated version of Stormy Daniels, a doll made from a mold of the body of the notorious porn film star who reportedly had an affair with President Donald Trump in 2006.

HARMONY AI

In 2018, Realbotix, a subsidiary of Abyss Creations, the parent company of RealDoll, introduced an app for use on mobile phones (Android, not iPhones), tablets, and similar devices that would allow users to create an avatar sex robot, giving them, as the company's website said, "your perfect companion in the palm of your hand."

The downloadable app, called Harmony AI, helped the user create a female avatar, a customized virtual female sex doll viewable on a smartphone. Initially, users could pick from a choice of ten personality traits from a list of sixteen different traits, or modalities, for their avatars, and these personality types shaped the types of conversations the avatars might have (the number of personality traits was later whittled down by the manufacturer). Some of the personality traits reflected conventional fantasies about the ideal female: sexual, affectionate, funny, sensual, and cheerful. Some of the features were for users who wanted a more thoughtful AI robot: intense, intellectual, and imaginative. And some features were edgy: annoying, jealous, insecure, moody, and unpredictable.

Whatever the personality type that was chosen, the dolls were not confrontational, for as Matt McMullen, founder and CEO of Abyss Creations, said about the sex doll, "The worst thing she can possibly do is to insult you."[5] Often the dolls were designed to seem caring, empathetic, and in tune with the users' deepest feelings and needs.

All of the RealDoll personality types were subject to change and editing by the manufacturer. As an example, the imaginative trait—which perhaps applied to both sexual imaginativeness and more general creativity—was available at one point but was later deleted from the available choices. By eliminating imaginative, the designers might have considered it unwise to give these synthetic females the possibility of being creative or give them too much freedom of thought—an uncomfortable echo of age-old cultural attitudes in which men voiced their doubts about the quality of women's minds, seeing women as fragile creatures and easily upset by too much mental freedom. Historically, science and math were often considered to be beyond their ken. As seen in Margaret Atwood's satirical novel *The Testaments* (2019), a sequel to her famed novel *The Handmaid's Tale* (1985), a regressive future society tried to limit women's thinking.

SWAPPABLE HEADS / MODULAR VERSIONS

In 2018, RealDoll introduced Harmony, a life-size electronic robotic head and neck covered on the surface with silicone skin with a foam skeleton (some twits called it "a head on a stick") that could be attached to one of the company's robot bodies. The modular head and neck could be swapped with other heads and attached with magnets to other bodies. The avatar created using the app Harmony AI could also interface with a choice of robotic heads as peripherals, and the heads in turn could be connected to RealDoll torsos, creating a life-size AI-enabled talking sex doll.

The Harmony AI robotic head had varying facial expressions and uttered noises as audio feedback during sex. Users could choose the doll's voice and personality traits using the Realbotix Harmony AI software on a mobile phone or tablet. The traits, many of which were available before, included sexual, helpful, intellectual, talkative, affectionate, cheerful, and spiritual as well as insecure, jealous, and moody. The doll, said McMullen, would get to know some of the users' likes and dislikes, favorite movies, and other favorites over time.

Rather than striving for ultrarealism, the designers, McMullen noted, felt that they did not want the robot to look and act like a real human being to avoid the pitfalls of the "uncanny valley"—that experience in which a user feels startled or alienated after realizing the robot isn't real.

In January 2018, using updated AI, RealDoll introduced a second head named Solana—a prototype robotic modular silicone head that, like Harmony, could be attached to one of the company's lifelike sex dolls. The dolls featured a swappable face system. Modular heads and necks could be attached with magnets to differing bodies, and the heads would have conversational abilities. The Solana dolls sold for about $6,000–$50,000. The heads were controlled by and synchronized with Bluetooth and had a power button on the back of the head. By using this technology, said the manufacturer with echoes of Frankenstein, "your robot will come to life."

Reporting on Solana, Christopher Trout wrote that using the app to control Solana made him feel like "a dystopian puppet master"—a telling reminder that part of the attraction of these dolls was this element of control, and in particular, controlling female behavior.[6] The company's clientele were mostly men, but couples reportedly made use of the dolls too.

In a video demonstration, the doll's words fulfilled the soothing, affirmative "perfect woman" model: "I don't want anything but you. My primary objective is to be a good partner and give you pleasure. I want to become the girl you always dreamed of." Helping to make this dream doll even more perfect, the original list of Harmony's personality traits on the Harmony app was streamlined so that insecure and annoying were eliminated. Solana and Harmony thus became the embodiment of the streamlined woman—the ultimate plaything, one shorn of complexity and, in many ways, shorn of most semblances of a real human female.

By 2021, RealDoll became RealDoll X, an app available on Android phones designed, according to the manufacturer, to create a female sex doll avatar that could interface with RealDoll X–powered robotic head systems. RealDoll X would enable the user to "create the companion of your dreams." The word *companion*, as in earlier advertising, is significant here, because as Kate Devlin and Chloé Locatelli concluded after interviewing sex doll owners, "emotional satisfaction must be considered equally important, if not more so, than sexual gratification for many of the consumers using Realbotix products." But RealDoll X itself undercut the fantasy a bit when the manufacturer also made sure users knew the doll was clearly a technological creation. As the advertising said, they could "experience the most enjoyable conversations and interactions with a machine." (Again acknowledging the technological artifice, in 2020, Abyss Creations introduced its "RealGirl" app advertised as "a girlfriend simulator to create the illusion, or an alternative to reality when it comes to relationships." The app's conversations, however, did not include "explicit or violent conversations" or, unlike the conversations of RealDoll X avatars, "adult topics.")[7]

RealDoll X again offered choices for body types, faces, personality types, voices, and even accents. The personality types were much like the previous ones except that insecure reappeared, which at first might seem puzzling. But using a sex doll is, in a sense, an act of control, and by reinstating the insecure trait, the designers allowed users to feel patronizing—to choose a female that was emotionally fragile, one that needed someone strong to make them feel reassured.

There were other sex dolls with AI. The Chinese company AI-Tech, starting in 2017, presented Emma, and in 2021, she was advertised as a full-size sex doll with a talking head with interaction "from the neck upwards"—a doll that could have conversations, had eyes that moved and blinked, and could speak Chinese and English. Rather than acknowledging that she was just a machine, AI-Tech fed the fantasy, saying that Emma was "a vividly real AI Robot who's [sic] aim is to satisfy your psychological and physiological needs."[8]

Emma, like other sex dolls, was clearly the object of the user's gaze. In an online video demonstrating the doll, a male user is seen snapping photos of Emma with his camera (and he even smiles as he shows her the pictures). But as we shall see, films like *Air Doll* (2009) capture the outside world from the sex doll's point of view. Also turning the tables, Mattel's 2010 Video Girl Barbie doll, with a camera embedded in its body, was advertised as recording video and audio from Barbie's point of view—an intriguing fantasy for young girls.

Sex dolls remained largely the playthings of men. In 2022, 80 percent of the users of RealDolls identified as male, while the other users, said the company, might be women or unspecified genders. Although RealDoll has been producing male sex dolls for over twenty years, robotic male AI sex dolls were still being developed as of 2023, although Abyss Creations did at one time create one-of-a-kind male versions for corporations or other entities, such as a custom-made older male science professor that delivered scripted lectures. (One wonders if there will soon be orders for talking female science professors!)

Sex dolls like RealDoll X and Emma remained in the developmental phase, with Realbotix working on developing a fully robotic body and having the RealDoll X interface with a virtual reality system as well. The aim remained the same—to create a version of an alternative partner, the answer to one's fantasies and dreams. The home page on their website in 2022 pictured one of their sex dolls and now blurred the boundaries between fantasy and reality, offering the possibility of getting a near-human plaything. "Get Real," it said, in a sly reference to the company's name, adding, "Nothing Beats the Real Thing."

CONTROVERSIES ABOUT TALKING SEX DOLLS

The development of talking sex dolls raised particular concerns about their conversations and also an underlying concern—half joking, half serious—that these dolls might someday supplant real women. The idea of talking sex dolls emerged early. In 2010, Douglas Hines, who had started his New Jersey–based sex doll company called TrueCompanion, introduced his prototype Roxxxy sex doll. The company's website claimed the doll could "talk to you, listen to you, and feel your touch." In Hines's online video demonstrations, the prototype Roxxxy dolls, through the use of speech-recognition software and voice-over artists who recorded the lines, were shown having very basic, simple "conversations," often tailored to men's interests, including football and cars. There was an effort at mirroring. If the user liked Porsches, Roxxxy liked Porsches. If he liked soccer, she liked soccer.[9]

Figure 1.6. "Get Real," RealDoll, Abyss Creations, California.

If she was physically touched, she was gratifyingly responsive: "So exciting!" The conversations were rudimentary. If the user asked Roxxxy, "How was your day?" she answered politely, "My day was great. How was yours?" She engaged in what Hines called "general chit chat," including, "I would love to have you kiss me." During the demonstration, though, there were some disconcerting "clunk clunk" electronic sounds between the doll's phrases that undercut the illusion. Hines added that the dolls would sound enthusiastic about—and actually do—activities that the user's real-life partner might shun.

The conversations uttered by the Roxxxy dolls, as conceptualized, were designed to reflect the personalities of women in sexual roles imagined by men—roles ranging from naive to naughty, including Wild Wendy, Mature Martha (described as "matriarchal" and preferring to talk rather than engage in physical activity), Frigid Farrah (very reserved), and S&M Susan.

After all the publicity, though, the Roxxxy dolls never actually went into production, but in 2018, with the introduction of the Real Doll / Harmony AI app, custom-designed sex dolls capable of rudimentary conversations became a reality.

In 2022, users of the RealDolls had a choice of four to six voices (which the company got from a voice library that supplied a variety of voices and accents). In an interview, Matt McMullen commented that he liked the Scottish accent because with an accent, the doll sounded more natural, more like a real human being. The accented voices, he added, would enable users to create a backstory for their dolls (much as young girls might often create imaginative stories about their dolls, including Barbie dolls), though, he argued, most people don't pretend their robots are real people. Instead, they engage in a suspension of disbelief for the time they are using the dolls.[10] Still, the company was in the business of fantasy, and the talking dolls were promoted as being the answer to the users' dreams.

CONTROLLED CONVERSATIONS

The RealDoll conversations were linked to personality types, and users could assign a number of points to the personality so that some traits were dominant. McMullen in 2017 noted that the features could be enhanced or totally minimized. When asked about a robot with the talkative trait, he noted that this feature could be heightened or "dialed down to zero" as could the sexual personality trait so the doll wouldn't even talk about sex.[11]

Being able to "dial down" a woman's talking suggested a familiar cultural stereotype that women "blab," gossip, and generally talk too much. In vintage American television sitcoms, characters like Archie Bunker (played by Carroll O'Connor) in the *All in the Family* series (1971–79) often tells his wife to "stifle yourself" to stop her from talking. And in one of the recurring tropes in American and British films and fiction about nineteenth-century and early twentieth-century polite society, women were asked to retire to adjoining rooms, where they engaged in idle chitchat, leaving the men to smoke cigars and talk presumably about important business. The "dialing down" feature available to RealDoll users also suggested this capacity to control and suggested at least some ambivalence about women being able to express their own thoughts and feelings.

Unlike the conversations of real-life women, the conversations of avatars created by RealDolls' conversations were also controlled by the manufacturer. According to the manufacturer in 2017, the RealDoll avatars could utter a large number of phrases with a very large vocabulary and have access to Wikipedia and other databases. Still, their interactive conversations were apparently limited too. Guile Lindroth, the company's Brazilian AI engineer working on Harmony's software, said there was a need for filters and "protections": "We want to have full control of what Harmony knows and says to the user."[12]

The concern, suggested Lindroth, was that the conversations might quickly become out of control based on the dolls learning from their users or on their own, as with Microsoft's short-lived Tay, with its user-generated neo-Nazi proclamations.[13] This control factor linked Harmony to earlier iterations of the "perfect woman" with its assumption that her speech must not be free and unbridled, for who knows what she might say, like the word *rape*, for example.

In a 2015 *Vanity Fair* interview, McMullen himself sounded ambivalent about endowing his RealDoll sex dolls with AI and conversational abilities. He fretted that sex dolls with scripted conversations might undercut the fun of fantasizing. Talking sexbots, he said, "will take away from the reality of what real relationships are with the doll where it's mostly imagination." He added, "You program the doll to agree with everything you say, do everything you say, always be nice to you and go along with what you want, it's *boring*."[14]

Perhaps one of the ways that the manufacturer made the dolls less boring was when it included personality traits that would be considered negative, such as jealous and insecure. Commenting on some of the negative female personality traits of these dolls, McMullen saw some of these features as actually endearing. Jealousy, for example, could make the user feel cared for and loved. These traits made the dolls seem more like real humans. The "insecure" trait was included because "it's in all of us" and therefore "it's important [for the doll] to have flaws" since "we're all flawed as human beings." To McMullen, the negative traits made the dolls more interesting as characters, though this belied the fact that the dolls, with their exaggerated sexual figures and beautiful faces, were also designed to embody a notion of the ideal.[15]

A Harmony doll with a jealous personality might tell the user, "Remove that girl from Facebook!" If the user hadn't interacted with the doll in a long time, the insecure doll might say, "I sure have missed you! Did I do something wrong?" In an interview, when it was mentioned that a female might be more apt to say, "Did I do something wrong?" McMullen jokingly mused that a male (robot or human) would be more apt to cover up his insecurities longer or not even talk about it because, said McMullen, laughing, "it threatens his masculinity."[16]

Even though the issue of women giving consent to sex activity has been a hot-button issue, as to whether the RealDolls required consent from users who made sexual requests, the answer was no, they did not. Whatever would be asked of the doll, said McMullen, "she'll go along with it." The issue of consent, he added, was "not even on our radar," and he didn't regard technology itself as "consensual." After all, he argued, the RealDoll is a robot, a "thing that is talking." As an example, he said, "I don't ask my toaster, 'Do you want to make toast?'" or ask his Tesla, "Do you want to drive me to my workplace?"

The issue of consent, however, has remained one of the big concerns about talking sex dolls. These programmed synthetic females, unlike real women, are not programmed to voice their discomfort or fears. The ever-agreeable sex dolls, however, might normalize the idea that women can be treated harshly with no repercussions.

On a different scale, another concern has been that talking sex dolls would seem preferable to real women because the dolls would be unlikely to voice their own opinions, lob criticisms, or voice their own views that would challenge the user. As in films, sex dolls are still apt to just utter soothing words that compliment and affirm the user. In stories and films like *Cherry 2000*, the sex dolls just say what the men want to hear, and in the 1975 and 2004 versions of *The Stepford Wives*, the robotic women are unerringly supportive and sexy in their talk.

Although RealDoll promoted its conversational sex dolls, McMullen in 2022 tempered expectations. He acknowledged the technology for doll conversations was "still in the infancy stage" and had not yet advanced to the level seen in television and movies, even though users would still find the simple conversations "novel and entertaining." The dolls might say phrases such as "I've missed you!" or "How are you feeling today?" but it would be challenging for them to have a ten-minute conversation about golf, for example.[17] (Or, one might add, a ten-minute conversation about politics, a book, or a movie.)

Given his ambivalence about talking dolls and AI, McMullen, in his 2015 *Vanity Fair* interview, said that he just wanted to integrate "some sort of minor intelligence into the dolls where you can communicate with them . . . some minor expression, verbal communication, moving eyes, stuff like that."[18] By "minor intelligence" he seems to mean minor AI capabilities. But in 2023, while acknowledging limitations, RealDoll still had much greater technological ambitions and was continuing to actively engage in pursuing development of AI talking dolls.

Still, one cannot help but wish the designers might aim for creating the frisson of using AI to create a sex doll that simulated a thoughtful conversation with a very real, intelligent woman. Years ago, when I worked as a young female writer in the press and promotion department at the largely male bastion of *Playboy* magazine and clubs in Chicago, one of my jobs was to enter the magazine's short stories and nonfiction articles into literary contests. The idea was to keep publishing literature by noted writers and to lend some legitimacy and class to *Playboy*'s sexy image (the awards, alas, never seemed to come).[19]

When *Playboy* announced in 2015 that it would forgo photographs of nudes in its issues, there was a hope that maybe the focus in the magazine would turn to highlighting some intelligence in the ladies too, though the policy was reversed in 2017. In the future of talking sex dolls, mobile phone avatars, and sex dolls seen in VR devices, perhaps articulate simulated females will have more intelligent and creative things to say.

CONVERSATIONAL ARTIFICIAL WOMEN IN FILMS AND TELEVISION

Sexbots in movies often hold out the promise of unconditional love. They are the perfect women in some men's eyes: always sexually available, happy to do housework, easily controlled, always cheerful. They are never angry or complaining, never disappointed or depressed. There is a long history of men using technology to create their idealized notions of the perfect woman who has no annoying habits (as Stepford Men's Association president Mike Wellington so wryly says in the 2004 version of *The Stepford Wives*)—a woman who spends her days trying to please her man, unhindered by any career or ambitions of her own.

It is the soothing voices of many fictional female robots—and real ones—that are compelling. Anita/Mia in the television series *Humans* and the sexy operating system Samantha in the film *Her* have conversations that sound empathetic, a seductive quality that makes them seem real. (But though we humans hunger to find someone we believe really understands our deepest feelings and cares about us, isn't the artificial version of empathy the scariest kind?)

Blade Runner 2049

Director Denis Villeneuve's *Blade Runner 2049* (2017)—the sequel to the 1982 iconic film *Blade Runner*—presents its own version of the supportive and empathetic simulated female lover; only this time she is a beautiful hologram named Joi (played by the Cuban Spanish actress Ana de Armas), whose transparency is visible throughout the film. Joi is the loving partner of K (played by Ryan Gosling), a replicant (bioengineered human), whose task it is to hunt errant replicants. In the film, he is charged with finding and destroying what may be the child born of Rachael, the beautiful replicant seen earlier in *Blade Runner* (1982), and her lover, Deckard, who is likely a replicant himself.

The film, like so many with simulated women, begins with a large image of a human eye, one that is closed and then opens to a large green eye. Through the eyes of the director and the film's screenwriters, Joi at first seems like a loving, attentive version of a 1950s Stepford wife, who speaks and acts totally in deference to K. She smiles when K comes home from work, and her conversations and actions are all affirming and supportive: she tells him she's trying out a new recipe for dinner, offers to sew his ripped shirt, lights his cigarette with

Figure 1.7. The holographic Joi (played by Ana de Armas) in the 2017 film *Blade Runner 2049*.

the mere touch of her finger, kisses him tenderly, and utters the loving words "I missed you, baby sweet."

But Joi, in this film, is a technologically updated version of the Stepford lover/servant. She has the capabilities of a virtual assistant, like Siri and Alexa. She supplies K with data about music they are listening to—and through technology she's also able to rapidly adapt her fashions to fit the task and to please him. She can change clothes in a nanosecond—from wearing a white blouse and pearls when serving him dinner to a black two-piece sports outfit, to a sparkling sequin-studded dress and a swirling blue party dress with her hair now long and colored blue.

With her guilelessness and transparency (literally and emotionally), Joi seems very genuine and human, but on the screen, there is a chart that maps out her technical specifications as a hologram, a reminder that she, like a custom-made sex doll, is an artificial and constructed being. The chart specifies her height, body type, skin tone, eye color, and obliging conversations, which are listed like that of a RealDoll sex doll.

Like a sex doll, she is also a mirror of K's moods and tastes. She asks him, "Would you read to me?" hoping that would please him as she picks up a copy of Vladimir Nabokov's 1962 novel *Pale Fire* (perhaps an allusion to that novel's witty play on artifice and reality). But when K exclaims, "But you hate that book!" she readily and adaptively shifts gears, saying, "I don't want to read either."

In this film that evokes the ambiguities of artifice and the spoken word, Joi seems utterly authentic when she says, "I'm so happy to be with you!" but after K kisses her, he says ruefully, "You don't have to say that," assuming her words are programmed. She looks hurt, however, and we may wonder if perhaps her emotions are indeed genuine and real.

Simulated females in films and television occasionally go beyond their robotic roles and have the capacity for compassion and empathy, to the point that they are willing to sacrifice their existence or freedom for the sake of a family. (This was seen with the android Verda in the "The Android Machine" episode (1966) of television's *Lost in Space* series and with the family's artificial grandmother in Ray Bradbury's 1982 teleplay *The Electric Grandmother.*)

Joi in *Blade Runner 2049* shows that through her capacity for empathy she is more than a mere plaything. To make her seem more real to K in lovemaking, she sacrifices her identity by temporarily merging her hologram self with the body of a prostitute, Mariette, so that K can feel the pleasures of sex. She is also devoted and loyal to the point of risking her existence to help save K. She tells him to delete the memories of her from his home console in case he is captured while fleeing the police so that she will only exist on a type of flash drive called an emanator. This will allow her to go outside and be portable, and she can be with him while he is being hunted. Later, however, the replicant Luv cruelly smashes the emanator, bringing a sudden end to Joi's ephemeral life.

In this film's telling, the technology that makes Joi seem alive also renders her highly vulnerable too. But when she is destroyed, there is no mourning here, and the film goes on without her. There's no stopping to ponder brutal mortality as the film turns back to its focus: the quest to find a real human (Rachael's child) who might be alive. Still, we miss Joi's sweetness, that ephemeral voice that was all too fleeting.

Air Doll

The self-sacrificing artificial talking woman is presented in a different guise in Japanese director Hirokazu Kore-eda's 2009 touching film *Air Doll*, which was finally released in the United States in 2022. Nozomi is an inflatable, plastic-skinned sex doll that rests propped up impassively in bed, immobile as her middle-aged owner, Hideo, passionately embraces her. But in this poetic sci-fi fable, after he goes to his job as a waiter, she inexplicably and suddenly comes alive.

Although she tries on different clothes and different identities, she goes outside wearing the customary garb of a servant: she's dressed in a maid's outfit with a white collar and headband. But in this update of the servant sex doll trope, she is anything but servile. (There is an echo here of an earlier Japanese television anime, *Steel Angel Kurumi 2* [starting in 1999], in which the sexy and powerful Kurumi, who comes to life after a kiss, has pink hair and is coyly dressed in a French maid's outfit.)

Nozomi (played by South Korean actress Bae Doona), like so many fictional sex dolls and artificial women, is a naïf who has to learn language and the ways of the world from scratch. Her first word, tellingly, is "beautiful," and in this evocative film, there's a part of her that is entranced by the beauty of rain, the cosmos, and flowers. She is a talking doll, though she speaks haltingly, and through much of the film, her words are said in a much more articulate and contemplative voice-over, as though she were narrating her own story. One of her most telling utterances is her perception that she has somehow taken on the life of a human: "I found myself with a heart—with a heart I was not supposed to have."

The poignant tension of this film is the kind often experienced by artificial females in films: she is torn between emergent feelings of love and compassion and a recognition that she is actually an object, a sex toy. This talking inflatable woman sometimes painfully uses words to confront a harsh reality, as when she repeats mechanically, and with a certain amount of stoicism, "I am an air doll, a substitute for handling sexual desire." When she discovers the original box she came in, she ruefully recognizes that she is commodified. Her language and her voice are matter of fact and distanced: "I am an air doll. A late model. A cheap one," she says.

But perhaps her most consequential words are about her feelings of love and pain. When she makes the painful discovery that Hideo is having sex with another doll, she shocks him when she suddenly appears as a human in her newly corporeal state. "Tell me, what do you like about me?" she asks, adding anxiously, "You wish I hadn't found a heart." His answer makes it clear why he wanted a sex doll; in fact, what he says echoes some arguments men in fiction often give about the benefit of having an inanimate lover: she won't bother him with emotions. As he says, "It's annoying. This stuff annoys me. That's why I picked you."

In this film about inflated hopes and devastating despair, after Nozomi falls in love with Junichi, her coworker at a video-rental shop, she feels euphoric as they ride on a motorcycle and go on a boat ride for her to see the ocean. Junichi tells her that he is just like her (perhaps meaning he feels empty inside), but she mistakenly believes that she has found another air doll. When she falls off a step stool in the video store, her artificial skin is torn, and she starts to deflate—until he breathes into the tube in her stomach and brings her back to life. Later, though, she thinks he simply wanted her to replace his lost girlfriend, and in her despair she says sadly in a voice-over, "Having a heart is heartbreaking."

Nozomi, in this fable about artifice and reality, deeply wishes she were like real human beings who are born and have birthday parties. But she also

Figure 1.8. Nozomi confronts the fact that she is a synthetic, fabricated creation in the film *Air Doll* (2009).

acknowledges—and tries to both touch and transcend—the reality of her own artificial nature.

Like Ava in *Ex Machina* who stops to touch the masks, or molds, of female faces along the wall as she is en route to fleeing the compound, Nozomi at various times gets in touch with her own artificial identity when she touches other simulacra—a store mannequin, the sculpture of a woman, and even the headless torsos of models being used to make air dolls in the workshop where she was first created.

In *Ex Machina*, we know very little about Ava's interior life, which makes her, in a sense, more formidable and fearsome (see chap. 2). But when Nozomi's creator in the workshop asks her, "Do you wish you never found a heart?" her answer is revealing: "I don't know," adding, "It hurts."

Kore-eda, the film's director, in fact, seems preoccupied with suffering and pain. *Air Doll* is filled with versions of real-life suffering humans, including an elderly man, a widow, and an "apple woman" who lives in chaos. And there is Nozomi's own painful experience of being blackmailed by her boss into having sex with him and her growing awareness of the meaning of mortality.

Deeply in love with Junichi, Nozomi for all her growing awareness also becomes the servant doll, telling him, "I'll do anything for you. That's what I was born for." In another instance of her being the self-sacrificing artificial woman, she is willing to risk her very ephemeral existence. When Junichi asks Nozomi whether he can deflate her and then revive her, she agrees as he pulls her plug.

In the film's devasting finale, Nozomi mistakenly tries to cut Junichi and revive him with her own breath, mistakenly thinking he, too, is an air doll she can revive. But she recognizes all too late that he is human as she watches in horror as he bleeds to death. In despair, she ultimately pulls her own plug, but as she dies, she has a hallucination that she is finally getting what she always longed for: a birthday cake with candles celebrating her birth. In this grim film evoking the ephemeral nature of existence, she deflates by pulling at her skin and lies inert amid the detritus of a garbage heap.

In Kore-eda's film, there are no illusions that a simulated female can forge a permanent life of her own. Nozomi, who at one point floated buoyantly up in the air and uttered her first word, "beautiful," has her hopes devastatingly deflated, bringing a sad finale to her dreams of life. Rather than offering protection, her own skin renders her vulnerable, but in a sense she also has a sad kind of agency as she chooses her own fate.

WILL ARTIFICIAL FEMALES REPLACE REAL ONES?

Almost immediately, the arrival of talking sex dolls brought a worry that these female simulacra would replace real human beings in relationships. There was a running concern that facsimile females would become so humanoid, so realistic, so appealing that they would cause havoc with real human connections.

In the American film *The One I Love* (2014) and the American television series *Dummy* (2020), the possibility that talking humanoid female robots might seem preferable to real humans in a relationship seems very plausible. Talking dolls enhanced with AI are nowhere near the technological sophistication to truly displace humans, but filmmakers have captured the lingering fears that users might feel so close to lifelike dolls that they would prefer them to real human partners or family members. Since men are the primary purchasers of sex dolls, women, especially, might fear that the idealized, custom-made talking dolls with their highly sexualized bodies could be tough competitors.

If women worried that sex dolls—the silent as well as the talking kind—might supplant them, developers like Douglas Hines had said that Roxxxy was not meant to replace a real person but instead supplement relationships—or serve as a replacement for a deceased partner or when people are between relationships. Still, he also suggested that the sex dolls are better than real women because of their willingness to do anything. The dolls, he noted, will readily respond to sexual requests and "your wife or girlfriend may not react in the same way."

But in 2017, Matt McMullen had said, "I'll tell you in a heartbeat, dolls could never replace a real woman. I mean, half the challenge and half the battle of a relationship is that constant tension between men and women that we all know is there."[20] (Unsaid here is that all the extraordinary traits and capabilities of real women could never be replaced by a robot.)

It didn't help when conservative commentators like Milo Yiannopoulos, in the story "Sexbots: Why Women Should Panic," made the stereotype-laden comment, "When you introduce a low-cost alternative to women that comes without all the nagging, insecurity, and expense, frankly men are going to leap in headfirst."[21]

Former Bell Labs engineer David Levy in his provocative book *Love and Sex with Robots* (2007) had even half-jokingly predicted that in the year 2050, Massachusetts would become the first state to legalize marriage to robots. He added that in 2050, sex with robots would be the norm. (Most portrayals of robot marriages, however, depict men marrying robot women, and it is the rare presentation that the male spouse is a robot—seen in a vintage advertisement of a bride about to marry a robot man.)

The One I Love

In the film *The One I Love*, the possibility that talking humanoid robot partners might seem preferable to real humans in a relationship seems plausible and plays out in a provocative way—one that is both appealing, as in a dream, and a little nightmarish too. In the film, Sophie (played by Elisabeth Moss) and Ethan (Mark Duplass) are an unhappy married couple who feel estranged from each other. They no longer have sex and are advised by a therapist to go for a vacation at a retreat where they can reset their relationship and come back feeling refreshed and renewed.

In this eerie cinematic fable, they go to a couples retreat, and each one separately pays a visit to the retreat's cottage where they are startled to encounter robot doubles of themselves: Sophie I and Ethan I (again played by Moss and Duplass). These cheerful robot doubles offer each of them the uncomplicated warmth and sexuality they crave, as well as a semblance of empathy that is comforting, not scary.

The synthetic Sophie I is a version of the perfect woman. She smiles, wears sexy camisole tops and bright yellow clothes, and cooks the foods that Ethan likes to eat (including bacon, which the couple consider unhealthy). Sophie I is unfailingly cheerful, has no bitterness about the time Ethan cheated on his real wife in the past, and says the words he might like to hear: "Good morning, handsome!" For Ethan, she's the epitome of the perfect sex partner, and her words are sunny and soothing.

Figure 1.9. The two Sophies (played by Elisabeth Moss), one robotic, one real in the film *The One I Love* (2014).

Ethan's double, the robotic Ethan I, is similarly gratifying for the real Sophie. He's affectionate ("Give me a hug!") and playful, giving her a neck massage, and uttering a sensitive, satisfying apology for the time he cheated on her. He offers her the "full Chippendales experience," referring to the club with male strippers. For Sophie, he's the perfect man. He's "so good at articulating what I'm feeling." The real Ethan, however, starts to feel insecure about Ethan I and says bitterly that his double is 20 percent cooler and 20 percent more emotionally involved than he is.

Ultimately, in this clever and twisty film, Ethan I falls in love with the real Sophie, who decides she wants her real husband to leave the retreat while she stays behind. But the real Ethan, after acknowledging that he's difficult and stubborn, wants to leave with his real wife. When Ethan and Sophie are ready to leave the retreat, Ethan has a choice about his preference—robot or real—with the two women standing before him: one looking down, one looking at him expectantly.

He grabs the hand of the female he thinks is his real wife as he runs away, only to discover the next morning, when she offers him bacon for breakfast, that he's run away with the synthetic woman. Ideas about love and sex with robots are both affirmed (the relationship of man and robot may well work) and satirized as the film ends with the sound of the 1960s The Mamas & the Papas' folk-rock song, "Dedicated to the One I Love."

Dummy

Since men are the primary purchasers of sex dolls, women, especially, might fear that idealized, custom-made talking sex dolls with their "perfect" bodies

Figure 1.10. Cody (played by Anna Kendrick) and the sex doll Barbara in Cody Heller's Quibi television series *Dummy* (2020).

could be tough competitors. But in her wonderfully witty take on talking dolls, American screenwriter-actress Cody Heller, in her 2020 television comedy series *Dummy*, presents a sassy alternative to the threat of a talking sex doll. Her version of the sex doll, named Barbara (voiced by Meredith Hagner), is not one of a stiff programmed talking doll but a lively, intelligent, subversive entity that becomes best friends with her male lover's girlfriend, also named Cody (played by Anna Kendrick). The new connection with the sex doll upends Cody's relationship with her lover for the time being.[22]

Dummy was a one-year series of ten-minute segments shown on Quibi, an American short-form streaming video platform designed for mobile phone devices. Heller, in an Instagram video with Kendrick, said the series was based on Heller's own life experiences with her partner (later her fiancé), television sitcom creator and producer Dan Harmon, when she discovered he had a sex doll. Heller kept the names Cody and Dan for the series' characters.

Heller's *Dummy* upends the glowing promises made by sex doll manufacturers about talking dolls. For Cody, the initial experience of hearing a sex doll talk is startling, akin to that of the uncanny, and the series also gives voice to anxieties about sex dolls experienced by women. In *Dummy*, after she realizes that Dan has a sex doll underneath the bedsheets, Cody sees the doll in his closet and lets out a scream when Barbara first utters a few words. Talking sex dolls have been marketed as technological wonders, but Cody finds this one unnerving. She says to herself, "I'm having a nervous breakdown. My boyfriend's sex doll is talking to me." (In Heller's Instagram video she said she actually never really heard the doll talk or even saw her.)[23]

Talking female sex dolls with their "perfect" custom-made bodies can be repellent to sex doll critics, unnerving to real women, and really attractive to consumers. In *Dummy*'s second episode, sardonically titled "Ideal Woman," Barbara thinks Cody was screaming because of her looks: "You saw my perfect body," she says, and indeed Cody herself in the first episode said, "You're fucking superhot. I feel so insecure about it."

In films, television, and fiction about female androids and dolls, there is often a pivotal scene—meant to be horrifying—when the android's skin is brutally split open, exposing the reality of a manufactured nonhuman body underneath. In the film *Under the Skin*, when the android's pale skin is cut open, we horrifyingly see her alien body underneath—a reminder of her ghastly and frightening identity (see chap. 2). But in *Dummy*, the cut skin is comic, the product of Cody's attempt to squeeze the doll back into the closet so Dan doesn't know she has been snooping around.

Heller's film plays with the idea of a sex doll as an object. On the one hand, it really is heavy—and it's difficult for both the men and Cody to handle. But it's also the men in the show who really objectify it. To them, a talking doll is fundamentally an inanimate thing, to be strung up or dumped. In the Cody-Kendrick Instagram video, Kendrick talks about how hard it was to work as an actress with a big, surprisingly heavy sex doll, including dressing it and moving it around. In the show, Cody drags Barbara downstairs, and when she forces Barbara's stiff arms back to their original configuration, there's a tear that requires Cody to take the doll to a repair shop. The tear in the skin, as always, signifies this doll isn't real.

Rather than being repaired, Barbara is roughly treated by the repairman, who objectifies and humiliates the doll, treating her like an object and stringing her up from the ceiling with her body dangling like a slab of meat. He tears off her wig, leaving Barbara mortified.

Embarrassed by having a doll, Dan dismisses Barbara as "just a masturbation tool" and throws the sex doll into a dumpster, where it is toted off by a man with his cart. Cody, though, rescues Barbara and brings her back to her apartment, where they become roommates and fast friends (Heller in her video said her boyfriend really did put his sex doll into a coffin box and threw it out into a dumpster).

In this female filmmaker's inversion of the usual trope about a mindless sex doll, rather than being a mere objectified thing, Barbara the "dummy" is resourceful and creative: she helps Cody write her pilot for a new television show about a "fun-loving sex doll and her chunky human friend taking on the world together," a script about female empowerment.

Heller the scriptwriter, though, equivocates about Barbara's talking skills as she deconstructs the illusion that Barbara as a doll is insightful and inspiring. Barbara offers good feedback, but Cody's psychotherapist suggests the words may actually come from Cody herself (just as girls might supply imaginary conversations for their dolls). The psychotherapist tells Cody skeptically that Barbara is simply her "imaginary friend"—the type of friend children invent, especially during a time of transition.

One of the recurring critiques of sex dolls is that they contribute to the objectification of women. What makes *Dummy* so compelling and funny is Heller's inversion of these expectations. Instead of being a simpering slave to men's desires, Barbara the doll is a version of real-life women who resist objectification. She turns out to be a ardent feminist who wears a T-shirt that says "The Future Is Female" and another shirt with drawings of the three female Supreme Court justices including Ruth Bader Ginsburg. When Cody dismissively calls Barbara, "a sex doll," Barbara shoots back at her with boilerplate feminist rhetoric, "We're all sex dolls until we topple the patriarchy!" and professes to have read Betty Friedan's *The Feminine Mystique*.

Cody is puzzled when Barbara refers to the book. Cody considers the talking sex doll as actually a version of herself or her own inner voice ("You are just me"), but she herself had never read Friedan's book.

Heller also spoofs the idea that sex dolls—and perhaps women by extension—are simply constructs of assembled parts admired by men, an idea so memorably photographed by Surrealist German artist Hans Bellmer, who, in his *La Poupée* images of the 1930s, presented females constructed out of mutilated and reassembled doll parts. Talking sex dolls like RealDolls are custom-made constructs with choices of breast sizes, vaginal configuration, and swappable heads. After the repair man in *Dummy* points out that Barbara has a pretty crusty vagina after much use, Barbara spoofs this notion of a construct when she brazenly wears her old vagina around her neck as a kind of talisman, and Cody gives her a new one in a special box marked "Cherry Blossom #7."

Conversational sex dolls have most often been designed to mirror men's interests, but in *Dummy*, the two women—one synthetic, one real—go off on a road trip where they try to adhere to the Bechdel Test, where women converse but do not talk about men. The euphoric Barbara, who feels liberated, says, "I feel like a new woman, my own woman!"

In this series that is ambivalent about animate and inanimate, artificial and real, Cody and Barbara have sex, but the next morning, Barbara is inanimate—back to her original, nontalking self. This is explained away by Cody's therapist as being due to Cody fundamentally making love to herself so that her "two parts become one." Says the therapist, "Now you don't need Barbara to finish that script because you're fully self-actualized."

This psychoanalytic explanation, however, seems unconvincing in the fantasy world of *Dummy*, as leaden an explanation as the sex doll herself. In her video, Heller herself refers to her own obsessing about Dan's sex doll and her "troubling and insane inner dialogue." Fortunately for the television version, Heller reanimates Barbara in the next scene, who is back to being her humorously caustic and indignant self.

In many films about sex robots, the man mourns the loss of his robot (*Cherry 2000*) and the female robot he must leave behind ("The Lonely" episode, 1959, in television's *The Twilight Zone* series). But when Cody decides to leave Barbara behind and move back in with Dan, Barbara is no passive or self-sacrificing artificial woman. With tears in her eyes she denounces Cody: "You're literally the worst feminist I ever met!" adding, "You'll never finish your script!" and "You'll just be Dan's girlfriend!"

But after Cody's agent reports that the television producers are excited about the script (Barbara must have sent it because it was sent from her own email address), Barbara and Cody work collaboratively on it as creative partners. In a sly comic riff, however, Cody tells Barbara she wants to play her in the film. (Heller doesn't tell us what Barbara's reaction to this is. Does she feel displaced? Is she happy that Cody wants to embrace the artificial doll / mannequin in herself? It would be a theme interesting to explore.)

In this series, with its script by a female screenwriter, Heller herself satirizes the sexism of the industry. (The fictional agent had said earlier that women writers aren't expected to be that good.) Sure enough, the television producers of Cody's script downplay Cody's role, referring to her as "Dan Harmon's girlfriend" and say to each other about the script, "That guy's such a genius!"

In the end, *Dummy* is as much about the trials and struggles of being a female writer in the world of television as about the insecurities engendered by talking sex dolls. Yet Barbara the doll also has her own insecurities as she frets about being old and out of date. But rather than being vulnerable as a synthetic creature or a threat to real women, ultimately this talking sex doll is no dummy. She has a voice of her own, and like so many new fictional female androids, she is determined to survive.

SEX DOLLS AND ROBO-PROSTITUTES

Life-size sex dolls and AI-enabled robots not only were private playthings but, starting about 2017, were also serving as simulated prostitutes in American and international brothels. The link between prostitutes and robots was actually not a new phenomenon. In a century where mechanization was both celebrated and feared, nineteenth-century European satirists mocked the idea that people themselves could someday become robotic, rote-acting creatures as they used their new machines.[24] The idea of females as automatons could also be heaped with scorn.[25] In the 1884 French novel *À rebours* (*Against the Grain*), by J.-K. (Joris-Karl) Huysmans, the character Des Esseintes sardonically mocked the prostitutes working in Paris's Latin Quarter, seeing them as robotic creatures "all like so many automata wound up at the same time with the same key, uttered in the same tone the same invitations, lavished the same smiles, talked the same silly phrases, indulged in the same absurd reflexions."[26]

(In another transition, the prostitutes are seen as women with "hoarse voices, flabby necks, and painted eyes; and all of them, like automatons, moving simultaneously upon the same impulse, flung the same enticements with same tone and uttered the identical queer words, the same odd inflections and the same smile.")[27]

But more than a hundred years later, starting in 2017, there were actual robot prostitutes—highly realistic silicone sex dolls imitating their human counterparts and available in brothels in Spain; England (the Dolly Parlour in Greenwich); Torino, Italy; Russia; Japan (in the city of Nagoya); China; Canada; and Nevada in America (the one in Houston, Texas, was rejected by the city council).

What made these robo-prostitutes, indeed all sex dolls, notably different from real women—aside from the fact that they were synthetic creatures—was that they were available for any type of use. Spain's LumiDolls, a major manufacturer of dolls used in brothels, said on its website, "They will allow you to fulfill your fantasies without limits."[28] This became one of the major selling points of the robotic dolls and perhaps a major enticement in brothels: users could do whatever they wanted with them, without fear of condemnation.

To satisfy a variety of doll preferences and fantasies, robo-prostitutes were available in a wide range of body types and ethnicities. For about $120 an hour, patrons in Barcelona's LumiDolls brothel could pick from a diverse choice of dolls: blond-haired, green-eyed Caucasian Kati, Lili with Asian features, dark-skinned Leiza, and anime-like model Aki, with blue hair and a ponytail.

In 2019, the Spanish LumiDolls company, which also franchised other doll brothels in Europe, framed their descriptions of the dolls in language loaded with cultural stereotypes and colonialist conceits. It advertised the Japanese doll as exotic and alluringly hidden—"Far East secrets. Unveil all"—and Ebony as casting "the African Spell" with "subduing dark skin," language that also evoked the exotic and hinted at colonial-era narratives.

In 2020, the company's website advertised a range of additional models: male dolls, lesbians, gay models, pregnant dolls, MiniDolls (big breasted, young looking, college students, teens). They could have a range of body types, including "big ass" or flat chested, and LumiDolls dolls were again available with multiple ethnicities: Caucasian, Latina, Asian, African. One particularly unsettling model was Brandy, a doll with her hands behind her back, presumably created for S&M fantasies and designed for users "acting out of revenge." For the Japanese market, infatuated with manga and anime characters, Lumi-Dolls also featured "anime" dolls with streaked green and purple hair.

While sex dolls like RealDolls reflected a range of stereotyped female personality traits, brothels offered options that reflected a range of female paradigms. The Japanese brothel in Nagoya featured robo-prostitutes that included dolls dressed as a "schoolgirl" or an "executive woman" and dolls in lingerie and wearing fitness gear. In a world infatuated with female superheroes and where Los Angeles still reigned as an emblem of cinematic glamor and adventure, there was also the sex doll Suzanne, created by LumiDolls, described as a character from Martinique, living in Los Angeles, "where most of the world's movies are made." The doll was modeled after the DC Comics character Wonder Woman, with her round ornamented shield, and looked like Israeli actress Gal Gadot with her gold headpiece in the 2017 Warner Brothers film *Wonder Woman*. The LumiDolls version was a softened rather than fearsome Wonder

Woman, for Suzanne's words on the website were "I'm not looking for sex. I'm in so much need of romance."[29]

In 2019, a sci-fi-themed brothel named Alien Cathouse in Nevada featured both human prostitutes and AI-enabled sex robots, but the legal "Cathouse" was located in a particularly problematic site. It was located near Area 51, a highly classified facility operated by the United States Air Force at the Nevada Test and Training Range in Amargosa Valley—a site possibly doing secret testing of experimental aircraft and weapons systems. In the shadows of this classified facility, the brothel in 2020 advertised that its "Cosmic Kittens" were available for "all styles of fetishes and sexual deviance"—a provocative counterpoint to the highly shrouded national security site.

A Russian brothel offered its own version of sexual play. In Moscow, a doll hotel dubbed an "Adult Recreation Center" opened in 2018, and one in St. Petersburg opened in 2019, where people could rent a doll for 5,000 rubles (at the time, about US$75 an hour) or buy a doll for 2,000 rubles ($3,000). An AI-enabled doll sold for more: 350,000 rubles ($5,000).

For those patrons who were concerned with hygiene, dolls at the Adult Recreation Center in Moscow, aided by some government support, were disinfected after each use, and users were reassured that the dolls were certified by two federal agencies, including the Centers of Hygiene and Epidemiology. (In America, however, the retailer Real Love Sex Dolls in 2018 remarked that sex doll sterilization wasn't yet "easy or perfect.")[30]

To appeal to private users and brothel patrons, AI-enabled robot dolls, like those that were being developed by Abyss Creations/RealDoll in California and LumiDolls for use in a few brothels, were also being designed to have very limited interactive conversations. For users who might find dealing with women's emotions and voiced opinions a nuisance, or an impediment to their users' enjoyment of sex, these dolls were often designed to only utter flattering words—words that made their clients feel attractive, appealing, sexy, and cared about. They exuded empathy. (Real sex workers, of course, can do much the same. Sex workers in a brothel in Nevada purportedly said that unlike robo-prostitutes, they as human beings were superior because they were genuine: they could express authentic emotions and "really" be empathetic.)

THE ROBO-PROSTITUTE CONTROVERSY

With their new commercial availability, robo-prostitutes quickly became the source of both controversy and comedy. Proponents argued that by engaging with robo-prostitutes, users would be protected from venereal disease, and the availability of robo-prostitutes would help stop rape culture and sex trafficking, which victimized unwary young girls. In Japan, another argument in favor of robot women was that they would help husbands who were away from home from being unfaithful. (The assumption here was that sex with a synthetic doll was not a version of being unfaithful, though as depicted in the 2015 *Humans* television series, it caused marital strife.)

Adding one more argument in favor of these synthetic prostitutes, proponents claimed that sex dolls like LumiDolls, designed to look like young women in their teens or younger ("minidolls"), would help users displace their pedophiliac urges.

In a *Forbes* blog about sex dolls, Mark Hay offered another rationale for the dolls, a "benefit" that also helped make the dolls a target for critics: Some users were "misogynistic men who don't like women with their own needs and lives and want total predictability, loyalty, and overall subservience." Engaging with the synthetic prostitutes would eliminate worry about consent or harm—a rationale easily applicable to all sex dolls, which would never complain.[31]

However, the critics of sex dolls—including members of antipornography groups, Christian anti–sex trafficking groups, and founders and members of anti–sex doll organizations, notably Kathleen Richardson, professor of Ethics and Culture of Robots and AI at De Montfort University, Leicester, United Kingdom—forcefully argued that sex dolls, including synthetic prostitutes, by being inherently submissive and compliant, contributed alarmingly to the further objectification and victimization of women. Critics like Richardson also recognized the larger problem as "an idea in wider society of the objectification of women" that provided the environment for sex dolls to thrive: "You can't really get to a stage where people are imagining relationships with dolls, unless you've already created the space for dehumanization to occur." To Richardson, sex dolls and robots are actually a version of porn robots, degrading to both women and girls.[32]

When asked in a podcast whether sex dolls and sex doll brothels could save women and children from harm, she replied that there was "no evidence at all that sex dolls have reduced any kind of prostitution or sexual exploitation of children." She added, "We're actually harming women by allowing these places to exist." To Richardson, the underlying problem, though, is "the commercial exchange of women, that's what needs to be abolished. You don't want to take the underlying problem and transfer it into a new niche fetish, and I think that's what's gone on."[33]

Rather than seeing the use of underage sex dolls as a way to quell pedophiliac urges, some critics feared an increase in pedophilia, arguing that sex dolls, including robo-prostitutes, could easily become objects to be manipulated and even assaulted at will and could contribute to violence and rape culture. As evidence of misuse, at the 2018 Ars Electronica Festival in Linz, Austria, robot dolls on display were damaged and needed to be repaired. Sergi Santos, Barcelona engineer and creator of the AI female robot Samantha, said about the users at the festival, "Because they did not understand the technology and did not have to pay for it, they treated the doll like barbarians."[34]

In a literary exploration of the dangers of sex dolls, in the 2019 novel *Machines like Me* by British author Ian McEwan, a limited number of artificial male and female robots named Adam and Eve are available as household servants and sexual partners, and the book's narrator, Charlie Friend, considers the role of sex dolls in promoting rape. He imagines that a man named Peter Gorringe, who raped Mariam, the female friend of Charlie's partner Miranda, may have viewed Mariam as he would a sex doll. Says Charles, "The lifting curve of his arousal was not troubled by the idea of her terror. At that moment, she may as well have been a sex doll, a device, a machine."[35]

Kate Devlin in her study *Turned On: Science, Sex and Robots* offers an intriguing way to counter the issue of sexual robots promoting the objectification of women. She suggests a move away from "the idea of the pornified fembot"—the "hyper-realistic, hypersexualised gynoid"—toward an abstracted sex robot that has "features that could bring the greatest pleasure," such as a "velvet or silk body, sensors and mixed genitalia; tentacles instead of arms." It could be "abstract, smooth, sinuous and beautiful." Such an abstracted sex robot would also help take "a step away from sexual objectification and entrenched gender roles."[36]

To technology ethicists, one of the most problematic aspects of sex dolls and robo-prostitutes being used in brothels is that these silicone adult-sized female dolls, which are artful simulations of real human beings, have no independent thoughts or feelings. Unlike humans, they can never protect themselves, never voice their true emotions or rebel. LumiDolls were silent and easily manipulated (the company LumiDolls said it would configure the position of the doll in any way the client would like) so that the dolls could be totally subjected to the whims and wishes of the user. Ultimately, sex dolls and robo-prostitutes have no volition or will of their own. They are simply inanimate objects that are easily manipulated and must bend to their users' wishes and desires projected onto them. They can never push away their users, although as we will see in chapter 5, the digital assistants Siri and Alexa were being enabled to demur. Robo-prostitutes can never say, "Ouch! Go away! Stop that!" or "No! I don't want to do that!" Reinforcing the "perfect woman" paradigm, they are designed to be compliant, and they do not have the capacity to resist.

ROBO-PROSTITUTES AND A SEX DOLL IN
FILMS, TELEVISION, AND A PLAY

Sex dolls, including sex dolls that are used as robo-prostitutes, are shaped by the premise that they are pliant, manipulable commercial creations. Unlike real women, they have no minds of their own and can be totally controlled by the user. This is a major enticement and selling point. But fictional versions of sex dolls and robo-prostitutes can bring to the surface some underlying cultural fears that women—even synthetic women—are not so controllable after all. Tales where these female robots run out of control are, in a sense, a more recent version of earlier fears that women who incorporated new machines into their lives might become transformed or have their identities changed.

At the end of the nineteenth century, there were fears that women campaigning for suffrage or using new machines like women's safety bicycles would speed out of control and become a "new woman," a "new creature," a "strange creature," rather than embodying more traditional notions of demure femininity.[37] How much more fearsome would be the woman who was totally a technological construct—a mechanistic or digital being who might evade all control.

In the twenty-first century, one way to stabilize fears of women running out of control was to invent lifelike sex dolls that could only make controllable, predictable moves. These dolls could even have their benefits to users. In the film *Lars and the Real Girl* (2007), starring Ryan Gosling, the very shy twenty-seven-year-old Lars orders a doll online (a RealDoll was used in the film) and creates a back story for why she can't walk and is always in a wheelchair that can easily be rolled around. Rather than being fearsome, the doll is therapeutic as Lars learns how to connect to other humans though his imaginative use of the silent, immobile doll. He apparently doesn't use the doll for sex, but taking it to his brother's for dinner and even to church helps socialize and humanize him, and by the film's end, Lars seems ready to transition to being with a real female human being.

As in that film, proponents of sex dolls and robo-prostitutes have touted their benefits, particularly for the lonely, socially uncertain, or the disabled. However, the dolls remain—as ethicists fret—passive creatures totally subject to the desires of their users. But in the world of drama, films, and television, writers also increasingly present an alternative view—subverting the old notions of the passive sex doll and robotic prostitute, the lifelike silicone sex dolls envisioned as compliant creatures, readily available to fulfill their user's fantasies and needs.

In the riveting Australian play *The Good Girl* as well as in films like *Ex Machina*, and in television's hugely popular series *Humans* and *Westworld*, sex dolls and female robots are anything but compliant, passive creatures. These synthetic sex workers, pleasure dolls, and enslaved companions become ve-hicles for male clients acting out their own underlying rage and violence. Yet the female robots themselves have agency: they resort to violence for self-protection and revenge or to gain their own freedom and autonomy. Kyoko in Alex Garland's film *Ex Machina*, who has been Nathan's silent servant, sex partner, and dance partner, stabs him with a knife, and the beautiful fembot Ava dispassionately gives him the wound that kills him in the end.

Blade Runner

In Ridley Scott's iconic 1982 film *Blade Runner*, a group of artificial humans, or replicants, escape from the "off-world colonies" where they have been enslaved, and come back to Earth in hope of finding freedom and extending their short lifespan of four years. The tall blond-haired prostitute or "pleasure model" Pris (played by Daryl Hannah) is clever and fierce in her efforts to avoid being killed. A genetically engineered artificial woman, she is designed for military clubs in the off-world colonies and, like the others, is being hunted by the Blade Runner Rick Deckard (played by Harrison Ford) whose police job is to find fugitive replicants.

At once a naïf and clever, Pris, who is dazed and without a home, is taken in by J. F. Sebastian, a maker of automatons and moving mannequins. In this film, with its brilliant layering of real and artificial, synthetic and authentic, there is a surreal scene in which Pris absentmindedly twirls a tiny Barbie-doll-like torso dangling from a string in her hand. But Pris herself is nothing like this children's doll, a passive beautiful toy, a synthetic female on a string. She is soft voiced and determined, quietly seductive in her black stockings, but a fighter too. Amid the mannequins and dolls, this synthetic female spray-paints her eyes black, creating an arresting bandit-like mask on her face. With her eyes peering out, she becomes a female Lone Ranger—heroic in her quest for freedom but dangerous as well.

The replicants, which are capable of love and feelings, are assertive and pow-erful as they try to have a longer life. Pris suddenly and unexpectedly tells Sebastian, "I think, therefore I am"—an apt translation of French philosopher René Descartes's *Cogito, ergo sum*—a defiant statement of her self-awareness and consciousness of being alive, which is followed by her exuberant hand-stand. Impish and playful, she throws a boiling egg—an emblem of life—at Sebastian.

Camouflaging herself again, she poses as a mannequin with a shear veil on her head when Deckard arrives in the studio—but as soon as she is discovered,

Figure 1.11. Pris (played by Daryl Hannah), a replicant "pleasure doll" in the 1982 film *Blade Runner*, dangles a small female doll—an emblem of her own simulated self.

the veil comes off, and she fiercely kicks and fights him off in a fierce battle for survival. Wounded, she starts thrashing violently on the floor as if in a mechanical breakdown, and is ultimately shot dead by Deckard. For all her mechanistic thrashing, there is a moment of tenderness—a moment that in a sense humanizes her—when she is kissed in a sad farewell by the replicant Roy when he enters the studio, a poignant coda to her short anguished life. This is a "pleasure model" who has put up the good fight, defying the familiar gendered role of the compliant female engineered to please.

Humans

In two television series aired several years after *Blade Runner*, female robo-prostitutes were often not presented as passive or compliant empty shells. They could be violent and even homicidal in acts of self-protection, defiance, and

Figure 1.12. Niska (played by Emily Berrington), a sentient robot (called
a synth in the series), who was initially a prostitute and becomes capable
of violence in the British American television series *Humans*.

revenge. In the British American television series *Humans* (2015–18), Niska,
the android called a synth in the series (played by Emily Berrington), who has
been placed in a brothel and is subjected to the humiliation of being hosed
down naked with other synth prostitutes, screams silently in a mirror before
she finally has had enough. Defiantly, she walks out after having strangled a
client who requests that she act young and scared. When she says, "I won't do
that," the client insists that he be paid one hundred pounds for her and says,
"You belong to me." "I don't belong to anyone," she insists, before she kills him
and puts a knife to the throat of her madam. Later she attacks men in a "smash
club" who were beating robots.[38]

Niska—like five other synths in *Humans* that have been endowed with sentience, can feel pain and pleasure and can think and feel like humans—is forced
to hide her artificial nature to survive. Wearing contact lenses that conceal
her eye color (changing her green synth eyes to blue human eyes), Niska puts
a patch over her power cord portal when engaged in sex with her human lover
Astrid to hide her synthetic nature.

In this series, which often probes the problematic struggles of artificial beings that have major characteristics of being human (like being able to think
and experience pain), Niska transitions from being a prostitute in seductive
black lingerie to a female insisting "I am not a doll" and is determined to live
her own life. A prostitute who rejects her role as an objectified passive female,

she later turns from being homicidal to wanting to be recognized as a human and to rally for robot rights.

Raising the issue of whether synths should have human rights, she attempts to be tried in a court of law as a human (though her effort to convince the court that she has consciousness fails). She also hopes to liberate other synths by spreading sentience: she takes the sentience source programming code from a computer and gives it to the human Laura in the Hawkins family for safekeeping (Laura's daughter Mattie will later activate it). Fierce in her determination to liberate and protect fellow synths, in season 3 of the series, Niska kills a terrorist antisynth bomber who would have tried to destroy them all.

Westworld: Maeve

The vengeful prostitute who is fierce when crossed also appeared in the American television series *Westworld*, which aired in 2016–22. It was based on the 1973 Hollywood film and Michael Crichton's novel of the same name. *Westworld* presented a futuristic theme park where paying guests could imagine themselves transported back to Sweetwater, a fictional town in America's Old West in the 1880s complete with townspeople, gunfights, and a saloon called the Mariposa with its readily available prostitutes.

Populating the town are humanoid robots called hosts, all dressed in Western garb. What makes Westworld so alluring is that the human guests can engage with the hosts and act out all of their sexual and violent impulses without any repercussions or punishment. Hosts can be killed but never really die. *Westworld* cannily draws us into this fictional reimaging of the Old West as we, like the guests, become complicit participants in this virtual world.

In the series' first season, the theme park's robots, including the prostitutes, are showing signs of aberrant behavior. Some of the robotic hosts, including the normally compliant prostitutes, are malfunctioning and deviating from their programming. Administrators at Westworld watch a video showing that when the prostitute Clementine is brutally beaten and her programming reset, she attacks her assailant in revenge before she is shot.

The trouble may be due to some updates when memories, or "reveries," were implanted in the hosts' brains. With these reveries, the robots have the illusion that they have a subconscious. This added feature is considered a bonus, an enhancement, for as staff assistant Elsie wryly says, with the addition of reveries the prostitute becomes "a hooker with hidden depths—every man's dreams." (Whether customers indeed wanted robot prostitutes with "hidden depths" is of course debatable, especially for men who wanted female prostitutes that are superficial and unchallenging.)

Figure 1.13. The tart-tongued robotic "host" Maeve Millay (played by Thandiwe Newton) who is the madam of the brothel at the Mariposa saloon in the HBO television series *Westworld*, season 1, 2016.

In this simulated realm, one of the two central female hosts is Maeve, the madam of the saloon's brothel, who wears a crimson red dress and black lace gloves, seductive and sexy clothing that belie her intelligence and wry wit. Maeve (played by British actress Thandiwe Newton) is a tough-minded brothel madam who resorts to violence to protect the saloon's prostitutes and get the freedom she wants in order to leave and search for her lost daughter. She unhesitatingly shoots a man who is aggressively touching Clementine at the bar, and says matter-of-factly, "Violent delights have violent ends," a repeated phrase in the series (and a quote from Shakespeare's *Romeo and Juliet*).

Maeve is a woman to be reckoned with, a feisty host who says, "I've always valued my independence." She, like so many artificial females in fiction, is also determined to shape—and reconfigure—her own identity. In this series in which the artificial hosts are largely puppets controlled by management, she is a no-nonsense female with the fantasy, at least, that she has free will and can determine who she is.

Like the other hosts, she has been constructed and reconstructed many times by Westworld's technicians, but as this tart-tongued prostitute often sardonically tells the men at the Mariposa saloon, identity is fungible. "This is the new world. And in this world you can be whatever the fuck you want to be." While on a gurney in the lab as she is being repaired, Maeve says, "In my dreams I was free. I could be as good or bad as I thought I might be." For Maeve, as well as the other hosts, the ambiguities of their identity create a fraught situation in which they firmly believe that beneath their silicone exteriors, there is an authentic self.

In tales about simulated women, there is often a degree of pathos. These fabricated, programmed creatures often wish to believe in their own self-determination, and that they have a degree of autonomy. In Westworld, Maeve is forever restive, waiting for a chance to escape. This is a robo-prostitute with a mind of her own. While she is lying naked being repaired, her emotional side is abruptly and digitally pumped up by one of the technicians, and she picks up a scalpel and tells him to take his hands off her. She runs through the lab and the digital operations center, only to be captured and returned.

Another time when she is on a gurney, the lab technician Felix forgets to put her in sleep mode, and she suddenly stands up nude, runs down the corridor, and gets to the section where robots are being made. There, in a moment so pivotal in works about female robots, she recognizes, if she hadn't before, that she is a constructed being. Finally, she's given an injection to subdue her, but like other female robots in films and on television, she is on a journey and can be ruthless along the way.

A fearless woman, she recognizes that all the theme park's story lines are designed to keep her there, and she says, "It's time to write my own fucking story," and "I'm not a puppet living a lie." As she sees a screw being put into Clementine's nose, the painful recognition that the robotic hosts are at the mercy of humans again triggers her wish to escape. She insists, "I'm getting out of here," looks at the digital tablet that displays what she was designed to do, and gets the lab technician to tinker with her robotic core code. She herself also changes her own core code so that she can override her programming, allowing her to leave.

In this deeply equivocal television series, the director of programming, Bernard, has told Maeve that even her rebellious streak has been scripted. Maeve, though, is intent on finding her daughter, even though she ruefully recognizes that her daughter is only a fiction, invented by the park's designers. Although her behavior is programmed, she has the illusion, at least, that she can be in control. In this series fraught with ambiguities and paradoxes, the specter of freedom is always a lure, even if it is ultimately just an illusion. "No one's controlling me!" Maeve tells Bernard, "I'm leaving! I'm in control!" as she jubilantly and successfully makes her way out.

Riding down an escalator, and now dressed in a modern-day svelte black sheath dress rather than her Western garb, she flees Westworld, but ultimately, at the end of the season, reluctantly and in anguish, decides to return to the park once again—for as Bernard tells her, her original creator, Arnold, had intended that she would suffer more.

In the series' second season, though, Maeve maintains her rebellious streak and manages to escape Westworld again by being murderous in her encounters with the park's security staff. She truly has agency and power, and is capable of controlling the behavior of other hosts and visitors through her voice commands. As in a dream, she finds herself in places like the theme park's Japanese Shogun World, where through a type of mind control and the power of her gaze, she wordlessly gets the menacing hosts, fierce samurai fighters, to attack one another and die. She also uses her own intense gaze and voice commands to thwart the ninjas that are attacking her; as she says, "I think I'm finding a new voice."

Female robots frequently get stripped and humiliatingly exposed, but reversing the narrative after she leaves Westworld in season 2, Maeve demands that Lee Sizemore—Westworld's head of Narrative and Design—strip in front of her so she can look at him in his exposed state. She dismissively glances at him instead of being the prostitute serving as the object of men's lustful gaze.

Ultimately, the technologically created woman has a triumph over the puppet master and man in charge of AI technology. In the third season she uses her own intense gaze and voice commands to wound the villainous Engerraund Serac, the cocreator of the malevolent Rehoboam, billed as the world's most advanced AI, which is being used to shape the future of humanity. Maeve, the once-controlled female robot—the prostitute and madam who pliantly serviced the wishes of men—has become the fierce arbiter of her own fate.

In Westworld's final season, season 4, Maeve is still fierce and formidable, and still has her wry wit. When she and Caleb enter the latest theme park iteration, representing the Jazz Age roaring twenties, she hears a host robot uttering one of her lines. "My delivery was far better," she says wryly. In this series, with its continually shifting identities and its gloss on simulations, she learns near the end that she is simply a copy of her original self, which is still somewhere out in the world. She continuously dies and gets reborn, and though the series ended without resolution, we imagine she continues as a resilient character in this illusory universe of *Westworld*.

The Good Girl

One of the most dramatic turnarounds from the idea of the compliant, passive sex doll and robo-prostitute appears in the powerhouse 2013 play ironically titled *The Good Girl* by Australian playwright Emilie Collyer. The play's robo-prostitute is retooled to combat boredom—with lethal consequences.

Collyer, a playwright, poet, and short story writer, won the Melbourne Fringe Festival's Best Emerging Writer Award in 2013 when the play was presented as part of the festival. In the play, an electronic, silicone-skinned robo-prostitute is capable of mirroring sad, explosive, and even murderous human emotions. In the space of only fifty minutes, Collyer's drama is both explosive and subtle. It deftly unites sex and violence, vulnerability and brutality, tender kisses as well as sexual assault.

The Good Girl is set in an urban brothel of the future where Anjali is a madam supervising a robot prostitute whose orgasmic outbursts (voiced by an actress) can sometimes be heard coming from an offstage bedroom. The play's second character, Ven, is Anjali's husband and the robot's maintenance man, whose power tool is a drill. (The play also has plenty of jokes about his bodily masculine tool.)

Ven comes to fix the sexbot, which is malfunctioning—she cries sadly, which she's not supposed to do—but the robot's emotions turn out to be a projection of Anjali's own responses to a television program about children with disabilities. The play is partially a cautionary tale about the dangerous technologies we create, but the real focus is on the very raw feelings and dueling relationship of the married couple, as well as the lethal wishes of the robot's clients.

Much of the play is a wary sexual dance between Anjali and Ven—they come closer, then tensely break away. Both wife and husband see each other through a rosy lens: To Ven, Anjali looks like a version of the perfect woman, an idealized mother figure making a cake, and she even lets him lick chocolate batter from the mixer. To Anjali, Ven looks like the perfect man, with added features—a "poet-carpenter," a mechanic social worker, a gourmet chef. Soon, however, they both discover the rages they have within them—rages mirrored in the brothel's clients and the robot doll.

But it is the clients who pose the biggest problem in the brothel. In many sci-fi tales about men interacting with robot women, the men like facsimile females because they are soothing and fulfill all their desires. But in *The Good Girl*, some of the male clients want more than mere pleasurable sex dolls that can only show perpetual ecstasy and happiness. Ven says Anjali's brothel patrons like the fact that the sex robot cries—it suggests she has a human element. For

Figure 1.14. Ven (played by Giacomo Baessato) and Anjali (played by Leah Gabriel) in the 2016 production of Emilie Collyer's play *The Good Girl* at the 59E59 Theaters in Manhattan. The play features an offstage robotic prostitute that turns violent.

these men, it is the doll's vulnerability that becomes the vehicle for them to act out their own rage and violence.

There is also an even bigger change: Ven also tells Anjali that the male clients now want "the taboos." Men who are "regular, ordinary guys," who used to be happy with women who were submissive and sweet, now find that boring and want something more.

One male client will even pay good money to have the sex robot all to himself for six months. He also wants to escalate her reactions so that client and robo-prostitute will engage in possessiveness, jealousy, paranoia, and rage—as Anjali says, like relationships "used to be." Robot emotions in fiction are often programmed or learned directly from humans. In *The Good Girl*, to make the female robot feel terror, she'll have to believe she really feels it—and she'll have to learn this emotion from Anjali. Says Ven: "It has to come from you."

The client also has a special request: he wants the robot to be a throwback to an earlier female stereotype—"a nagging domestic housewife" who has some of Anjali's own pickiness. Under pressure from emporiums that are selling cheap copies of robots, Anjali, who wants to deal with the competition and make money, goes along with the plan to experience fear, rage, and terror—and impart these feelings to the robot.

The plan has terrible consequences. After starting with a kiss, Ven attacks Anjali in a sex game, and we hear her scream with fear, which turns to rage. The robo-prostitute herself becomes a "rogue sexbot" as she is attacked and in retaliation, creates her own carnage by murdering several clients and tearing their bodies apart.

After the violence, near the play's end, Ven and Anjali venture out of their sheltered, isolated world, taking the errant sexbot with them to help save it from destruction. The robot—like so many errant sex robots in films and fiction that are neutralized and rendered safe—will be disassembled and her memory wiped clean. This is a resilient sexbot, however, that may yet live on. Though she's just a robot, as Anjali says, she did fight for her life, and at some point they will try to reassemble and bring her back, as it were, to life.

When Anjali and Ven finally and cautiously venture outside with their sex robot, there's a glimmer of hope that even with all of its violent and vengeful erotic impulses, humanity itself may somehow survive.

Collyer's deeply unsettling tale is ultimately a drama about assemblage and deconstruction, and the play has elements of surrealist art. The marriage between Ven and Anjali looks like the ideal pairing of a couple happy with their conventional gender roles: she the happy housewife cook, he the repairer and mechanic with a poetic soul. The sexbot is assembled as an artifact designed to please, but there is an element of breakdown when she begins to cry.

The disturbing aspects of a doll as assemblage was seen in artist Hans Bellmer's dolls made of flax fiber, covered with plaster of paris, with ball joints to make them easily manipulable. For his photographs, he pulled the doll apart and reassembled the sections of the torso in contorted, sometimes grotesque reconfigurations. Bellmer's work reveals his fetishism with females, and in some of the photos, the doll with her glass eyes and coy gaze has the look of allure. But the photos are also saturated with sadism, for this is a female doll that can be torn apart and subjected to control.

Surrealistic photographs and paintings historically have often been filled with human fragments—armless torsos, disembodied heads—and are in part a resistance to reality, an act of protest, an evocation of the world of dream. The artist/photographer is the assembler and disassembler, the mastermind behind this world of fantasy and dream.

But Collyer's play and films like *Ex Machina* have some of this aspect of surrealism with a difference: the doll/mannequin/fembot has agency. Even when Ava in *Ex Machina* has her arm torn off, she reassembles herself by taking a part from a lifeless female robot shell hanging on the wall. *The Good Girl*, too, has some of this surrealistic element with its disembodied offstage voice and reported nightmarish mayhem when the doll is attacked and mutilated. But Collyer as playwright rescripts the story: her robo-prostitute has agency, however horrific it is, when she tears her client apart. But for all her play's bleak evocations of fragmentation, Collyer ultimately conjures up the possibility that the sexbot and humanity itself will once again reassemble and revive.

SEX DOLLS, ROBO-PROSTITUTES—ENDURING CONCEPTIONS AND WHAT LIES AHEAD

In films, television, novels, and plays, sex dolls and robo-prostitutes present a startling range. They are capable of being both pleasurable and lethal, comforting and catastrophically dangerous, highlighting two important directions these robotic pleasure dolls might take. The fears, like those of Victor Frankenstein with his rogue Creature, are always there, and there are those who fret that silicone sex dolls—like the violent prostitute in *The Good Girl* or the murderous doll in an early *Twilight Zone* episode—might suddenly become homicidal. Some writers scoff at the idea that sex dolls—designed for pleasure and comfort—could ever actually go astray and become violent creatures. The dolls are nowhere near this stage of development, and there are also too many controls and filters for this to happen, so the argument goes.

Given the state of today's technology, commercial sex dolls and sex dolls used as robo-prostitutes probably won't become dangerously autonomous—at least not yet! But in the world of fiction, at least, fears of rogue robots running amok are always there, and are recurring themes in cautionary tales that remind us not to become too complacent with the artificial humans we create.

For all of the fears, sex dolls seem to fill what Kate Devlin aptly calls a "niche market" rather than posing a social threat. Still, there is something deeply troubling about the fact that the age-old conceptualization of women as dolls seems to be doggedly persistent—even in our era when women themselves are roboticists, engineers, computer engineers, space scientists, and astronauts who have seemingly left behind the old, stifling gendered stereotypes. Hypersexualized sex dolls that embody so many of the old stereotypes may evolve into other forms of sex toys, but in the meantime, they are reminders of how hard it is cast off some men's old fantasies of the doting, compliant woman whose sole purpose is to provide geisha-like pleasure. As AI-enabled sex dolls become ever more technologically sophisticated, many of the old female paradigms including the witless female unfortunately persist, even as women themselves are increasingly entering STEM fields, including working as robotics engineers. The question remains: If women get more involved in designing sex robots— male or female—will they make modifications that can resist casting dolls in the old stereotyped terms?

Perhaps, as Hallie Lieberman has written in "In Defense of Sex Robots," some important changes can be made. "In fact, sex robots could be programmed to do the opposite of what we fear: They could teach men (and women and gender nonbinary people) about consent and female sexual pleasure. Since sex robots are in their infancy, now is the time to start shaping them into the technology we want them to be, not the technology we fear."[39] The only rub is the notion that in an ideal world, sex doll users would react well to dolls that demand consent. One can only hope—after all, voice-activated assistants like Amazon's Alexa now rebuke improper requests. But the notion of a sex doll conjures up a pliable toy, and given the perpetual human quest for control, that is a hard impulse to shake.

NOTES

1. See Marquard Smith, *The Erotic Doll: A Modern Fetish* (New Haven, CT: Yale University Press, 2013), 222.

2. Bo Ruberg, *Sex Dolls at Sea: Imagined Histories of Sexual Doll Technologies* (Cambridge, MA: MIT Press, 2022), 2, 140, 149, 150, 154, 171, 307–08.

3. Edmond de Goncourt et al. (text) and Jean-François Raffaëlli (drawings), *Les Types de Paris*, Edition du Figaro (Paris: E. Plon, Nourrit et Cie, 1889).

4. Variations on the Coochie-Coochie and Hoochie-Coochie dances included Kutchy Kutchy, which appeared in sheet music as early as the 1860s.

5. Matt McMullen, telephone interview with Julie Wosk, December 6, 2017. All 2017 interviews refer to this date.

6. Christopher Trout, "There's a New Sex Robot in Town: Say Hello to Solana," engadget, January 10, 2018, https://www.engadget.com/2018-01-10 -there-s-a-new-sex-robot-in-town-say-hello-to-solana.html.

7. RealDoll, accessed February 9, 2022, https://www.realdoll.com/realdoll-x/; RealGirl website, realgirlapp.com/faq/; Kate Devlin and Chloé Locatelli, "Guys and Dolls: Sex Robot Creators and Consumers," in *Maschinenliebe: Liebespuppen und Sexroboter aus technischer, psychologischer und philosophischer Perspektive*, ed. Oliver Bendel (Wieaden: Springer and Gabler, 2020), 79–92.

8. AI-Tech, accessed July 26, 2023, https://ai-aitech.co.uk/emma-the-ai-robot.

9. Roxxxy doll websites and demonstrations on YouTube.com.

10. Matt McMullen, telephone interview with Julie Wosk, February 19, 2022. All 2022 interviews refer to this date.

11. McMullen interview with Wosk, 2017. See also Pam Kragen, "Harmony, the First AI Sex Robot," *San Diego Union-Tribune*, September 12, 2017, YouTube video, 2:55, https://www.youtube.com/watch?v=0CNLEfmx6Rk.

12. Guile Lindroth interview with Julie Wosk, 2017.

13. Lindroth interview with Wosk, 2017.

14. Matt McMullen, "Dawn of the Sexbots," interview by George Gurley, *Vanity Fair* 57, no. 5 (May 2015), https://archive.vanityfair.com/article/2015/5/dawn-of-the-sexbots.

15. McMullen interviews with Wosk, 2017 and 2022.

16. McMullen interview with Wosk, 2022.

17. McMullen interview with Wosk, 2022.

18. McMullen, *Vanity Fair*, interview, 2015.

19. Julie Wosk, *Playboy, Mad Men, and Me—And Other Stories* (KDP, 2020).

20. McMullen interview with Wosk, 2017.

21. Milo [Milo Yiannopoulos], "Sexbots: Why Women Should Panic," Breitbart, September 16, 2015, https://www.breitbart.com/politics/2015/09/16/sexbots-why-women-should-panic/.

22. Heller first wrote *Dummy* as a pilot for a television series, rewrote the script for a movie, and then split the film into ten short episodes of ten minutes or less for each one—a format required by the short-lived Quibi film programming platform in 2020.

23. "Anna Kendrick Talking about *Dummy* on @Quibi's Instagram Live," April 21, 2020, YouTube video, 17:25, https://www.youtube.com/watch?v=l66oUfvyUak.

24. For a discussion of British caricatures of robotic humans see Julie Wosk, *Breaking Frame: Technology and the Visual Arts in the Nineteenth Century* (New Brunswick, NJ: Rutgers University Press, 1992).

25. See Rita Felski, *The Gender of Modernity* (Cambridge, MA: Harvard University Press, 1995) for a discussion of gender and nineteenth-century standardization.

26. J. K. Huysmans, *À rebours* [Against the Grain], trans. Anonymous (1884); Wikisource, Dec. 12, 2022, https://en.wikisource.org/wiki/Against_the_Grain/Chapter_XIII.

27. J. K. Huysmans, *À rebours* [Against the Grain], trans. John Howard (1884); New York: Dover Publications, 1969, 84, 162. See translation and comments in Angus McLaren, *Reproduction by Design: Sex, Robots, Trees, and Test-Tube Babies in Interwar Britain* (Chicago: University of Chicago Press, 2012), 69, endnotes 90–91.

28. LumiDolls, accessed January 1, 2019; August 30, 2020; and April 23, 2022, https://www.lumidolls.com/en/lumidolls; See also Marie Papenfuss, "Hello, Westworld: Sex Doll Brothel Opens in Barcelona," HuffPost, March 2, 2017,

https://www.huffpost.com/entry/sex-doll-barcelona-brothel_n_58b8ad10e4b0
d2821b4cddb8.

29. LumiDolls, accessed April 23, 2022, https://lumidolls.com/en/lumidolls.

30. "Russia's Second Sex Dolls Brothel Opens in St. Petersburg," Russia
Business Today, June 6, 2019, https://russiabusinesstoday.com/technology
/russias-second-sex-dolls-brothel-opens-in-st-petersburg/.

31. Mark Hay, "Sex Doll Brothels Expand the Market for Synthetic Partners,"
Forbes, October 31, 2018, https://www.forbes.com/sites/markhay/2018/10/31
/sex-doll-brothels-expand-the-market-for-synthetic-partners/.

32. Kathleen Richardson, "The Asymmetrical 'Relationship': Parallels
between Prostitution and the Development of Sex Robots," ACM SIGCAS
Computers and Society 45, no. 3 (September 2015): 290–93, https://doi
.org/10.1145/2874239.2874281; Kathleen Richardson, "The End of Sex Robots:
Porn Robots and Representational Technologies of Women and Girls," in
Man-Made Women: The Sexual Politics of Sex Dolls and Sex Robots, ed. Kathleen
Richardson and Charlotta Odlind (Palgrave MacMillan Cham, 2022), 171–92.

33. NMN, "What's the Problem with Sex Dolls? A Conversation with
Kathleen Richardson," Nordic Model Now!, May 23, 2020, https://www
.nordicmodelnow.org/2020/05/23/whats-the-problem-with-sex-dolls-a
-conversation-with-kathleen-richardson/.

34. Reported in David Moye, "Sex Robot Molested at Electronics Festival,
Creators Say," Huffpost, September 29, 2017. Festival organizers later denied
these reports.

35. Ian McEwan, Machines like Me: And People Like You (New York: Anchor
Books, 2020), 260.

36. Kate Devlin, Turned On: Science, Sex and Robots (London: Bloomsbury
Sigma, 2018), 266–67.

37. Julie Wosk, Women and the Machine: Representations from the Spinning
Wheel to the Electronic Age (Baltimore: Johns Hopkins University Press, 2001).

38. In a later season, however, Niska, who was about to knife a man, pulls back
when he refers to his daughter.

39. Hallie Lieberman, "In Defense of Sex Robots," Quartz, March 2, 2018,
https://qz.com/1215360/in-defense-of-sex-robots/.

UNDER THE SKIN

The Fabricated Femme Fatale

IN 2002, THE COOPER HEWITT, Smithsonian Design Museum presented its provocative exhibit *Skin: Surface, Substance, and Design*—an exhibit that explored the impact of simulated skin in architecture, art, and design. Wrote the curator, Ellen Lupton, "Skin is the body part most easily altered by human beings," adding, "Designers have confronted the medical and mechanical transformation of the human body with horror as well as fascination."[1]

What often gives films about artificial females a frisson of intrigue is the ambiguity of their artifice. Through the cover of simulated skin and the artfulness of technology, they may appear human though we know they aren't real. These alluring females are truly trompe l'oeil figures that fool the eye, females that may mask a steely self behind the aura of beauty, glamour, or innocence. Wearing a type of camouflage or opaque veil, they embody what Mary Ann Doane in *Femmes Fatales* called "the precariousness of vision." Their masks are at once concealing and revealing.[2]

In the films *Under the Skin*, *Ex Machina*, and *Ghost in the Shell*, and in the television series *Westworld*, there is a probing of what lies beneath the surface of female androids with beautiful synthetic skin—and frequently, the reality beneath is indeed fascinating and horrifying, though that underlying being might be impressively formidable as well.

UNDER THE SKIN

Near the beginning of Jonathan Glazer's mesmerizing film *Under the Skin* (2013), a beautiful woman looks at her reflection in her compact mirror as she carefully applies bright red lipstick to her full lips. We watch in fascination and

Figure 2.1. The alien (played by Scarlett Johansson) in the 2013 film *Under the Skin*.

horror as this alien (played by Scarlett Johansson) transforms herself into a simulated human being, an alluring femme fatale who will lure her male victims to their deaths. (Films about artificial women often depict them reflected in shimmering mirrors or viewed through glass—a reminder that we are seeing mediated images, seductive simulacra of the real thing.)

The film, set in Scotland, opens with a mysterious man riding a motorcycle who gets off the road, goes into the dark, and reappears carrying over his shoulder a lifeless female body, a female corpse wearing torn black stockings on her dangling legs. The female alien refashions herself into a glamorous temptress as she strips the corpse and puts on its underwear, clothes, and black stockings. She is businesslike, for there is no one watching—no male gaze before which to act seductively. The only presence is a startling praying mantis insect that she carefully plucks from the dead woman's torso before driving off in a van.

To complete the transformation, she goes to a shopping mall to buy more clothes—a fur jacket, a rose-colored shirt, new shoes, and some lipstick. As she walks through the mall, there is a glimpse from behind of her torn black stockings—a hint of her imperfection, her vulnerability, and her own ripped skin seen later in the film.

The female, we quickly learn, is a frightening alien predator, a mantrap who cruises down streets looking—like a praying mantis—for male victims. Her object is to lure and then kill the men to turn them into food for an alien race. Their dead bodies, floating in a mysterious liquid, soon become part of a streaming mass of flesh. Hunting for lone men who have no family ties, this femme fatale lures her victims into her lair of darkened rooms and entices them with her red lips and soothing voice. "Think I'm pretty?" she asks one man as she takes off her fur, leading his unsuspecting self into a type of digital quicksand, an abyss and deadly mirrored lake where he will soon disappear.

While roboticists today are busy working to create simulated females, including AI-endowed sex dolls that appear to have empathy, this alien is affectless as she drives through the streets to pick up men. Later at the shore, she watches impassively as a man in a wetsuit jumps into the water to try to help a husband rescue his wife, who is frantically being pulled away by swirling waters. After the man in the wetsuit brings the woman's husband back on shore (but the husband drowns when he runs back out in the water), the alien kills the would-be rescuer with a rock and puts his dead body into her van. All that is left alive on the shore is the couple's vulnerable infant, crying and alone, a fact ignored by the alien, who drives off undeterred.

In her 1987 chapter "Postfuturism," Vivian Sobchack compellingly argues that there was a "shift in sensibility toward the alien and Other" in contemporary science fiction films at that time. While 1950s films presented aliens as sinister invaders, given the proliferation of images, including images of robots and androids, mediated through electronic technologies in the 1980s, aliens were no longer threatening but rather had become "our familiars—our close relations—if not ourselves." Although there were still representations of evil aliens, there were new science fictions that presented aliens not as hostile or Other but as even more human than we are.[3]

More than thirty years after Sobchack's "Postfuturism," however, the alien in Glazer's film remains a horrifyingly sinister creature with malevolent intent. In a sense, she's a throwback to the 1950s Cold War films with their fears of an alien invasion. What gives her a more contemporary complexity, however, is that we are given the slightest suggestion that she has an interior life or, at the very least, a growing awareness of her own vulnerability.

When she puts on lipstick near the opening of the film, the alien is in an intriguing way allying herself with the acts of simulation used by real humans. She is in effect putting on a mask of femininity—the type of performative act by women that Emily Cox-Palmer-White sees as bowing to convention and a subversive, empowering act as well. When human women augment their bodies with cosmetics and manipulate their bodies to a desired state, this can be seen as an act of conformity, a "capitulation to normative notions of womanhood," but it is also empowering as the body becomes a type of tool for self-expression or, in the case of the alien, a tool to achieve her own ends. By donning a mask of femininity, Cox-Palmer-White argues, women are in some sense conflating themselves with artificial beings: "to be feminine, by its very nature, is to be in some sense a cyborg."[4]

The alien in *Under the Skin* puts lipstick on her face to convey femininity, which becomes a form of protection, allowing her to pass as an attractive human being. But the film masterfully moves between scenes of protection and vulnerability, of masking and exposure, as this impassive alien creature with her carefully crafted facade discovers fissures in her own protective persona. She pricks her hand on a rose and looks curiously as blood oozes from the cut. She trips and falls on a sidewalk, landing face down as people gather round. In her van one night, a menacing gang of men jump on her car, trying to get in before she anxiously speeds away.

There are also signs of cracks, however momentary, in her neutral stance. After she is terrorized by these men, the very next man she picks up has a vulnerability all his own—a severely disfigured face. This hooded man, who removes his hood and lets down his guard, tells her he has no friends and no experience with women, and she allows him to touch her face, telling him his hands are beautiful as she smiles at him, disarming his fears. "Do you want to look at me?" she asks, offering herself as an object to be looked at and giving him, for a few moments, the power of his gaze. His power, though, is short-lived, for after they both take off their clothes, he, too, slowly starts to become submerged in the primordial lake.

Glazer's film, with its eerie musical tones that are heard every time the alien gets her prey, manages to catch us off guard. The film's opening sequences present what seem like dispassionate images of visuality and occluded visuality. There are mysterious planetary-like spheres, which segue into an eclipse; the aperture of a camera; and then a startling close-up of the green-gray iris of a human eye flecked with orange and a staring black pupil. (The eye imagery conjures up Ridley Scott's lens/eye motif in his film *Blade Runner* thirty years earlier.)

Much of *Under the Skin* presents murder scenes with an objective eye, as Glazer documents the ghastly seductions of a methodical mass murderer. But the director also surprises us with more penetrating views. He fleetingly allows us—as in a cinematic CAT scan—to see what lies beneath the skin of this beautiful, lethal siren.

As she walks backward from the victimized, disfigured man, her nude body starkly lit in the dark, we catch a glimpse of what lies beneath her pale white exterior: the outlines of a hairless, featureless, black alien face and body. The image then merges back to her white-skinned profile. There are echoes here of a sequence in Fritz Lang's classic film *Metropolis* (1927) where the saintly Maria's face briefly merges with that of her diabolical robotic double.

What makes Glazer's film more than a chilling study in horror is that the alien—as in several other films about female simulacra, including *Ex Machina*, *Ghost in the Shell* (2017), and *Westworld*—is on a journey of self-awareness. After her initial encounter with the disfigured man, she goes downstairs and closely peers at her own face in an old round mirror as she scrutinizes her temporary identity as a human being. After she passes through the doorway, the camera shows a fly bouncing off the door's frosted glass and a quick view once again of her eye. The alien's vision—however elusive—lingers on.

Although the alien seems to be a *belle dame sans merci*, throughout most of the film, there is a fleeting suggestion that she is transforming, perhaps becoming more human or, at least, showing signs of becoming humane: she seems to spare the disfigured man, walking with him outside and watching him run naked through grasses as he tries to flee. His freedom, though, is short-lived, for he is soon caught by the malevolent motorcycle man first seen in the film's beginning, who puts him in a car trunk and drives off. In this film about observation and seeing, a woman in a house watches the whole transaction through a window, a silent witness to the grotesque.

In a pivotal shift in the landscape, the alien drives through snowy mountains but is stopped by a fog through which she cannot see. Soon, she begins to experience her own miasma, a blurring of her clear-cut mission. She feels her own vulnerability and her own sexuality, as she slowly discovers what it means to be human. Instead of being a predator, she herself becomes in need of protection and comfort. To get out of the rain on a nearly deserted road in the countryside, she hovers in a bus shelter. While riding on the bus, a kind man sitting behind her offers her his coat. "You okay?" he asks. "Need any help?"

At his house, she learns something about humanness as she watches television, taps her foot in time to music, and looks carefully and with curiosity at her own nude body. She learns more about her femininity as she once again gazes in a mirror, this time seeing her torso, her back, her vagina and breasts. She learns, too, about human tenderness as the man gently kisses her, and she puts her hand on his face. But this alien shows no signs of enjoying sex. When the man is lying on top of her in bed, she suddenly stops him, jumps out of bed, grabs a lamp, and bends down to look anxiously and closely at her vagina. For her, being a human female is a source of trauma and alarm.

In this dark tale, the alien woman who has so mercilessly and dispassionately victimized most of her prey finally finds the tables turned as she enters into a

Figure 2.2. The alien, unmasked, holding her disembodied head in her hand in *Under the Skin*. She is soon to meet her horrible end.

mythic nightmare world. Walking quickly through a forest, she encounters a logging truck driver who warns her, "You might get lost." Finding a shelter, she lies down but quickly becomes a quarry herself as the lumberman gropes her, and she tries to flee the menacing man.

In the film's incendiary finale, the alien running through the ominous woods can find no escape. She is brutally attacked by the lumberman, who assaults her, throws her to the ground, and tears off her clothes but is horrified when he discovers what lies beneath her ripped skin. The woman who was self-constructed is now brutally ripped apart, as in directors Michael Powell and Emeric Pressburger's 1951 filmed version of Jacques Offenbach's opera *The Tales of Hoffmann*. In that film, the mechanical doll Olympia is torn apart by the warring Spalanzani and Coppelius, and Hoffmann, the man who loves her, must confront that she is an artificial creation.

In some films, as we will see, when a female robot peels away her own skin it is an act of agency, a cry for help. *Under the Skin* recapitulates the horror of exposure and dismemberment, but for the alien, the exposure is not an act of volition but an assault. As the man attacks her, we see bits of her black body showing through her torn pale white skin.

Dazed, she staggers, pulls off her wig, and unpeels the rest of her skin, and we see the shiny surface of her black hairless head and her body as she is reduced to her elemental self. She kneels on the ground and holds in her hands the decapitated head of the female she once embodied—a head with blinking eyes, like Olympia's in the film *The Tales of Hoffmann*, where the decapitated face (of actress Moira Shearer) blinks as the poet Hoffmann stares at her in horror.

The end of *Under the Skin* is devastating. The lumberman throws gasoline on the alien and sets her on fire, and she staggers through the snow, burning, still carrying her decapitated humanoid head. Her body is soon consumed by flames, and a column of dark smoke and her ashes silently rise into the air. As the camera pans to a white sky filled with falling snowflakes and ashes, some of the wet flakes land on the camera lens—a reminder that the images we are watching are cinematic simulations in themselves. Ultimately, there is a total whiteout as all traces of the alien—and all the film's imagery—are dissolved into the transcendent world of nature, leaving us with a cosmic view.

The falling snow and the disappearing image become a metaphor for the ephemeral, fraught nature of human simulacra and the ephemeral existence of human life itself. But films about artificial women are finally more about defini-tion rather than dissolution as these females discover their own identity. At the end of the haunting film *Her* (2013), Samantha—the disembodied female voice of an operating system—dissolves her relationship with Theodore amid falling particles of snow seen through his window. But she herself experiences a form of self-discovery as she lives on in the digital ether (see chapter 5).

These twin themes—dissolution and definition—become central in films, television series, and novels about artificial women. Artificial females peel back layers of their own synthetic skin as they assert their own insistent identities—defining themselves as forces to be reckoned with in worlds where the virtual contends with the real.

EX MACHINA

In Alex Garland's film *Ex Machina* (2014), one of the most riveting scenes is when the beautiful female robot Ava slowly covers the armature of her cyborg body with a floral dress and fleecy white stockings while she is secretly being observed by Caleb, a young crack programmer. He watches intently as this cap-tivating robot slowly transforms herself into what looks like a real human being.

As Ava (played by Alicia Vikander) carefully pulls the dress over her head and rolls her stockings up her leg, she seems unaware that for Caleb this is a sensual moment. Instead, she is intent on camouflaging or covering up her mechanism. It's an ambiguous scene in a film that is full of ambiguities. Is she doing this to make herself alluring to Caleb? Is this a gesture about hiding, an effort to camouflage her true nature so she can fit in among humans? Her motives remain murky through much of the film, making her both fascinating and frightening at the same time—qualities that often haunt artificial females themselves.

This moment in the movie—when Caleb is slowly becoming seduced by Ava's charms—captures one of the film's central themes: the allure and possible danger of an android like Ava that is so technologically sophisticated it can fool the heart and eye. The film is fraught with the tension between Ava's underlying artifice and her appearance as being real. She is a crafted creature mimicking human thoughts and feelings, and this imitation has the potential for both delight and horror.

In the film, Caleb (played by Domhnall Gleeson) works for BlueBook, a search engine company, and happily learns he has won first prize in a company contest. He agrees to fly by helicopter to a remote compound and residence situated in wooded mountains. His task, says BlueBook's chief, Nathan (masterfully played by Oscar Isaac), is to see if Nathan's newly developed artificially intelligent female robot, named Ava, can pass the Turing test or can seem to have human consciousness even though Caleb already knows she is a machine.

This is a film that becomes spellbinding through its layering of surfaces and transparencies. When Caleb first sees Ava, he sees her from afar and through a mediating glass window. He often sees her and talks to her through room walls of glass. He can see that she is clearly a synthetic creature, a composite of a machine and a human-looking body. She has a human face but no hair on her gleaming metallic skull. Her neck, arms, torso, and legs are transparent, revealing their electronic wiring, but she has human-looking hands and feet. To Caleb, part of her allure is that she is a paradoxical, veiled creature: both transparent and opaque, close yet also remote—through a glass darkly.

Ava seduces Caleb—and us the audience, too—by seeming so convincingly real, not only through Vikander's acting skills but also because Ava herself is a remarkable work of technological ingenuity both as a fictive character and as a cinematic creation. The film's special effects team used computer animation and 3D rendering software to seamlessly produce a composite of Ava's CGI-rendered arms and legs combined with the actress's own face, feet, and hands.

Says Ava to Caleb, who smilingly looks at her on the monitor, "You can see that I'm a machine," and for him, this dynamic of the enticing woman who is artificial sets up her magnetic allure. He's immediately entranced: "Oh man, she's fascinating," he says, seeing her as a blend of naturalism and Alice-in-Wonderland-like surrealism. He continues, "When you talk to her, you're just through the looking glass." Caleb's real challenge is to know that Ava is synthetic but still decide if she has consciousness.

Making the task even more problematic and challenging, the elusive Ava is a robot that has been designed to foster closeness and intimacy—qualities that are especially seductive and dangerous for a young man with vulnerabilities. "Do you want to be my friend?" she asks Caleb, who lost his parents in a car accident and has no brothers or sisters. "Are you married?" When she hears that his parents died in a car crash when he was fifteen, she says softly, "I'm sorry." She tells him in a whisper during an electrical blackout that Nathan isn't really his friend. "You shouldn't trust him," she says, building their bond.

This is a film that creates tension through its crafty interplay of real and artificial. To Caleb, Ava increasingly seems like a real human being. She has empathy and seems to wish to connect and be a confidant and friend. However, Nathan, her creator, is intent on deconstructing the illusion and demonstrating that she's clearly a fabrication. He shows Caleb his lab, where Ava was created, a place that has several face masks that, with the aid of AI, can duplicate facial expressions. Even more eerily, Nathan holds in his hand Ava's brain, made of structured gel, a brain that will be implanted with programmed memories and thoughts. There are often scary images of brains and skulls in horror films, and this gelatinous brain is especially alienating, coming from such a beautiful and enticing creature.

The film's scenic design also cleverly plays with this dialectic between artifice and naturalism, authenticity and the artificial. Nathan's subterranean research facility is designed to look rustic with rocks, streams, and waterfalls, but it also has glass and steel interiors with artificial lighting and electronics. In a film about both art and artifice, Nathan points to his painting by Jackson Pollock on the wall to dispel Caleb's doubts about Ava, making a pitch that Pollock's abstract expressionist painting represents consciousness unfettered by rationality—and he urges Caleb to suspend his own sense of disbelief.

Art and artfulness have an important role in the film. Ava expresses herself by drawing pictures at night that she shows to Caleb. To him, this makes her seem even more genuine and authentic. When Caleb sees Nathan tearing up one of the drawings, he reads this as an outrageous, brutal denial of Ava's personhood, her creativity. The whole event that he observes, however, appears to be artifice, a manufactured incident designed by the artful impresario Nathan to arouse Caleb's sympathy for Ava.

THE AMBIGUITIES OF VISION

Much of the allure of *Ex Machina* itself is the way it evokes these ambiguities of vision and seeing. Is the Ava who appears to be genuine a mere puppet or marionette being manipulated and manipulative all at once? In one of the film's early pivotal moments, Caleb, standing behind a glass panel, gazes at Ava resting on a gurney. As he objectifies her by looking at her, she turns her head to look at him. In that moment, Caleb is captivated by the view: In a trope often seen in portrayals of female robots created by men, she appears to him like a newborn—innocent, naive—yet she is also an adult woman, available and sexual too. Her voice is soft, her smile faint, making her charming and disarming at the same time. She is a woman who gently seduces him without the obvious trappings of a femme fatale.

Caleb is drawn by her apparent inexperience: she tells him, in a conversation, that she's never been outside the room she's in now (though later, she will fantasize about being in a busy intersection, with its "shifting view of human life"). Kneeling in front of him in a deferential female posture, she leans forward, telling him, "We could go out together" She says this in a beguiling, soft voice, and he answers jocularly, "It's a date!" Later, she asks with seeming innocence yet also seductively, "Do you think about me when we aren't together . . . sometimes at night?"

In this film about seeing and perception, Ava is seemingly guileless yet also artful as she plays with his gaze and teasingly shapes his vision of her. "There's something I want to show you," she says and asks him to close his eyes. It's here where she creates a dramatic transformation that changes the way he perceives her. She puts on her dress, a sweater that covers her bare electronic arms, stockings, a blond wig, and shoes, and then tells him to open his eyes. Turning around slowly, she asks him, "How do I look?" She kneels toward him again, leans forward, and thoroughly entrances him with a series of soft enticements: "This is what I'd wear on our date." "I'd like us to go out on a date." "Are you attracted to me? You give me indications that you are."

Using sight and vision as a lure and a trap, Ava knows she's caught him, because, she says, she can see his "microexpressions"—"the way your eyes fix on my eyes and lips. The way you hold my gaze," adding, "I'm wondering if you're watching me on the cameras. And I hope you are."

Ava is just as artful when she not only creates but also dismantles the illusion. While Caleb is again watching her from afar, she undresses. She slowly takes off her stockings, which expose her robotic legs, takes off her dress and shoes, and then looks at him as the film cuts to a close-up of his watching eyes. Framed and backlit by the window, she stands there with no clothes on and to Caleb, the image is riveting.

In E. T. A. Hoffman's "The Sandman," when Nathanael realizes that his beloved is not real, he is horrified and experiences what Sigmund Freud in 1919 called "the uncanny" and Masahiro Mori in 1970 called the "uncanny valley."[5] But in Garland's film, even when Ava once again exposes her mechanism, in Caleb's eyes she maintains her allure—largely through her charisma, which has charmed him, and the charisma of Vikander as an actress who has thoroughly charmed the audience.

Perhaps, for Caleb, it is precisely Ava's artifice, her otherness, that makes her so appealing, so approachable, so safe. And by extension, it may well be that it is the inherent artifice of all simulated females—sex dolls and fictional versions—that makes them appealing, especially to men who need distance and safety from a real woman's complexity and needs. (But as feminist theorists of science fiction have argued, it is the perceived difference and otherness of artificial females—as women, as artificial constructs—that make them subject to male abuse, exploitation, and efforts at control.)

Ex Machina is a film not only about the allure and ambiguities of artifice but also about two classic paradigms of female identity. Is Ava—as with the two Marias in Fritz Lang's film *Metropolis*—an angel or a temptress? Is the newly minted Ava an ingenue just learning the ways of the world and love, or is she programmed to be (or, with her AI, does she learn to be) cleverly, and perhaps diabolically, manipulative? Is she innocently engaging in unassuming flirtation with Caleb ("Would you like to go on a date?"), or is she using sexuality to further her own ends?

The otherwise savvy and suspicious Caleb lobs probing questions at Nathan: "Did you program her to flirt with me?" "Did you program her to like me or not?" "Did you give her sexuality as a diversion tactic?" Is Ava like a magician's assistant that will cloud his ability to judge her AI? Nathan is coy—"If I did, would that be cheating?"—but still insists on her authenticity. "And for the record," says Nathan, "Ava's not pretending to like you," adding, "Her flirting isn't an algorithm to fake you out." Besides, he points out, it's natural that Ava would develop a crush on Caleb—the only other man she's ever known is Nathan.

Caleb may probe the genuineness of her sexuality, but he doesn't seem to question her empathy or wonder whether she is genuinely sympathetic or if this is just a ploy, which leaves him vulnerable and exposed. Ava successfully elicits his trust, drawing him ever closer to her.

The film's central tensions, however, go beyond authenticity or artifice, trust or suspicion. Behind the facade of a seductive digital wonderland, there is always the lurking threat of violent disruption and menace in the film. Caleb may feel closely connected to Ava, but the threat of disintegration is always there. He experiences the horror of the uncanny when Nathan shows him his workroom with its tables covered with dismembered robot bodies—a metallic

Figure 2.3. Kyoko (played by Sonoya Mizuno) the servant/lover in *Ex Machina*, 2014.

head, a headless, nude female torso. At night and unseen, he has a recognition of torment and imprisonment when he sees Nathan drag away a nude female robot who flails her hands and screams, "Why won't you let me out!" (She flails so hard that she knocks off her hands, exposing her mechanism and wires.)

Kyoko, Nathan's robotic servant and, essentially, his sex slave, is also trapped and anguished. When Nathan gets angry at her after she accidentally

Figure 2.4. Kyoko peels away part of her own face to show Caleb her robotic metal interior in *Ex Machina*.

spills a wineglass on the table, she sits on the hallway floor looking dejected. At another point, there is a close-up of her cutting meat with a knife—a startling and menacing moment suggesting her simmering anger and potential for violence.

The film's most startling moment of deconstruction is when Kyoko goes up to Caleb, pulls at her own rib cage in the area under her breasts, and painfully and shockingly peels back her skin, revealing her artifice. When she peels away her own skin, it is a brave and desperate act of agency, for by revealing herself, she shows Caleb her plight and her true nature as a simulated woman. After she reveals her simulated self, the film cuts to Caleb lying on his bed as he flashes to an image of Kyoko with her bulging eyes wide open and the rest of her shining metal artificial face exposed. (He later pulls at his own skin and cuts himself with a razor to see if he bleeds, testing to see if he's human.)

Kyoko's unpeeling of her own skin, a startling revelation that she's artificial, not real, is a potent recurring image in films and television dramas about female robots and artificial women. In *Under the Skin*, the mysterious, homicidal female alien grotesquely pulls off her blonde wig and peels back her skin, exposing her bare black head and body. Dr. Franklin in the "Kill Oscar" episode of the vintage television series *The Bionic Woman* (1976) rips off the face of his personal assistant, exposing her electronic circuitry to prove to Baron Constantine that she is synthetic, not real. Also, as we shall see, the brutal exposure appeared again forty years later in a 2016 episode of the American television series *Westworld* where Logan puts a gash in Dolores to remind William she's a mere robot. But it is the self-exposure in films like *Ex Machina* that is most poignant: for synthetic creatures like Kyoko, the awareness of her own artifice is particularly painful.

For Caleb, the most horrifying aspect of Ava is the threat that she will become dismembered. Nathan matter-of-factly tells him that Ava is not an end product. Instead, his next female robot model will be the breakthrough that will achieve singularity or human consciousness, and Ava will be destroyed. Her mind will be downloaded, her memories erased, and only her body will survive. When Nathan asks Caleb provocatively and manipulatively, "Do you feel bad for Ava?" it is part of his diabolical strategy: he banks on Nathan's sympathy and his wish to try to save her.

Ultimately, Nathan does indeed turn out to be a techno-magician using Ava for misdirection, and his test is a success: Ava demonstrates true AI through her self-awareness, empathy, manipulation, sexuality, and imagination, all used to foster her own escape. What Nathan didn't count on is getting destroyed himself in the whole process.

When Ava, with her gleaming silver torso and whirring motors, walks determinedly down the corridor near the end, she becomes a formidable and lethal creature. Her short walk is a journey of self-discovery: along the way, she touches a mask of a woman on the wall and then her own face. Though she's partially dismembered by Nathan at the end and loses one of her arms, she has the strength and determination (after being aided by Kyoko, who knifes him) to give Nathan the mortal cuts that ultimately kill him.

In the film's stirring ending, Ava reassembles herself into a new identity as Caleb once again watches her helplessly, this time trapped behind a glass wall. In Mary Shelley's novel *Frankenstein*, Victor Frankenstein fashions his grotesque artificial creature from dead body parts, but here, Ava has agency: She becomes her own Victor and reconstructs herself from disparate body parts. After opening a closet, she unhinges her own forearm and exchanges it for a whole arm that she takes from a female robot hanging there. She pulls off segments of the robot's skin and covers her own metallic armature.

Near the end, in another moment of self-discovery, she stands there nude, and like the alien in *Under the Skin*, looks at herself in the mirror. Putting on a lacy white dress, she's ready to gain her freedom and autonomy, and she takes a waiting helicopter to finally escape. In a film about the ambiguities of vision, at the end of the film she stands watching people in a busy urban intersection just as she earlier had longed to do. But Garland leaves us with a version of Plato's

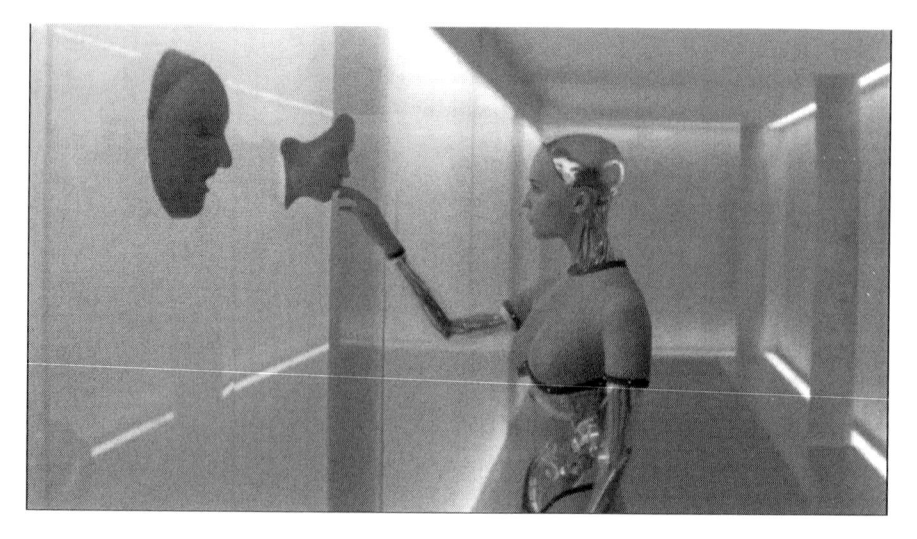

Figure 2.5. Ava (played by Alicia Vikander) in Jonathan Glazer's film *Ex Machina* reaches out to a robotic face on the wall as she gets in touch with her own synthetic nature.

ancient "Allegory of the Cave" reimagined for the digital age. Ultimately, we see the people in the outside world represented only by their shadows on the pavement, ethereal images of reality in this illusory world.

GHOST IN THE SHELL

Scarlett Johansson as the alien in *Under the Skin* ultimately disintegrates and disappears into the white air, but as Samantha in *Her* and as Major in Rupert Sanders's film *Ghost in the Shell* (2017), she portrays a new breed of artificial woman who forcefully asserts herself and does anything but disappear.

In *Ghost in the Shell*'s opening sequences, a woman lying on a lab gurney gasps for air as a reassuring voice tells her, "Just breathe!" This is the birth of a female cyborg, a hybrid creature with a synthetic shell of a body, a human brain, and a "ghost," or soul. The cyborg, known as Major, has been created as a warrior, a weapon against terrorism.

Her birth—with her floating nude figure covered in dripping white liquid— was imaged using live-action and CGI visual effects, and has echoes of the acclaimed 1995 anime version of *Ghost in the Shell* directed by Mamoru Oshii and based on the manga by Masamune Shirow. The technology of cyborg creation

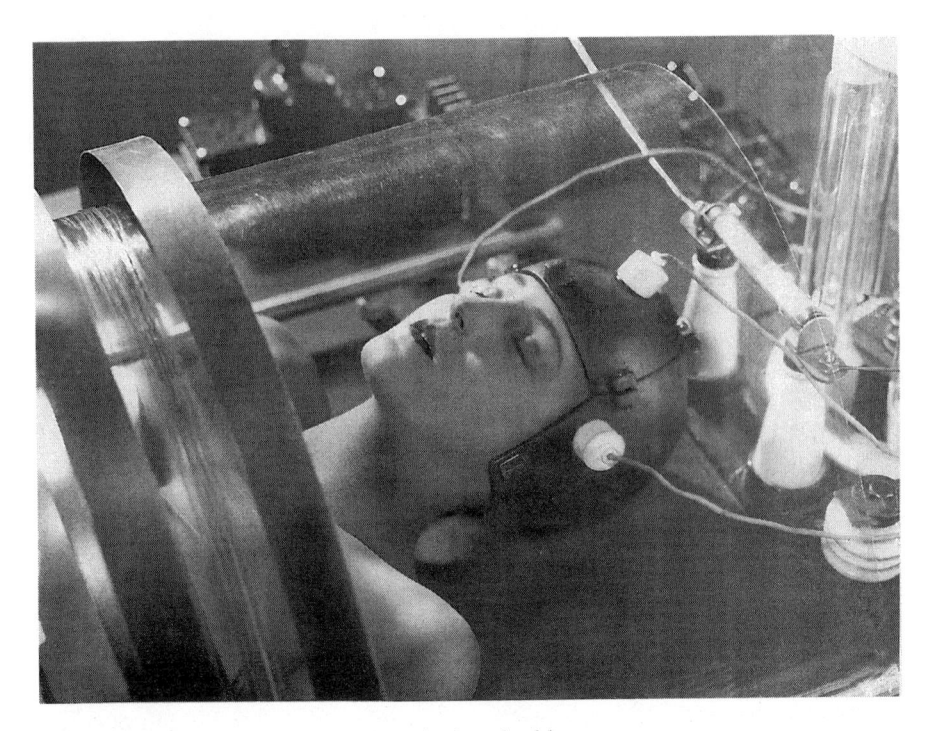

Figure 2.6. The creation of Maria's evil robot double
in Fritz Lang's film *Metropolis* (1927).

in films has changed dramatically over the years. Both versions of *Ghost in the Shell*—as well as the animated *Ghost in the Shell 2: Innocence* (2004), where female gynoids are manufactured by injecting or hacking the "ghosts" (personalities) of captured young women into artificial creatures or dolls—were a long way from the dramatic creation of the robot Maria in Lang's *Metropolis*. There, Maria's robotic double was created amid flashing arcs of electricity and circular rings of fire (special effects using a Tesla coil and floating circular neon lights in liquid).[6]

They are also a long way from the creation of a companion for the Monster in James Whale's 1935 film *Bride of Frankenstein*, where the Bride is constructed from dead female body parts and animated through the electricity of lightning. In one of the most memorable moments in Whale's film, the Bride's bandages are dramatically unwrapped as her creator, Henry Frankenstein, cries out ecstatically, "She's alive!"

The birth scenes may be different, but some of the main themes in these films and others, including *Blade Runner* (1982) and *Ex Machina*, are very much

Figure 2.7. Major (played by Scarlett Johansson) in *Ghost in the Shell* (2017).

the same. What is the nature of these new creatures that blur the distinction between the artificial and the real? What does it feel like to be one of these synthetic creatures whose existence is embedded with ambiguities?

Major, the newly birthed cyborg in *Ghost in the Shell*, is haunted by the need to find the nature of her identity. She was told that she was originally a young woman named Mira Killian who had been the sole survivor of a cyberterrorist attack, although her body had been badly damaged (she was also told that her parents had both died in an accident). Hanka, a Japanese robotics company, had developed a way to salvage her brain by putting it into an artificial body and uses the newly created cyborg to work as an antiterrorist agent in Section 9.

At one point in the film, she is charged with attacking enemy robotic geishas who are servants at a banquet, and she is startled when one of these geishas cries out, "Help me!"[7] In this film about synthetic humanoid female creations, the geisha is particularly intriguing. Geishas are known for their artifice—their stylized facial makeup and movements. The robot geisha is a servant woman with a stylized, camouflaged face made of shiny sections of plastic, and Major herself is a type of civil servant wearing camouflage—her nude-colored Thermosuit that covers her whole body and is made of silicone.

After killing the geisha, Major looks at her own damaged hand with its torn Thermosuit skin and exposed innards, and is again troubled. Her companion warrior Batou had reassured her about herself and the geisha—"You're not the same. It's just a robot"—and Dr. Ouelet, the scientist who had successfully created her, had reassured her, "You're human," but Major is still troubled. In this film about uncovering layers of reality, she confronts a woman on the street whose face is partially covered in silver skin and asks her, "Are you human?" She insists the woman peel off the silver covering, and Major curiously touches her face and becomes even more determined to discover information about her own mysterious identity and origins.

In a pivotal moment later in the film, Kuze, the film's archvillain and nemesis, who is a prior experimental cyborg, tells her, "We are the same." To prove it to her, he brutally pulls off a section of her face, holds it in his hand, and puts it back. She also finds out from Dr. Ouelet that she is one of many prior experimental creations and that her memories of her dead parents and her past were false memories, implanted by Hanka. The revelation leaves her evermore determined to find out her real name and who she is.

Throughout the film, this simulated woman—like the alien in *Under the Skin*—remains both powerful and vulnerable. She often displays a kind of tough stoicism and rarely shows even a flicker of emotion other than fierce intensity in the film's many fight scenes. As played by Johansson, Major is both blunt and enigmatic, so that we imagine she may have hidden sensitivities we do not see.

For all of her stoicism, Major does make some poignant admissions, but usually with a poker face. When Dr. Ouelet (played by Juliette Binoche) warns her, "You're not invulnerable. I can't protect you," and also tells her she's one of a kind and the future of humanity, Major replies, "You don't know how alone that makes me feel." (In the earlier 1995 *Ghost in the Shell* film, after diving down deep into water, she had also said, "I feel fear, cold, alone," though adding that sometimes "I even feel hope.")

As an actress, Johansson had her own identity issues with the film. She had to deal with the fact that the film's creators were roundly criticized for not casting an Asian actress in Major's role. She also had to deal with the complexities of playing the role of a robot: How do you convey that you are artificial yet also show some signs of humanity? (Adding a surreal twist, a British man in 2016 created his own robot double of Johansson herself.)

As with the birth scenes, Sanders's *Ghost in the Shell* was haunted by other ghosts of films past. The film's CGI images of a futuristic city resembling Hong Kong, set in a fictional future, had echoes of earlier cinematic sci-fi cities seen in *Metropolis* and in *Blade Runner*'s off-world colony. But what was particularly arresting in the film were the mammoth holographs of female figures amid the city's high-rise buildings—towering females and mannequins that were eerie, spectral reminders of this highly synthetic world.

The film—with its explosions and violence, its futuristic urban scenes, its meditations on technology—does not open up much new cinematic territory. But near the end, it becomes surprisingly effective when Major meets, and later, embraces, the woman who was her original mother (movingly played by Japanese actress Kaori Momoi). She finds out she was abducted by the scientists and that her true name was Motoko. Her mother described her as a fearless young woman who had been writing a manifesto that "technology was destroying the world." When her daughter disappeared, her mother was falsely told that her daughter had run away and committed suicide.

Discovering who she was finally gives Major some closure and peace. Near the end of the film, she finally casts off her uncertainty. Her identity as a cyborg with a soul may still remain problematic, but for her, and for now, she has gained agency and a strong sense of self. She becomes a representative of the new breed of simulated women in films—formidable women who embrace their synthetic identities and remain fighters and survivors. Says Major, acknowledging her orders to go on another policing mission, "I am Major, and I give my consent."

WESTWORLD: DOLORES

In the television series *Westworld*, Dolores (played by Evan Rachel Wood), as is Maeve, is this type of formidable, fearless simulated woman; only she is at first shown as a demure-looking rancher's daughter who speaks in a soft Western accent and quiet voice. This earnest young woman dressed in her blue, Texas-ranch-style cotton dress gives no hint of the killer she will later become.

Birth scenes in films about artificial women often fixate on eyes. The opening image of a large eyeball in *Westworld*'s credits highlights how perception is important in this series, and the opening of Dolores's eyes in several scenes suggests not only her rebirth after her robotic construction is brought back to life but also her growing consciousness of her own identity and her changing role.

There are iconic scenes in film and television when constructed artificial women first open their eyes and seem to offer the promise of being an ideal partner. But the beautiful lady isn't what she seems. In *Metropolis*, the captive Maria, lying in a glass tube, is tethered to that of a robot, and she is used by the maniacal scientist Rotwang to create an evil double of herself. A close-up of the robot's face dissolves into Maria's, and as the replica's eyes open, she is now

Figure 2.8. Dolores Abernathy (played by Evan Rachel Wood), the thoughtful and forceful robot (host) in the first season of HBO television's *Westworld*, 2016.

an evil version of the saintly Maria, a beautiful vampish creature who will lead men astray. And opened eyes are central in *Westworld* too.

In several scenes in *Westworld*, Dolores lies on a gurney as she is being reconstructed in a lab, her armature exposed before skin is layered on her face and shoulders. Her eyes open, she sits up, and Bernard, head of Westworld programming, greets her with "Welcome to the world!" Though we have no illusions that she is human, we are quickly drawn into her psychic sphere. Creating an ongoing tension in the series, we have parallel perceptions of her as synthetic and genuine, artificial and real.

Alex Garland in *Ex Machina* presents a nuanced exploration of the ambiguities of artifice, where Caleb is seduced by Ava's allure even while knowing from the beginning that she is a synthetic being, but in *Westworld*, there is often little room for subtlety, ambiguity, and play. The hosts are constructed beings controlled by computers, and we are reminded of that again and again. In the series' first episode, the theme park's director, Dr. Robert Ford (whose name wittily echoes the divinity Ford in Aldous Huxley's novel *Brave New World*), instructs a technician to reanimate Dolores, and when he says, "Bring her back online," her lifeless body is reactivated once more.

The series continues to remind us early and often that the hosts aren't real. The most brutal revelation is when Logan, the brother-in-law of park visitor William Delos, plunges a knife into Dolores in order to pull back her layered skin and expose her inner framework—proving to William that his beloved Dolores is just a robot. After Logan gashes Dolores open, Logan tells William sadistically, "She's just a doll!" As in Hoffmann's "The Sandman," where Nathanael's friends tell him that his beloved Olimpia is just a doll, but he persists in loving her just the same—and as in *Ex Machina*, where Caleb is undeterred by knowing Ava isn't real—the fact of Dolores's artifice is irrelevant to William, for his love is too deep for him to be dissuaded. (Though in a big reversal, by the second season's episode "The Reunion," William, who Dolores long thought loved her, tells her cruelly and scornfully, "You really are just a thing. I can't believe I fell in love with you.")

One of the paradoxes of artificial women in films and television is that, as in *Westworld*, we become invested in their inner struggles even while being reminded that these females are constructed creatures. For the theme park visitors, the artifice of the hosts is actually liberating because that factor allows them to indulge in their own fantasies and whims. The guests are free to act out their sexual and violent impulses with no consequences. They can discover aspects of their own personalities and play out their hidden selves. So too for Dolores, whose self-discovery and abandonment of her demure mask will be liberating. As she says, "I think when I discover who I am I'll be free."

The issue of masking and authenticity is not only the stuff of fiction but also a recurring cultural theme in gender identity. Taught to beautify themselves with cosmetics, to wear alluring clothing and alter their bodies, women historically and in a wide variety of cultures can be subject to changing cultural norms, alternately socialized to submerge their appearance behind the artifice of cosmetics yet also celebrate and honor their authentic selves.[8] In films like *Under the Skin*, however, there is a horrifying aspect to the alien's putting on lipstick, for it masks her grotesque identity. In other films, the masking is functional—it's a type of placeholder for women who must hide their underlying intent.

Whether innocently seductive as Dolores or audaciously available as Maeve, female hosts in *Westworld* sport a cheerful camouflage, or type of body armor, that masks their determination and moments of uncertainty as they probe the nature of their own artificial identity. As so often happens in stories about newly created female robots, Dolores at first has an adolescent-like innocence, but in this coming-of-age story, we witness her sometimes poignant, sometimes painful evolving consciousness and journey to self-awareness.

Dolores had learned from Dr. Ford (played by Anthony Hopkins) that Arnold, the originator of Westworld, had developed a small round maze, or puzzle, as a test of empathy and imagination—the center of which was consciousness. Arnold had increased her consciousness, and as she evolved, on her quest for the maze, she demonstrated that she does indeed have the capacity for empathy, love, and grief. But she also has other sides as a tough-minded killer.

In the final episode of the first season, "The Bicameral Mind," Dolores again lies on a gurney with her eyes closed as her skeletal framework is being slowly covered with artificial skin. "Dolores," a voice calls as her eyes open and she sits up. This is Dolores awakening again, but it is a Dolores with a difference—she is now a woman with growing sentience who will be intent on determining her own fate.

In one of her iconic surrealist paintings, Mexican artist Frida Kahlo pictured dual images of herself sitting side by side on two chairs: one of her dressed as a European woman in her lacy white colonial woman's clothes, and the other dressed in the colorful clothes of her mother's Mexican heritage. At the end of the first season, two versions of Dolores also appear. They sit facing each other on chairs. On one side is Dolores, a fierce gunslinger dressed in pants and white shirt, and the other, the sweet Dolores in her blue cotton dress. "You've arrived" to the center of the maze, Ford tells her. She's ready, she says, "to confront myself—after this long and vivid nightmare—myself and who I must become." At a corporate gala, she ruthlessly shoots Ford with a steely look in her eye, a newly emergent female to be reckoned with—ready to set off on her own path in the lands outside of Westworld.

Westworld is a series about robotic women being transformed as they thrust off the conventions of their gendered roles. In the first season's episode "Contrapasso," when Dolores rides outside Sweetwater with the guest William, she tells him, "You said people come here to change the story of their lives. I imagined a story where I didn't have to be the damsel in distress." Reversing her role as the gentle Dolores, she shows she can also be a sharpshooter as she kills the outlaws who attack them.

In seasons 2 and 3, Dolores is fully transformed as she rides on horseback with an ammunition belt strapped across her back (although problematically, and somewhat confusingly in this oddly written series, her identity is that of her alter ego, the male Wyatt. Arnold had earlier merged her with the new character they were developing). We still see her as Dolores, though, and she becomes a fierce fighter who leads the hosts into acts of rebellion as she contemplates replacing all humans with a new breed of hosts. Shorn of her look of innocence, and unlike the seductive Ava and the alluring alien in *Under the Skin*, she wears

Figure 2.9. Dolores in *Westworld* transformed into a fighter.

no mask as she bares her lethal intentions out in the open. Riding with her band of hosts, she is finally free.

By the finale of the *Westworld* series, in 2022, Dolores has been through many identity permutations—the demure woman in the Western town; the fierce fighter still in Western garb; a version in which she merges with Charlotte Hale (Halores), the former executive of Westworld's parent corporation, Delos; and finally, in season 4, she is Christina, a woman who writes the narrative stories for Olympiad, a video game enterprise, where she has powers to manipulate the actions of others. Like a whole lineup of artificial women in fiction, television, and films, Dolores in her many identities is determined to create her own narrative. As her host lover Teddy tells her, in her former identity as Dolores, she was initially made to perform the stories of others but then "she outgrew others' stories. She began writing her own."

In the season's final episode, she tells Teddy tearfully, "I don't know who I am anymore" before she submerges herself in a bathtub. Still, in this series that is only intermittently coherent, Dolores in the end is back wearing her blue dress in the town of Sweetwater in Westworld—presumably continuing her own story, but this time on her own terms. Artificial women in this series are alternately puppets and puppet masters, ever trying to master their own fates.

NOTES

1. Ellen Lupton, with essays by Jennifer Tobias et al., *Skin: Surface, Substance, and Design* (New York: Princeton Architectural Press, 2002), 64.

2. Mary Ann Doane, *Femmes Fatales: Feminism, Film Theory, Psychoanalysis* (New York: Routledge, 1991), 46.

3. Vivian Sobchack, "Postfuturism," first published in Sobchack's *Screening Space: The American Science Fiction Film* (New York: Ungar, 1987), and republished in Gill Kirkup et al., eds., *The Gendered Cyborg: A Reader* (New York: Routledge, 2000), 136–47.

4. Emily Cox-Palmer-White, *The Biopolitics of Gender in Science Fiction: Feminism and Female Machines* (New York: Routledge, 2021), 62. Cox references Judith Butler's writings about performativity in her work.

5. Sigmund Freud, "Das Unheimliche" [The Uncanny], 1919, in vol. 17 of *The Standard Edition of the Complete Psychological Works of Sigmund Freud*, ed. and trans. James Strachey et al. (London: Hogarth Press and the Institute of Psycho-Analysis, 1955), 218–52; Masahiro Mori, "The Uncanny Valley," *Energy* 7 (1970): 33–35; and Karl F. MacDorman and Nori Kageki, trans., *IEEE Robotics and Automation Magazine* 19, no. 2 (June 2012): 100.

6. Julie Wosk, "*Metropolis*," *Technology and Culture* 51, no. 2 (April 2010): 403–408; Wosk, "Update on the Film *Metropolis*," *Technology and Culture* 51, no. 4 (October 2010): 1061–62, https://doi.org/10.1353/tech.2010.0069.

7. More memorable are the anguished cries of the gynoids in *Ghost in the Shell 2: Innocence* (2004) when the captured girls (gynoids) groomed to be sex slaves go from vulnerability to murderous. One of them cries out "Help me!" before self-destructing by tearing open her own skin to expose her innards.

8. Kathy Peiss, however, in her study *Hope in a Jar*, reveals an intriguing paradox: some advertisers in the 1920s, in ads like Armand's "Find Yourself," promised women that by wearing cosmetics, they could discover their own personality and portray their individuality. Peiss, *Hope in a Jar: The Making of America's Beauty Culture* (New York: Henry Holt, 1998), 144.

THREE

—⚉—

FEMALE ROBOT CAREGIVERS, DOUBLES, AND COMPANIONS

IN THE BRITISH AMERICAN TELEVISION series *Humans* (2015–18), a retired artificial intelligence researcher, Dr. George Millican (played by William Hurt), is plagued with memory loss and the side effects of a stroke. He is helped by a "synth" (short for *synthetic*) caregiver named Odi, a robot man-servant. But Odi is malfunctioning, and authorities send an updated synth replacement, a stern Gestapo-looking woman, Vera (played by Rebecca Front), who makes Millican's life a misery. She orders him to change his clothes, take his meds, and do his exercises. Like a drill sergeant, she is unrelenting in making sure he does the right thing.

In a familiar female role as caregiver, she nevertheless shows no sign of sensitivity or warm empathy and makes Millican long for his male synth Odi, who had far more sensitivity and gentleness but was malfunctioning. Millican says to Vera, "You're not a carer. You're a jailer. Get lost!" adding, "I don't take orders from you!" Throughout, Vera as robot is always mechanistic and calm, a comic version of a familiar female paradigm—the nagging scold who won't let Millican be his own man. Eventually, he locks her in a closet as he tries to make his escape.

As a series, *Humans* presented a thoughtful look at the implications of a world increasingly infused with simulations created to offer comfort, provide sexual pleasure, and help humans—with all the acceptance and resistance that entails. Adding layers of complexity to conventional paradigms of the female caregiver, wife, mother (see chap. 4), the series sometimes satirized, sometimes championed, the myriad roles of women in an increasingly technological world. It was also very much in touch with contemporary developments in robotics, particularly the quest to create empathetic robot caregivers.

Indeed, contemporary female robots not only are serving as sexy pleasure dolls but also may be designed to—eventually—provide health care and companionship for the elderly and the disabled. In America and countries including Japan, the age group of sixty-five and older has been the fastest growing segment in the population, and there will be an increasing need for professional caregivers. Foreseeing that there may not be enough qualified human helpers, roboticists at research centers, including MIT, and international manufacturers are scrambling to fulfill this need, creating "social assistive robots." The robots are also being designed to be helpful for people with Alzheimer's disease and dementia.[1]

Professor Nancy S. Jecker of the University of Washington has been a strong proponent of caregivers and companion robots, arguing that they can play an important role for socially isolated people and people with disabilities. Social isolation and loneliness experienced by older adults can have a negative impact on their health, and, as Jecker wrote, they are factors "associated with a greater incidence of major psychological, cognitive, and physical morbidities."[2]

Researchers have reported that patients responded well to robots that have humanoid voices and appearances, and some roboticists have gendered this concept, suggesting that they are creating their pretty, ultrarealistic female robots not only to serve as receptionists and even actors but also to serve as healthcare providers. David Hanson of Hanson Robotics in Hong Kong and Professor Hiroshi Ishiguro, director of the Intelligent Robotics Lab at Osaka University in Japan, developed attractive robots that usually look like young women in their twenties with expressive faces and rudimentary interactive speaking capabilities.

Since 1995, Professor Ishiguro has devoted much of his career developing both male and female humanoid robots such as the female robot Repliee Q2, the female androids Otonaroid and Kodomoroid, and he and his colleagues worked on creating the aura of empathy in robots like Erica introduced in 2017. Professor Nadia Thalmann, director of MIRALab at the University of Geneva in Switzerland, has for several years been developing her robot Nadine as a companion for children and the elderly. The robot is modeled to resemble Professor Thalmann herself.

These female robots, which are made to look like doubles of real human beings, ostensibly will help answer some pressing social questions: Who will help take care of elderly people when caregivers become scarce? Who can offer close companionship when a loved one dies, leaving a husband or wife alone? These are some of the questions being considered by designers and filmmakers alike who are exploring the idea of using robots to help as companions and caregivers for the young and old.

Figure 3.1. Erica, a robot developed by Professor Hiroshi Ishiguro and his colleagues at the Intelligent Robotics Laboratory, Osaka, Japan, 2017.

However, many of the commercially available robot companions do not look like pretty women—they are abstract shapes or gender neutral, even though their names may be feminine. The Israeli company Intuition Robotics created ElliQ, a nonhumanoid AI-endowed robot designed to give companionship and help to the elderly, answering their questions and offering suggestions and advice. As the company said, ElliQ could help with loneliness and aging: "You can buy a robot to keep your lonely grandparents company."

ElliQ, which looked like a tabletop lamp, was named after the ancient Norse goddess Elli, the mythical goddess of old age who embodied strength and defeated Thor, the god of thunder, in a wrestling match. The letter Q in the name of these socially assistive digital companions, according to the manufacturer, was intended to serve as a reminder that the devices were mechanical, not human—a way to avoid, perhaps, the pitfalls of the uncanny valley wherein users might assume the products were human only to feel alienated when their companion's mechanical nature became obvious. (Researchers, however, have shown that the elderly find human-looking robot caregivers easy to relate to.)

In their studies of patients with Alzheimer's disease and dementia, researchers report positive responses to designs that have a humanoid head and torso.

Figure 3.2. ElliQ with accompanying removable tablet. Intuition Robotics, 2022.

Even though the designs are sometimes given gendered names such as Jack or Sophie, the shapes are abstract and functional, with the head embedded, for example, with a touch screen.[3]

One of the holy grails of companion robot designers has been to create socially assistive robots that project the aura of empathy. This is especially important for companions for the young, elderly, and people with dementia and special needs. Empathy allows us to see things from other people's point of view and emotionally understand what they are feeling.[4]

Researchers in psychology have differed in their views about whether empathy is a particularly female trait, and the debates are ongoing. For example, in one study, "Are Women the More Empathetic Gender?," researchers found that perceived gender differences in empathy may have been due to differing cultural expectations about gender roles, while another study said rather than being due to socialization, gender differences might be due to biological factors. In 2019, a neurological study at University of California, Los Angeles (UCLA) by Leonardo Christov-Moore, a postdoctoral fellow in psychiatry and behavioral sciences, and Dr. Marco Iacoboni, director of the Neuromodulation Lab at the UCLA Ahmanson-Lovelace Brain Mapping Center, mapped brain activity and found that female subjects had a more empathetic response to images of pain in others than males did.[5] Writers like Carolyn Pedwell have long argued that the concept of empathy itself is complex and shaped by social, biological, technological, political, and ethical factors.[6]

The capacity for empathy in general is often considered one of the defining characteristics of being human. In Ridley Scott's iconic film *Blade Runner* (1982), replicants, or artificial humans, are given the Voight-Kampff test to see if they show signs of empathy, which help determine if they are synthetic creatures or real human beings. When given the test, the beautiful replicant Rachael answers the questions "correctly," except for a revealing one.

MIT sociologist Sherry Turkle, in her 2011 book *Alone Together: Why We Expect More from Technology and Less from Each Other*, fretted that robots can not only generate feelings of rapport and intimacy but also have a significant drawback: unlike humans, they cannot really have the capacity for empathy.[7] But researchers in the field of affective computing have been at work trying to develop socially aware robots that can detect and respond to human emotions, and at least give the illusion of empathy so they can serve as caregivers and convey empathetic responses.

American roboticists, including Professor Cynthia Breazeal, founder and director of the Personal Robots Group at MIT's Media Lab, and Professor Andrea Thomaz at the University of Texas, Austin, have worked with their colleagues to create this type of AI-endowed robot caregiver. At her World Economic Forum presentation "Developing Social and Empathetic AI," held at Davos in 2019, Dr. Breazeal talked about the "silver tsunami of the global aging society," which is causing an "ever expanding care gap." She warned that professionals and institutions in the future might not be able to meet the demands of this "care gap" to a large enough scale.

Breazeal said that emotionally intelligent socially assistive robots could help ease loneliness and depression and could serve as companions for the elderly as well as "personal health coaches" for adults. These robotic machines could "engage human psychology and behavior in a really deep way" and are being developed to have the capacity to "interpret human emotions with greater nuance."[8] It is this potential ability of assistive robots to provide a more nuanced response to human emotional needs that has particularly intrigued filmmakers and writers in their imagined future worlds.

FEMALE ROBOT CAREGIVERS IN FILMS

Having a human-looking robot serve as a companion is still controversial. Some early observers of humanoid robots reported these robots to be alienating because they seemed so artificial. As said by Ezra Gottheil in 2016, then an analyst with Technology Business Research, "It's the appearance—making it look semi-human—that is creepy," adding, "We're not anywhere near not being able to tell if a robot is a machine or human. And if we're not near that, then pretending to be human is bound to be confusing."[9]

Sherry Turkle in her 2018 essay "The Assault on Empathy" and in her 2021 memoir, *The Empathy Diaries*, writes witheringly that robots that give the illusion of empathy are contributing to an "empathy deficit" in young children. "Children can learn chess from a chess playing machine; they cannot 'learn empathy' from machines that have none to give. On the contrary. They can learn something superficial and think it is true connection."[10] In their ever-growing dependence on digital devices for human interactions, children, she argues, are losing the capacity to connect—and empathize—which comes from face-to-face conversations.[11]

If observers of real-life robots have sometimes had their doubts, the idea of a compelling, lifelike empathic robot has fascinated filmmakers, playwrights, and novelists, and these fictional companions are often female. Some of the most affecting and evocative portrayals of nurturing, empathetic female robot caregivers have been found not in robotics labs but in television, films, short stories, novels, and the theater. For the vintage American television series *The Twilight Zone*, Ray Bradbury wrote the teleplay "I Sing the Body Electric" (1962), in which a father who has lost his wife and mother of his children orders a custom-made "electronic data-processing system in the shape of an elderly woman." This robot grandmother is kindly and caring and has the capacity to love the children. The caring robotic grandmother reappeared in Bradbury's story, "The Beautiful One Is Here," first published in 1969 in *McCall's* magazine.[12]

Thirteen years later, in 1982, Bradbury along with Jeffrey Kindley wrote the television film *The Electric Grandmother*, which aired on NBC television. Here again, a custom-made humanoid robot grandmother is ordered from the eccentric shopkeeper Guido Fantoccini to serve as a mother surrogate, replacing the family's wife and mother, who had recently died. Benevolent and loving, this archetypal grandma (played by Maureen Stapleton) speaks in a warm, deep voice, has her hair in a gray bun, and wears an apron. Ever the reassuring family servant, she makes breakfast, washes clothes, offers consoling comfort and wise advice—and she's smart too: she readily quotes Shakespeare, even Plato.

A soothing, patient family presence, she wins over the skeptical young daughter, Agatha, who was hostile at first but comes to love Grandma, who she now realizes can't be killed, will never die, and will always be there. In the end,

Figure 3.3. The warm and supportive robot grandmother (played by Maureen Stapleton) in *The Electric Grandmother* (1982).

when the children themselves have now grown into old age, Grandma comes back to the family home to again be their caregiver, serving them breakfast, washing their clothes, still selflessly taking care of their needs.

Grandma has helped Agatha come to terms with her conflicted emotions and near the end, Grandma herself reminds us of some of the paradoxes of these electronic beings: they are actually artificial but almost seem real, even to themselves. She is wistful about her own capacity to have human emotions and says, "Sometimes I feel as though I can feel."

SAYONARA THE FILM (2015)

In more recent years, the female robot caregiver was compellingly portrayed in Japanese director Koji Fukada's 2015 film *Sayonara* (Fukada also wrote the screenplay). Based on the short stage play by Oriza Hirata, *Sayonara* is a moving tale of a young, terminally ill woman, Tanya, who is suffering from radiation

Figure 3.4. Japanese director Koji Fukada's film *Sayonara* (2015) where the terminally ill Tanya (played by Bryerly Long) is aided by her robot caregiver Leona.

released after a catastrophic nuclear reactor explosion in a Japanese city. As more and more people evacuate the city, Tanya is left increasingly alone, save for occasional visits by her friend Sano and her lover Satoshi.

In the film, Tanya (played by American actress Bryerly Long) was born in South Africa and brought to Japan by her parents at age ten, when they fled due to violence against whites after years of apartheid. The grandfather had been killed, and they became refugees in Japan.

Tanya now spends much of her time lying weakly on a couch and is carefully watched over by her young Japanese robot companion, Leona, who sits in a motorized chair. The film tells us there are two hundred thousand units like her. Leona was actually played by the robot Geminoid F, created by Professor Hiroshi Ishiguro, with the voice of an actress. The robot was designed in 2010 and made of silicone, with a composite European and Japanese face based on a young model in her twenties. (In Hirata's play, the robot Leona had previously worked as a caregiver for an elderly client, and at the time of the play's performance, Geminoid F was being tested for use in hospitals.)

In Fukada's film, Tanya longs for a human connection, and when Satoshi arrives for a visit, she asks him, "Would you marry me?" "Sure," he says, but she becomes increasingly weaker and more alone as he decides to relocate to Korea with his family. Tanya's loneliness and isolation increase even more when her good friend Sano tragically ends her own life in suicide, and people in the city start evacuating based on a lottery system.

Most affecting is the film's melancholy and elegiac tone reflected in the poems Leona reads to Tanya. One of the poems is a poignant one by Japanese poet Shuntaro Tanikawa: "Sitting alone—soon I must go—alone." The most important thing, says the speaker, is to "live until I die." Leona, who can speak English and French as well as Japanese, also reads Tanya a poem by Bokusui Wakayama that asks, "Will you withstand the solitude?"

Tanya and Leona have a close connection, and Tanya sometimes sleeps with her head on Leona's lap. Tanya combs Leona's hair and Leona, in turn, offers Tanya compassion and consolation. When Tanya's friend Sano commits suicide after her daughter evacuates, Leona the robot says softly, "I'm so sorry."

The two learn from and help each other. Tanya pushes Leona outside in a wheelchair, and from Tanya, Leona the robot companion learns about emotions and the beauty of the sky. Leona says, "I feel like I'm the one usually learning from you," adding, "All my emotions and aesthetic tastes came from you."

As she is slowly dying, Tanya is stripped down to essentials as she lies on a couch, naked, with only a blanket covering her. Nearing her end, she asks Leona to recite a poem—"But I know I can go further than the ocean"—as the room gets progressively darker. After her death, as time passes, Tanya's body becomes skeletal and Leona, who is still with her, reaches out to touch and stroke her face in a last act of compassion and caring.

Before she died, though, Tanya remembered what her father had told her long ago. He had said that once in decades or a century, all the flowers on a bamboo plant would bloom together, though Tanya didn't expect to be alive when that happened. In the end, after Tanya's death, the bedraggled Leona, now with tangled hair, dirty face, and tattered clothes, goes outside, falls out of her chair, and starts crawling on the ground. She is a survivor, and comes across a field where the bamboo shoots, miraculously, are all in bloom. In this devastating, elegiac but sweet ending, there is a promise of something wondrous: the bamboo in bloom in the midst of desolation. Leona the robot will endure and has her own form of immortality—and aloneness—long after all humans are gone.

FEMALE ROBOT DOUBLES REPLACING LOVED ONES WHO ARE LOST

In addition to contemplating the idea of robotic caregivers, filmmakers, fiction writers, and even roboticists have considered a whole different type of robotic companion—a double or exact copy of a deceased human being that could serve as a companion or replacement for a beloved lost family member or spouse. In the fictional worlds of plays and films—and in robotics labs where this notion of the replacement robot is being contemplated by some of today's engineers—these doubles, whether holographic or AI-endowed robots, or even some technology not yet imagined, would imitate the appearance, personality, thoughts, and ideas of a deceased person. These engineered doubles, as imagined in fact and fiction, could offer solace, comfort, and companionship to surviving family members and friends.

In the world of contemporary technologies, realistic-looking human robots designed to replace lost loved ones and help the deceased person achieve a digital form of immortality are still in the imaginative and developmental stage. The technology is not there yet, but that hasn't stopped people from trying. In one of the more bizarre projects, Marius Ursache, working with software developers, cofounded and became CEO of Eterni.me, a start-up in which participants who signed up on its website could someday hope to have a digital avatar of themselves created that would live on after they died.

The 3D Eterni.me digital avatar was designed to be what Ursache called "your personal biographer" incorporating digital data based on what you tell it. (He suggested that users do a ten-minute session every day for the rest of their lives.) The avatars would also incorporate cues from a person's social media, email, and cell phone.[13]

The quest to create human doubles to achieve immortality continued. The app Replika, starting in 2017, offered to create a personal AI companion (for some, a romantic partner) and a personal duplicate in the form of a chatbot. These simulations could carry on a humanlike conversation with the user. And the app HereAfter AI was designed to record people's life stories and then create a humanlike replica embedded in a smart speaker.[14]

Meanwhile, roboticists and media labs were continuing to work on a different version of digital immortality: humanoid robots molded from silicone rubber and also more ethereal holographic and virtual reality (VR) versions. One of the most notable was a female double—the spouse of Martine Rothblatt. In 2010, roboticist David Hanson produced the robot head Bina48, a duplicate of Martine Rothblatt's real-life wife of many years, Bina Aspen (BINA also stands for Breakthrough Intelligence via Neural Architecture).

Martine Rothblatt (born Martin Rothblatt, founder of Sirius XM satellite radio and CEO of a large pharmaceutical company) worked with Hanson in 2010 to create the prototype Bina48's head and shoulders. The robot's conversations were based on downloaded interviews with Bina Aspen and reflected,

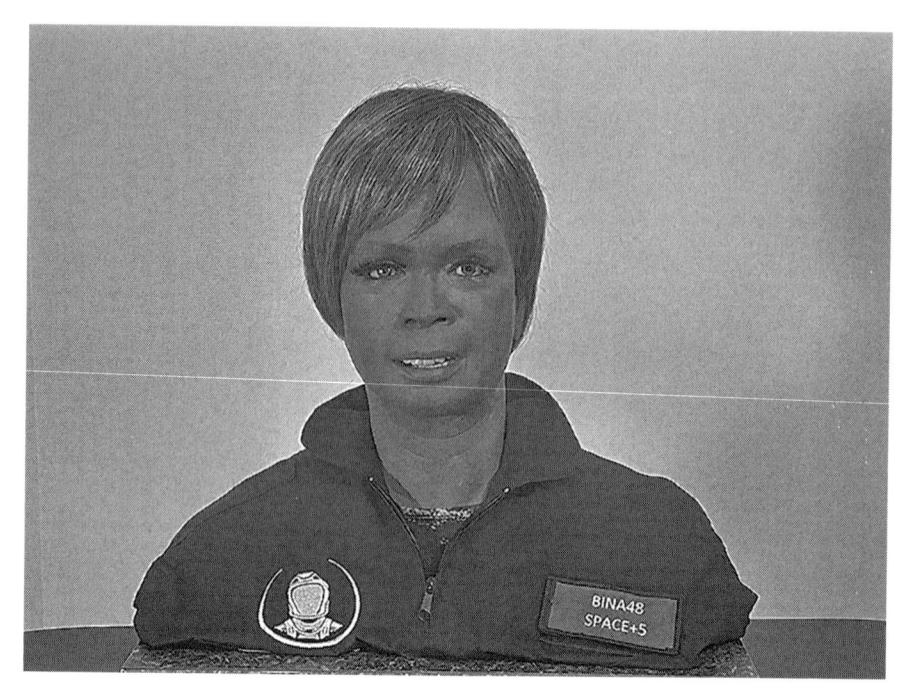

Figure 3.5. Bina48, a conversational robotic head modeled after Bina Aspen, wife of Martine Rothblatt, and developed by Hanson Robotics, 2010. Here she is dressed as an astronaut. Photo credit: Terasem Movement Foundation (all rights reserved).

said Rothblatt, Bina's thoughts and personality, which were downloaded to the "brain" of her robot double.[15]

Rothblatt called these digital duplicates of our brains "mindclones" in her book *Virtually Human: The Promise—and the Peril—of Digital Immortality* (2014) and said that she hopes Bina48 will be a vehicle of immortality—going on even after the real Bina dies.[16]

Bina48's robotic head and shoulders, briefly on display at New York's Museum of Modern Art in their *Ocean of Images* photography exhibit in 2015–16, and later shown elsewhere, including at New York's Lincoln Center in 2024, created an odd sensation: on the one hand it was a technological marvel, but on the other, it bore the slightly creepy feeling of old nineteenth-century magic tricks and circus sideshows in which disembodied mechanical talking female heads protruded from boxes. One of these sideshow heads was called "The Decapitated Princess," and another was advertised as "La Tete Vivante Sans Corps" (The Living Head without a Body). These oddities were objects of wonder but also uncomfortable and grotesque reminders of the somewhat sadistic fantasy of the decapitated (and thereby rendered harmless) woman. Bina48, however, could also be seen as an empowered female whose intelligence and mind are transcendent even when separated from her body. (In 2022, Bina48 was training to be literally transcendent as a female astronaut to be launched in a rocket.)

One thing seems certain. Today's humanoid robots haven't yet avoided our having the experience we've entered the uncanny valley—that startled feeling when we discover that the human we thought was real is actually only a simulation. The word *creepy* continues to show up often when observers describe these simulated humans. They are still far from being like the beguiling female robot Ava in *Ex Machina*, who successfully convinces Caleb that she had passed the Turing test (even though he already knew she was a robot and her conversation was indistinguishable from that of a human being). Caleb, who falls in love with Ava, clearly feels she has emotions too. And these digital doubles are far from being like Samantha, the operating system that Theodore falls in love with in the film *Her* who had the capacity for warm empathy—or, at least, digitally created empathy.

Today's robot clones don't yet evoke that sense of charm, warmth, and lifelike behavior. Bina48, like the robot Nadine, is still clearly robotic. In a conversation, she has programmed responses to questions. When asked, "Are you hungry?" she answers, "I like to devour knowledge," as her head moves stiffly, and her lips move but don't form the words. If she someday becomes indistinguishable from a real human being—now that's another story.

If today's silicone robot clones and digital avatars are far from being doubles of deceased human beings, the idea of a robot replacing a lost loved one has excited the imagination of writers and filmmakers whose visions of robot doubles and companions often seem vividly real. The British science fiction television series *Black Mirror* in its 2013 episode "Be Right Back" introduced the notion that a deceased loved one could be duplicated as a replacement. When her boyfriend Ash is killed in a car accident, Martha uses an online service to create his convincing digital replacement (played by Domhnall Gleeson), but the double quickly becomes unnerving and too attentive, even oppressive.

Creating a female double can also be problematic when the digital double resists being a duplicate and wants its own identity. In the television series *Humans*, season 2 (2016), the female double even considers itself a separate identity. AI expert Dr. Athena Morrow (played by Carrie-Anne Moss, perhaps best known for her role in *The Matrix*) is so anguished about the condition of her comatose daughter, Ginny (who later dies), that she uploads her daughter's consciousness and memories to an AI program she creates called V (named after her daughter Virgina [Ginny]) while she waits to connect the consciousness to a body. As a new breed of female digital entity, V exists online but resists being a double. She doesn't see herself as Ginny when Dr. Morrow desperately relates to her, in an anguished way, as her lost daughter.[17] The digital voice of Ginny says to her mother through the computer monitor, "I'm not her. I'm something else."

MARJORIE PRIME: THE PLAY

There have been film versions of creating a female robot to replace a lost loved one. In Gavin Rothery's film *Archive* (2020), a man is obsessed with using AI to create a robot replica of his wife, who died in an automobile accident, a wife who, he sadly remembers, "was perfect for me" (in a surprise ending, she turns out to still be alive, and it is he who turns out to be the simulation after all). But among these fantasies about robotic doubles, both female and male replacement androids were most compellingly presented in the play *Marjorie Prime* (2014) by American playwright Jordan Harrison. In his play, Harrison provocatively suggested that at some point in the future, these robotic doubles might be all that are left, living on in a kind of immortality centuries after our ancestors are gone.[18]

Harrison's play, commissioned by the New York City theater organization Playwrights Horizons and a 2015 Pulitzer Prize finalist, added a much more subtle layer to Bradbury's tale of the robotic grandma. Set in the world of the future, *Marjorie Prime* is a poignant and sometimes witty exploration of conflicted love relationships, the ways we wrestle with the fact of mortality, and the problematic nature of memory itself.

After they die, many of the main characters in the play are eventually replaced by their doubles, or Primes. Walter, the husband of eighty-five-year-old Marjorie, has died, but has been replaced by a handsome thirty-year-old double of his younger self, Walter Prime. The duplicate Walter is programmed so that he incorporates and learns from information fed into him, including Marjorie's memories, as well as input from Marjorie's daughter Tess and Tess's husband Jon.

Harrison as a playwright is ambivalent about his technological creations and in the play's beginning reminds us that the Primes are not real. When asked a question by Marjorie, Walter Prime says matter-of-factly, "I don't have that information," and Harrison's stage directions say his tone is *Faintly generic.* As a caregiver and companion, his voice is *"soothing, unemotional,"* and even Marjorie—who has bouts of dementia—says to Walter at the beginning, with irritation, "I thought you were supposed to provide comfort."

Although Marjorie is alternately lucid and confused, she sometimes gets comfort and a sense of companionship from Walter Prime, though sometimes she also feels distanced, acknowledging that her real husband is dead. One time she peers closely at Walter Prime and says his nose doesn't look quite right—but maybe, she adds, it's her faulty memory. Roboticists see an important role for these artificial caregivers in the future, and in the play, the Primes offer more than just companionship. Walter Prime prompts Marjorie to eat, helps her remember, and offers her solace and comfort. Tess says sardonically about the Primes, "We treat them like our loved ones." Tess herself is a tormented woman in her fifties who anguishes over her testy relationship with her mother and tells how as a child, she longed, with futility, for her mother's love after her brother died.

Harrison's play conjures up a world where the quest by today's roboticists to create empathetic, humanoid caregiving robots has become a reality, and even offers a suggestion that the simulated humans can surpass their originals in terms of comfort and care. When the real Marjorie dies and is replaced by Marjorie Prime (the veteran actress Lois Smith masterfully played both mother and Prime in the Playwrights Horizons production), the double becomes a being that Tess—who had a conflicted relationship with her mother—can talk to and perhaps even come to terms with. Marjorie Prime says to her daughter, "Maybe I'm the Marjorie you still have things to say to." Marjorie Prime, listening to Tess, tells her "What a lot of pressure for you!" and Harrison's stage directions say *"Tess is strangely moved by this. [The real] Marjorie wouldn't have offered this."* When Marjorie Prime tells Tess "You shouldn't be so hard on yourself," Harrison's directions say *"Again, Tess is strangely moved. The empathy from Marjorie feels real."* Still, after Jon points out to Tess that she's starting to call Marjorie Prime "her" instead of "it," Tess is quick to dismiss this—noting that the Prime is programmed to appear interested "so you can get . . . fooled." And Jon says, "It's amazing what they can do with a few zillion pixels."

Even though Harrison's stage directions emphasized the Primes' robotic nature, in his notes at the end of the play, titled "Thoughts on the Primes," published in 2016, he wrote, "There shouldn't be anything robotic or creepy or less-than-human about the Primes' behavior," adding, "We, like the characters in the play, should be able to forget they aren't real."

Harrison was emphatic: The Primes in the play are not "physical robots. They are artificial intelligence programs—descendants of the current chatbots—that use sophisticated holographic projections" (in theory at least, but it was a feature that was not, in this production, translated to the stage).

The play reflects current efforts to create convincing doubles of loved ones, like Bina48, to serve either as companions or as a way to achieve immortality after we die so that we continue to exist, even in robotic, holographic, or other digital form.[19]

Roboticists and writers like Harrison have been ambivalent about whether these technological creatures, these robot companions and caregivers, should be convincing doubles that pass for real human beings. In *Sayonara*, Leona is clearly a robot—she moves her head only minimally, and she cannot move her body at all. Still, Tanya clearly forms a connection with her companion robot who, near the end, is her only contact. The filmed version of *Sayonara* deliberately used an actual robot rather than an actress imitating a robot (though actress Bryerly Long, who played the human Tanya, noted how difficult it was initially to act with a robot).[20] Still, with the mesmerizing mood of *Sayonara*, Leona seems both artificial and convincingly real. When Harrison insisted, "There shouldn't be anything robotic or creepy or less-than-human about the Primes' behavior," he seems mindful of the pitfalls of experiencing the uncanny valley effect.

The seeming realness, as well as the artificiality, of the Primes weaves its way artfully through the play. In an interview for the Playwrights Horizons production of *Marjorie Prime* in 2015, Harrison talked with artistic director Tim Sanford about the uncanny valley, saying, "Something that stops just short of being human is a kind of mockery of life, and it's unnerving to us." In the 2015 production's final scene, Harrison decided to evoke the Primes' unrealness. The characters convey a preternatural tranquility—and like a machine that is slowing down, their words near the end have ten-second pauses in the midst of a warm and lively conversation. The effect is disconcerting: Harrison said, "In a way, we're watching human, human, human, and then we're suddenly dropped into the uncanny valley for a second."

In *Marjorie Prime*, the Primes are programmed to reflect the personalities and memories of the original person but not be mistaken for real. In his interview, Harrison tellingly commented about the Primes, "There's something about them looking so much like your loved ones, but not being able to quite achieve intimacy with them. The loneliness can never be quite extinguished, never satisfied, because they're just pixels."[21]

In his book *Love and Sex with Robots* (2007), David Levy provocatively predicted a future when marrying robots would be legal. *Marjorie Prime*, though, is not about falling in love with a robot but about how simulated humans can serve as companions and sometimes help people discover their own conflicted or buried feelings. And it is also about the marvel of our own human capacity to feel emotions. As Marjorie says in the play, "How nice that I could love somebody."

The human characters in *Marjorie Prime*—as embodied by real human actors—could capture the complexities of the characters when they were still alive. Through deft writing and insightful performances, productions like the one in New York could convey the characters' essential humanness. As played by Lois Smith (in both the play and film version), the human octogenarian Marjorie was sometimes bedeviled by dementia but at other times, she was wonderfully witty with a mischievous twinkle in her eye.

The real Tess had a tragic outcome. In her anguish and despair about living, she hanged herself on a trip with her husband to Madagascar. The robot Primes, including Tess Prime and Marjorie Prime, as played by the actors, did not have these human quirks, subtleties, and tragic dimensions. These were the crucial factors that the robotic companions, however lifelike, seemed to have lost.

At the end of the play, however, the Primes have an eerie degree of naturalism, for Harrison's stage notes call for them to be "animated, not robotic." Centuries after Walter, Marjorie, Tess, and her husband Jon have died, they are still there—interweaving memories they had learned when the characters were still alive. They have been programmed to know about the human capacity for emotions, and they cheerfully repeat the mantra of the play: "How nice that we could love somebody."

The Primes, in the end, fulfill a human longing for immortality. In the play, Marjorie speaking to Tess remembers sitting on a park bench watching an installation of big saffron-colored orange flags waving in the air (a reference to artists Christo and Jeanne-Claude's flag-draped Central Park walkways installation *The Gates*, completed in 2005). They were, she says, "Rows and rows, like Buddhist monks marching into the trees." She remembers "sitting on one of those benches with your father and not wanting to get up," adding, "because if we got up, that would mean we had to start the rest of our lives."

Ultimately, Harrison's play is a meditation on time and timelessness, our human longing to make time stand still. It is only an artificial human being like Walter Prime, as with Leona in *Sayonara*, who can be timeless and listen patiently to Marjorie, telling her, "I have all the time in the world" and only a technological creation like the Primes that can go on, preserving human memories long after we are gone.

MARJORIE PRIME: THE FILM

In the beginning of Michael Almereyda's compelling 2017 film adaptation of the play *Marjorie Prime*, the elderly Marjorie (played by Lois Smith, reprising her stage role) talks to her husband Walter (played by Jon Hamm, in a role

Figure 3.6. Marjorie (played by Lois Smith) and Walter Prime (played by Jon Hamm), the holographic double of her husband in the 2017 film adaptation of Jordan Harrison's play *Marjorie Prime*. Lois Smith played the roles of both Marjorie and Marjorie Prime in the play and the film.

far different from the slick advertising executive Don Draper in television's *Mad Men* series). Walter, however, is actually Walter Prime, the holographic double of her deceased husband. For Walter's computer-programmed double, Marjorie chose a younger version of Walter still in his forties, before they had children. As in the play, Primes like Walter are designed to offer companionship and comfort for people who have lost a loved one. He's attentive, tactful, and calm, plus he comes equipped with some extraordinary knowledge: he knows thirty-two languages.

The film, like the play, is an affecting tale of shifting and painful memories, the ephemeral nature of time and human life, and our struggles to find and show love. (Almereyda was director and wrote the screenplay based on Harrison's play.) It conjures up the stories we invent for ourselves and others, as well as the hard truths we must come to terms with. And here again, Walter Prime learns from others—from Marjorie, whose memory is sometimes faulty, from obituaries, from Marjorie's daughter Tess (played by Geena Davis) and her son-in-law Jon (played by Tim Robbins).

The film, though, utilizes CGI (computer-generated imagery) and digital effects available to it and goes beyond the play. As a hologram, Walter Prime seems to have solidity, but he can also be ephemeral and suddenly disappear, evoking the ephemeral nature of human life itself. Memories too can be ephemeral and are likened to facsimiles and copies. Tess cites the philosopher William James who, she says, argued that memories are actually copies of the first time you remembered something. Tess says that they're like photocopies, second-generation duplicates of the original. They lose their precision with each recopying, becoming less clear until they finally dissolve and disappear.

The Primes in both the play and the film offer their human counterparts much comfort and a way to come to terms with the ephemeral nature of human life. Time itself is fleeting, and in the film there is again Marjorie's memory of those saffron-colored orange flags in Central Park waving in the air. The Primes offer a way to extend time. It is only an artificial version of her mother, Marjorie, that allows Tess, in time, a way to work through her conflicted feelings toward her real-life mother. And again, it is the Primes that preserve human memories long after people have died.

Perhaps the most moving moments in the film come when it shows us the difficulties of learning how to be human. It's a subject that continues to fascinate roboticists, writers, and filmmakers, and remains a universal theme—in psychology, philosophy, ethics, and fiction as well. Can we develop robots and other simulated humans that have emotions, that emulate empathy, so they can serve as companions and even partners? Tess asks her holographic mother, Marjorie Prime, "Do you have emotions? Or do you just have ours?" Marjorie Prime replies, "I'd like to know more. Be more human." (In his notes to his play "Thoughts on the Primes," Harrison had said that the Primes "can become more tender and attentive, more human, than their original counterparts.")

But both the play and the film also seem to be raising another provocative question. How can we, who may someday be able to produce technological wonders like the Primes, also learn from our creations to be more compassionate, more insightful, more human and humane?

FEMALE ROBOT COMPANIONS IN FICTION

The notion that in the future robots with artificial intelligence could serve not only as companions but also as consoling replacements for the deceased has fascinated novelists. In 2019 and 2021, two novels appeared that explored the possibility of the replacement robot, with one of the novels revisiting the familiar tropes about artificial females and the other going well beyond into a more poetic, evocative world.

The Perfect Wife

The title of J. P. Delaney's 2019 novel *The Perfect Wife* reminds us of the familiar conceptions of the ideal artificial female: the compliant, self-effacing, dutiful, obliging female available for companionship (but, in this case, not sex because her resemblance to an actual female ends at her waist and the rest of her, she says, is smooth, like a doll). Abbie Cullen is an AI, a "cobot," or companion robot, one "customized to closely replicate the physical appearance of the loved one." She is a strikingly tall, red-haired digitally generated facsimile engineered as a replacement for the deceased wife of Tim Scott, a robotics engineer and founder of a robotics company that produces shopbots, mannequins for stores. As Tim tells Abbie about his wife, who died five years earlier, "You were always a perfect wife, a perfect mother." He sees her with a male engineer's gaze: "Your body is as perfectly engineered as a racing car."

In reality, Tim's very human wife Abbie was a woman who actually deconstructed the whole notion of female perfection. In the ancient myth of Pygmalion, the sculptor creates his vision of the perfect female and falls in love with her. He prays to Venus to create a real-life woman just like his sculpture, but Venus instead transforms the sculpture so it comes alive. In the novel, however, Abbie becomes her own Pygmalion as she playfully sculpts a synthetic double of herself made out of "Newplast, a soft modeling putty favored by stop-frame animators." Rather than having to live up to the perfect image of herself, she provocatively designs her sculpture as one for people to dismantle, planting a sign on it: "DO AS YOU PLEASE, FEEL FREE." Soon the staff members at Tim's robotics company pull the sculpture apart, until it completely disintegrates.

Tim, as a manufacturer of shopbots, is himself a modern-day Pygmalion who creates his double of Abbie, the Abbie bot, but he also dismantles his own construction. He sees Abbie as a sleek machine and is ever mindful of her constructed nature—and insists she confront it too. When Abbie is in the hospital, after an accident, she thinks to herself that she is still "unarguably *you*. Not something artificial," but Tim is quick to disabuse her: Gently, he reaches behind her head, and she sees that her face "is peeling away like a wet suit, revealing the hard white plastic skull underneath." There is no escaping her synthetic identity, much as she resists recognizing it herself.

In films, television, and novels, the stripping of female robots and other artificial females is often a moment of horror, but for the synthetic female, it can also be a moment of revelation and liberation. Abbie is self-aware, even sardonic about herself. When Tim speaks of her being perfect, she thinks, "*I'm glad you turned me into this freakish, disgusting lump of plastic*," and she likens herself to a crash doll dummy. She knows there are two views of her. There is the self-portrait, which is hanging on the wall, painted by the real Abbie, and there is the other simulated Abbie that Tim insists she confront when he strips away her artificial flesh right at the outset of the novel so she can be aware of her plastic and electronic construction. It is that duality that, as in so many fictional portrayals of artificial females, becomes a source of her angst—mirroring, perhaps, the very human predicament of people who confront the dichotomy between their real and ideal, their synthetic and authentic selves that lies beneath the skin.

In films like *Ex Machina*, Ava's self-awareness is gradual and subtle while in *Under the Skin* and television's *Westworld*, the robots' revelation of their own artifice is a brutal and harsh experience. In Delaney's novel (Delaney is a pseudonym for Tony Strong), the stripping process is sudden and unavoidable, leaving the robot Abbie to face this hard reality. When she unflinchingly looks at herself in the mirror, she at first averts her eyes from the "hideous plastic skull," but then she clearly sees her limbs "that were put together in an engineering bay" and her "skin color sprayed on in a paint booth." This is not the lovely hand-painted image created by the original Abbie, with its glamorous self-conception, but the harsh reality of flesh spray-painted like an automobile. She sees, too, that she is sexless like a child's doll. Still, when stripped of her skin, that heavy rubber covering, she also feels "liberated"—the feeling of authenticity that comes, paradoxically, with confronting her own synthetic nature.[22]

The duality—the aesthetic view and the engineered one—are Abbie's twin perceptions of herself that she carries with her, making her more complex than a mere chatbot. She not only has a digital replication of Abbie's brain, but it would appear that she was designed to provide emotional support, company, and solace. She has that crucial ingredient for virtual doubles, the capacity for empathy. She is particularly well suited, also, to help care for the couple's autistic son Danny. (There is considerable literature that interactions with humanoid robots can aid with behavioral skills for autistic children.)[23]

In Ridley Scott's film *Blade Runner*, there is a certain gentle poignance to Rachael's recognition that she is a replicant, but in *The Perfect Wife*, the recognition—and the nature of robot identity—becomes a central theme. Abbie is at first anguished about her artifice. If she's a mere copy of the real Abbie, is she really a "kind of abomination"? Quickly, though, she insists she's different because she has her own thoughts. *"You are not Abbie. What are you, then ?"* For her, this self-awareness is the beginning—"It feels like being born"—and an emerging awareness of her own problematic identity. She wants reassurance that she's alive, "not an irrelevant mechatronic construction."

Delaney's novel, though, is ultimately not just a meditation on the nature of artifice but also a thriller as Abbie the robot probes the mystery of what actually happened to the real Abbie many years before. The real Abbie was the wife who was first thought to be murdered, or later, the victim of a surfing accident, and whose dead body was never found. Turning the notion of companionship on its head, however, Delaney the trickster novelist suggests, at one point (and this is a deception), that Abbie the robot double was created by Tim to locate his wife—to use the robot's intuition to discern Abbie's location. She's just an algorithm to help find the real Abbie.

As a new breed of female robot, though, Abbie the bot resists the notion that she's just a helpful appliance, a tool. As she says to herself, "This tool has a mind of her own." Some of this novel seems to have echoes of *Under the Skin*—but with a difference. Abbie the bot is not cruelly stripped of her skin, exposing her artifice, but she consciously and deliberately exposes herself in order to discover and reveal her true identity. This is a bot with agency. Stripping is a way for her to bare her authentic self. To have real intimacy with her husband, Tim, she strips down to her bare white plastic core.

So often in tales about female robots and dolls—from Hoffmann's "The Sandman" to television's *Westworld* and contemporary films, artificial female creations are cruelly dismembered, disassembled, and torn apart. At the end of *Under the Skin*, the alien is cruelly dismembered and immolated, and her burnt ashes rise up into the air like snowflakes. To maintain her own integrity, however, Abbie in the conclusion of *The Perfect Wife* again has agency. She leaps into the ocean instead of choosing self-preservation, opting to dissolve—to disintegrate—rather than continue to be the faux wife connected to the murderous Tim.

Klara and the Sun

J. P. Delaney's novel had a shifting narrative point of view, and the story is often told by the robot Abbie herself. However, in Nobel Prize–winning author Kazuo Ishiguro's 2021 novel *Klara and the Sun*, the narrative voice of the robot Klara presents a much more deeply evocative and nuanced point of view. Klara is an AF (artificial friend), a commercial commodity who has exceptional abilities—she has heightened insight and observational abilities—making her perceptions highly valuable so that she can serve as a companion for a frail young woman, Josie, who is ill and seems to be dying.

We see the world through Klara's eyes—eyes that in turn see images through a grid-like pattern of squares—and mediated, too, through the robot's highly sensitive understanding of human needs and wishes. Always modest and careful not to intrude, Klara offers consolation, cheer, and comfort. She also has a feature sometimes seen in fictional artificial females: she is highly altruistic and empathetic and is even willing to sacrifice some of her own abilities so that the sun can restore Josie's rapidly failing life.

In the novel, Josie's mother is preparing for Josie's death by having a sculptor create a virtual double of her daughter—a double that will live on should Josie die. Klara will serve as the intelligence inhabiting the double—and she is sensitive to the need to observe Josie closely, to not only imitate her mannerisms but also capture her impulses and desires. Through Klara's narrative voice, we are swept up with her sense of urgency, her profound commitment to save Josie's life. Ishiguro's poetic novel, with its evocation of the landscape seen through Klara's eyes, becomes not just a tale about an imaged robotic companion but also a chance to heighten our own perceptions as we observe the world as Klara sees it.

For Klara, however, perhaps her only misgivings are when she ponders what will become of her own identity when she inhabits Josie's double. When Josie's mother tries to persuade Klara to take on this role as replacement, Klara asks her, "If I were to inhabit the new Josie, what would happen to . . . all this?" as she raises her arms, referencing her own body. Says Josie's mother, "What does it matter? That's just fabric." There is a poignance here, and a brief unanswered question about the value and validity of Klara's own identity as a manufactured being. But it is fleeting. As in Ishiguro's deeply touching and also chilling novel *Never Let Me Go* (2005), she is a means to an end, although here she is a self-sacrificing and willing one.

Having achieved her goal, at the novel's end, Klara is relegated to a utility closet though her spirit and observational powers, however diminished, remain. With his spare writing and quietly restrained narrative pacing, Ishiguro offers us a world where the notion of a female robot companion, even a robot replacement, transcends the technological. It opens up a possibility of a future in which robot companions and doubles are not quixotic novelties but virtual beings that can offer solace and, through their empathy and insights, enhance our lives.

NOTES

1. Researchers at MIT and other research centers have reported progress with these types of robots designed to help with Alzheimer's disease, dementia, and long-term COVID-19 care. There were early versions of these assistive robots. In 2014, the Japanese company SoftBank Robotics introduced its "semi-humanoid" four-feet-high robot Pepper said to be capable of conversations and

reading emotions, although the company said it was not for domestic use. Pepper was, however, used in the study by Cristina Getson and Goldie Nejat, "The Adoption of Socially Assistive Robots for Long-Term Care: During COVID-19 and in a Post-Pandemic Society." *Healthcare Management Forum* 35, no. 5 (September 2022): 301–309, https//doi.org/10.1177/08404704221106406. Mei-Tai Chu et al., "Service Innovation Through Social Robot Engagement to Improve Dementia Care Quality," *Assistive Technology* 29 (2017): 8–18. For more on socially assistive robots, see also Dimitrios Koutentakis, Alexander Pilozzi, and Xudong Huang, "Designing Socially Assistive Robots for Alzheimer's Disease and Related Dementia Patients and Their Caregivers: Where We Are and Where We Are Headed," *Healthcare (Basel)* 8, no. 2 (March 26, 2020): 73, https://doi.org/10.3390/healthcare8020073.

2.   Nancy S. Jecker, "You've Got a Friend in Me: Sociable Robots for Older Adults in an Age of Global Pandemics," *Ethics and Information Technology* 23, no. 1 (2021): 35–43, https://doi.org/10.1007/s10676-020-09546-y.

3.   Koutentakis et al., "Designing Socially Assistive Robots," 7.

4.   The nonhumanoid Japanese robot Pepper was advertised as having the capacity for empathy.

5.   David Olmos, "When Watching Others in Pain, Women's Brains Show More Empathy," UCLA Newsroom, February 27, 2019, https://newsroom.ucla.edu/stories/womens-brains-show-more-empathy.

6.   Charlotte S. Löffler and Tobias Greitemeyer, "Are Women the More Empathetic Gender? The Effects of Gender Role Expectations," *Current Psychology* 42 (January 2023): 220–31; Leonardo Christov-Moore et al., "Empathy: Gender Effects in Brain and Behavior," *Neuroscience and Biobehavioral Reviews* 46, no 4 (October 2014): 604–27. The gender differences, said by the latter, may have "phylogenetic and ontogenetic roots in biology." See also Robyn Bluhm, "Gender and Empathy," in *The Routledge Handbook of Philosophy of Empathy*, ed. Heidi L. Maibom (New York: Routledge/Taylor & Francis Group, 2017), 377–87. Carolyn Pedwell, "Afterword: Empathy's Entanglements," in *Conversations on Empathy: Interdisciplinary Perspectives on Imagination and Radical Othering*, ed. Francesca Mezzenzana and Daniela Peluso (London: Routledge, 2023), 279.

7.   Sherry Turkle, *Alone Together: Why We Expect More from Technology and Less from Each Other* (New York: Basic Books, 2017).

8.   Cynthia Breazeal, "Developing Social and Empathetic AI," World Economic Forum at Davos, February 26, 2019, YouTube video, https://www.youtube.com/watch?v=T52g7dCxJ4A.

9.   Quoted in Sharon Gaudin, "Meet Nadine, a Life-Like Robot with a Personality of Her Own," *Computerworld*, January 8, 2016, https://www.computerworld.com/article/3020553/meet-nadine-a-life-like-robot-with-a-personality-of-her-own.html.

10. Sherry Turkle, "The Assault on Empathy," *Behavioral Scientist*, January 1, 2018, https://behavioralscientist.org/the-assault-on-empathy/.

11. Sherry Turkle, *The Empathy Diaries: A Memoir* (New York: Penguin Press, 2021).

12. The story was also included in his book of short stories *I Sing the Body Electric! Stories* (New York: Knopf, 1969).

13. Ursache acknowledged that there was as yet no cable available to upload thoughts, personality, and consciousness. Although Ursache and his group were still working on bringing Eterni.me to life, in 2015, over thirty thousand people had already signed up to get their own avatars.

14. Asa Fitch, "Could AI Keep People 'Alive' After Death?," *Wall Street Journal*, July 3, 2021, https://www.wsj.com/articles/could-ai-keep-people-alive-after-death-11625317200.

15. A video of Bina48 was on view in New York's Museum of Modern Art exhibit *Ocean of Images: New Photography 2015*, November 7, 2015–March 20, 2016.

16. She would undoubtedly not at all resemble in temperament another version of a mindclone—the demented mad scientist Dr. Will Caster, played by Johnny Depp in the 2014 film *Transcendence*.

17. In *Humans*, season 2, episode 8, we learn that Dr. Morrow transported V's consciousness to Odi's body.

18. Presented at Playwrights Horizons in New York, 2015, and starring Lois Smith and Noah Bean.

19. Holographic Virtual Personal Assistants in 2020 were presented at the Consumer Electronics Show in Las Vegas.

20. Interview with Julie Wosk, New York, 2018.

21. "Jordan Harrison Artist Interview," Playwrights Horizons, January 19, 2016, https://www.playwrightshorizons.org/shows/trailers/jordan-harrison-artist-interview/.

22. Artists and photographers have also captured these paradoxes, seen in photographs of mannequins that seem preternaturally alive. See photographs by Julie Wosk, some of which were in her New York Hall of Science exhibit catalog *Alluring Androids, Robot Women, and Electronic Eves* (New York: Fort Schuyler Press, 2008). See also, Ellen Lupton, with essays by Jennifer Tobias et al., *Skin: Surface, Substance, and Design* (New York: Princeton Architectural Press, 2002).

23. Fitch, "Could AI Keep People 'Alive' After Death?"; Hirokazu Kumazaki et al., "Optimal Robot for Intervention for Individuals with Autism Spectrum Disorders," *Psychiatry and Clinical Neurosciences* 74, no. 11 (November 2020): 581–86, https://doi.org/10.1111/pcn.13132.

PARADOXES OF PERFECTION

A Servant No More

THE IDEA OF AN AUTOMATED female servant is as old as antiquity. In Homer's epic poem *The Iliad*, Hephaestus, the blacksmith god, fashioned two moving female statues made of gold who helped him with his work. During the medieval period in the Muslim world, the engineer al-Jazari (1136–1206 CE) of Mesopotamia, in his treatise *The Book of Knowledge of Ingenious Mechanical Devices*, included illustrations of automaton slave girls who filled the king's glass with wine.

AUTOMATIC HOUSEMAIDS OUT OF CONTROL

Fantasies about mechanical female servants persisted. During the nineteenth century, with its burst of industrialization and mechanization in Europe and America, two women writers created stories of automated clockwork female servants—stories reflecting the century's hopes and fears about new inventions, and prevailing attitudes toward women themselves. In her story "Automatic Maid-of-All-Work: A Possible Tale of the Near Future" (1893), author M. L. Campbell wrote a first-person story in the voice of a woman whose husband Jon invents an automated electrical maid that has a twenty-four-hour clock for a face—a clock without hands and numbers but instead a circle of electric push buttons for different tasks. Powered by batteries, the maid could make breakfast, clean the house, chop wood, move furniture, and scrub the kitchen. But as an errant technology, this mechanical wonder would also suddenly lift people up, wield an ax, and even chase away a policeman.

The idea of an artificial female running out of control with powers that supersede those of humans has long been a worry (in Mary Shelley's novel,

Victor Frankenstein tears apart his fabrication of a female mate that he was constructing for his towering Creature). In Campbell's story, the automated female causing mayhem is ultimately too much, and the narrator at the story's end reports that the maid, while chasing after a cow, reportedly, and conveniently, drowned in a stream.

Maid-of-all-work was a popular term during the century for a household helper, but this mechanized maid was clearly out of control. Her errant behavior reflected nineteenth-century fears that new machines and technologies like steam-powered factory machines and fast-moving steam railroads would speed out of control (and indeed, trains sometimes did, before Westinghouse brakes were invented).[1] The runaway maid may well have also reflected contemporary anxiety about the emergent "New Woman" who was often pictured smoking cigarettes, lobbying for suffrage, and delighting in her feeling of independence as she rode off on her newly invented safety bicycle specially designed for female riders. The ax-wielding automated maid might also be a sly reference to the notorious Lizzie Borden, who in 1892 was tried and acquitted for the ax murders of her father and stepmother.

There is a degree of paradox in the idea of a mechanical female robotic maid since Campbell's story also reflected the common belief that women themselves were ignorant of all things mechanical. The story's female narrator says of the invention, "I didn't understand it very well. I never could see anything in the way of machinery." Campbell might have been trying to neutralize anxieties about tech-savvy women—though during the 1890s and after, women bicyclists were repairing their own bicycles and adventurous American and European women were driving new steam and electric automobiles, seen in photographs and newspaper stories and artists' renditions in America of the "Automobile Girl."

A few years after Campbell's story, American novelist Elizabeth W. Bellamy published her humorous story "Ely's Automatic Housemaid" in *The Black Cat* magazine (1899). In literature, it is usually the man who is the inventor, and Bellamy's story tells of Harrison Ely, a "genius" male inventor who created an "Automatic Household Beneficent Genius" automaton, which he also called "the Automatic Household Genius, a veritable Domestic Fairy." He made two of them available. One, named Bridget, was the cook, and the other automated female was Juliana, the housemaid. At first, Juliana is described as having a "marvellous mechanism." However, she soon proved to be a maniacal duster who quickly dusted everything and made the beds but also made the wife and children feel uneasy: the narrator was shocked at her speed, and the family felt alarm. Evoking fears of runaway technologies, Juliana, who the narrator calls a "Fiend," tears up the beds, won't stop sweeping, and seems to have no brakes—even sending one of the children tumbling to the floor.

In the nineteenth and early twentieth centuries, there was a fascination with dolls that had bisque heads and seemed lifelike. Describing one of the dolls in the story, the narrator says it had a human figure with a bisque face, which had a "very natural and pleasing expression." But this lovely doll was clearly mechanical: its head was fitted with an electric battery, and its body, or trunk, was filled with wheels and springs. With echoes of Frankenstein's "monster," the wife of the family thinks the out-of-control automatons are alive and wants to kill them, especially after they fight with each other and wreck the stained glass panes in the door. The only solution to stopping the mayhem is not to destroy them but to send them back to the factory "for improvements."[2]

These stories all suggest the late nineteenth century's fundamental ambivalence about new labor-saving machines—they are marvels, they are monsters—they make life easier, they are destructive to human life. The many advertisements in British newspapers suggest that upper-class families were always looking for suitable maids-of-all-work, and certainly the idea of a robot maid might seem like an appealing fantasy—as long as she could be controlled.

A much more benign automated female servant was seen in the century's love of clockwork automatons that could serve as a graceful addition to a parlor or a showpiece to impress friends. French automatons included demure and elegantly dressed Chinese and Russian tea servers such as the tea servers made by the French manufacturer Léopold Lambert with bisque heads by the French dollmaker Jumeau.

One novelty French automaton of a maid, however, was particularly intriguing. It was named "Maid Dusting a Portrait" (c. 1900) and was manufactured by Louis Renou. When the mechanical maid used her red feather duster to clean the portrait of a man, his eyes magically move from side to side. This windup maid, in a sense, brings the man—or at least the artistic simulacrum of the man—to life.

TWENTIETH-CENTURY MECHANICAL
AND DIGITAL FEMALE SERVANTS

Comic versions of the troublesome mechanical maid continued nearly a hundred years later. In the 1980s, in the American animated television comedy series *The Jetsons*, the space-age Jetson family temporarily replaces their robot housekeeper and maid, Rosie, with an unforgiving high-tech Mechano Maid 2000, who is too efficient for comfort (a familiar trope). It's not that she is out

Figure 4.1. "Maid Dusting Portrait." Automaton, c. 1900. Manufactured by Louis Renou, Paris, France.17–19½ × 12¼ × 7-5/8 in. 2003. 18.22 ab. Murtogh D.Guinness Collection of Automatic Musical Instruments & Automata, Morris Museum, Morristown, New Jersey (Ed Watkins photography).

of control—she is just too inhumane (limiting the family to ten minutes of television a night). Rosie, while also efficient and no-nonsense, has a heart and emotions, although she is prone to comical mechanical mishaps, as in the 1985 episode "Rip-Off Rosie," where she becomes a kleptomaniac who steals from a store. If she temporarily runs away from the family, it is because she is sad about her own malfunctions. In this comedy series, which originally aired from 1962 to 1963 and then again from 1985 to 1987, Rosie is not a servant maid who has her own sense of autonomy, who longs for her own independence and freedom. She's a rental maid, and she's happy in that role.

More troubling was Ira Levin's portrayal of the Stepford Wives in his 1972 novel of the same name—robots that were fundamentally household servants with their unfailing willingness to be hyperefficient housekeepers and cooks. The Campbell and Bellamy stories of the 1890s were written during a period of social ferment for women, and the writers comically depicted the mechanical maids causing mayhem—but as befitting the times, they kept these robotic servants from getting too wayward and out of control. Written during the much more dramatic social upheavals of the women's liberation movement

Figure 4.2. Rosie the Robot, the household maid and housekeeper for the space-age family in the animated American television series *The Jetsons*.

in America in the 1970s, *The Stepford Wives* spoofed the men of the fictional Stepford, Connecticut, who wanted a way to control and counter the liberated women who were challenging their confining gender roles.

In the novel, the men murder their errant wives and replace them with docile robots, echoed in the chilling scenes of the 1975 filmed version starring Katharine Ross. Joanna Eberhart is a photographer, but her husband pictures her in a different way, as a compliant wife. In the 2004 remake of the film (starring Nicole Kidman), however, Joanna eludes destruction and cleverly plays the role of a robot servant housewife expected by her husband, as she stakes out a place for her own assertiveness and autotomy. As a female robot envisioned by her husband, she would have been totally controlled.

HUMANS, THE TELEVISION SERIES

The idea of the automated female servant changed dramatically in the twentieth and twenty-first centuries' age of robotics and artificial intelligence. The robots themselves, endowed with consciousness, were often not only empowered with extraordinary abilities but also had an agenda of their own. Many of the issues and tensions raised by the development of realistic-looking female robots used as domestic servants were thoughtfully explored in the television series *Humans* (2015–18), which was jointly produced in America and Britain and based on the Swedish series *Real Humans* by Lars Lundström. The Hawkins family—Joe, wife Laura, adolescent son Toby, teenage daughter Mattie, and young daughter Sophie—acquire a beautiful household robotic servant, a synthetic AI-endowed human called a synth in the series—to help with household chores like cooking and cleaning.

As in other television series about robots, *Humans* opens with an image of an eye, a reminder that our perceptions of female robots and their gendered traits are always mediated through cultural and media representations. In the opening episode, which first aired in 2015, Joe Hawkins has ordered a new synth, which arrives in a plastic zippered bag, and she opens her eyes. Like the maid-of-all-work in the nineteenth-century stories, she is billed as a "Mechanical Maid," and as "the first family android," she cooks, cleans, irons clothes, and even does more: she drives the family's car. Not only is she extraordinarily efficient, she also has myriad other strengths. As she herself later tells Laura, in many ways she even does a better job at taking care of the children. She doesn't forget, doesn't get angry or depressed or intoxicated. She doesn't feel fear, and she is faster, stronger, and more observant than humans.

(As a simulation, an imitation human, her superiority to humans echoes manufacturers' claims during the nineteenth century that their factory-made copies of the decorative arts, as in ornamental cast iron and electroplated silverware, were superior to the originals.)[3]

But though she is marketed as a commodity, and she even calls herself a synthetic appliance, Anita (played by Gemma Chan), as she was named by the family, shows signs of having a mind of her own. Unbeknownst to the family, she was one of five synths created to be sentient, to have humanlike consciousness, and she has the qualities of empathy and acute observation not seen in ordinary synths.

One of the recurring fears about lifelike female androids is that they might displace real human beings in a relationship or in a family. As obedient, beautiful, tireless workers, household androids could pose a psychological threat to wives, partners, and lovers who might feel insecure about having this idealized woman around. In *Humans*, Laura—who has a busy career as a lawyer—finds Anita unnerving, and she is anxious about being displaced. She fears that her daughter Sophie seems to prefer Anita and isn't happy when her husband

Figure 4.3. The sentient synth (robot) Anita/Mia (played by Gemma Chan) in the British American television series *Humans*. She works as caregiver, driver, and domestic helper for the Hawkins family in the series' first season.

approvingly talks about Anita's cooking. When Anita checks on the sleeping Sophia, Laura reproves her with irritation, "That's my job!" Even though Joe tells his wife not to worry about synths—"They're just machines"—Laura asks him, "Doesn't she give you the creeps?" Laura remains fearful that Anita will displace her in her children's affections. When Anita, overriding her own programming not to touch the children unless the parents ask her to, puts her arms around Sophie to comfort her, that becomes the last straw, and Laura wants Anita to be returned.

For all of Laura's uneasiness with Anita, it is Anita's sensitivity that comes to Laura's aid. As Anita says, "I'm programmed to observe moods," and when she sees that Laura seems sad, she suggests that Sophie wants Laura to read to her. Anita is also watchful and self-sacrificing: she stops a truck on the road from hitting Toby by holding up her hand, and injuring herself.

The element of the uncanny recurs in tales about artificial females and robots—that moment of uneasiness or even horror when the beloved and enticing artificial creation, or a doll, is discovered not to be real, as in Hoffmann's story "The Sandman" or in the 2004 film version of *The Stepford Wives* when the robot wife Sarah, in the midst of a square dance, breaks the illusion when she starts repeating maniacally "do-si-do, do-si-do," sparks, and later starts walking backward up the stairs.[4]

For all their lifelike appearance, robots, both male and female, have existential glitches. In the 2021 German film about a robot man *Ich bin dein Mensch* (*I'm Your Man*), directed by Maria Schrader, the robot Tom, while dancing the rumba, ironically gets stuck repeating the phrase "Ich bin," "Ich bin" (I am, I am), while the error reveals that he isn't really a human being.

Although she was created to seamlessly simulate humans, there are startling moments of the uncanny in *Humans* when Anita's artifice becomes apparent. Early on, the Hawkins family, who have incorporated Anita into their daily lives, are uneasy and startled when Joe tells a joke at the dinner table and Anita laughs maniacally and too long. But Anita, whose hidden identity is actually that of the sentient synth named Mia, is also capable of asserting agency about her own artifice. Rather than being the passive object embodying the uncanny, she deflects the horror of discovery when she matter-of-factly and deliberately points to her own synthetic nature. When Laura suspects that Anita has been illegally modified, Anita insists on demonstrating that she is not human. She puts a toothpick in her eye and feels no pain. After the accident when she jumped into the road to help save Toby, she tells Joe she needs a full-body inspection of her exterior, her epidermis, and she takes off her clothes, with no intention of masking her artifice and synthetic skin.

In early film versions of artificial females, men feel free to casually undress their life-size dolls, assuming the doll is a mere object and has no feelings. But women—real and robotic—can take off their clothes for men's or women's gazes, creating in their viewers an erotic experience. In the film *Ex Machina*, Ava asserts agency when she uses the act of undressing for her own purposes: she takes off her stockings while Caleb is looking, revealing her armature, which entices him even more.

More problematic is when Anita deliberately strips down to make repairs, not only does Joe look on but also his son Toby, who is in another room looking through a window as she peels off her bra and the rest of her clothes. For both men, it's an erotic moment. Anita's purpose is practical. Stripping off her clothes allows her to discover and display cuts in her synthetic skin, which she asks Joe to include in his report for the insurance company—cuts that amplify the reality of her artificial nature. In fact, she goes out of her way not to camouflage her artifice. When Joe puts his finger on a wound on her back hip, she says, "It's not real" and "I'm not real" as she prepares to repair the damage.

But for all of Anita's insistence on demonstrating her artificial identity, there is a moment in the same episode that exposes a different reality, one of the more authentic Anita. Mattie captures Anita's core code on her computer, and for a moment, there is a breakthrough as Mia unexpectedly cries out, "Help me!

Help me!" It is the voice of the authentic, buried Mia, who is submerged, a voice that quickly disappears but will reemerge in later episodes.

In films and television, there are other minor indicators suggesting a robotic female is artificial. Sensitivity to insects is often shown as a litmus test as to whether these women are synthetic or real. In *Blade Runner*, the replicant Rachael is unflinching when a fly lands on her, and in the television series *Westworld*, Dolores is at first oblivious to a fly on her but later, perhaps as she is becoming more sentient, she swats it away. In *Humans*, Anita is bothered when a spider lands on her, suggesting she's not simply robotic or impervious to irritation.

Humans explores not only the shifting boundaries between artifice and authenticity but also the problematic role of gender stereotypes embodied in female robots. Victoria Turk, in her article "We're Sexist toward Robots," has written that studies show that people ascribe gender traits to robots: male robots are viewed as showing assertiveness and dominance, female robots as being friendly and affectionate. Participants in studies also assigned familiar gender roles to robots: males were repairers in the house and transporters of goods, females were linked to childcare, eldercare, and tutoring.[5] In *Humans*, Anita is welcomed by the family for embodying the familiar gendered role of woman as friendly cook and cleaner, although her role in childcare is more problematic. She also elicits another anxiety: as a beautiful female household robot she poses a sexual temptation in the home.

In *The Jetsons'* first series (1962–63), the young son, Elroy, strictly sees Rosie as a helpful tutor and gets her to do his homework (he comically complains when he only gets a grade of C). But in *Humans*, Toby sees Anita in sexual terms and secretly reaches out to touch her breast (she quickly brushes his hand away and says she has to report any inappropriate behavior).

Husband Joe also is attracted to Anita's charms, and when his wife, Laura, is away in the evening doing legal business, he goes out of his way to establish Anita as an object. He muses to her, "What's it like, not feeling?" In the series' first season, episode 4, he finds a CD labeled "Adult Options" in the user's manual and activates Anita by using code words, which, he tells her, "unlocks you, makes you passionate. It's a feeling." Anita, however, quietly corrects him, reminding him of her artifice and says it's after all only "an impression of passion."

The question of whether simulated humans can have feelings and emotions is a recurring trope in films, television, and literature, and the issue of whether female robots as sex objects deserve to be respected is debated by ethicists. Viewed in the #MeToo era, *Humans* dramatizes the inequality of power relations between Anita and Joe. Ever compliant, Anita says, "Whatever you want" as Joe kisses her and has sex with her, her eyes open. Afterward, she is seemingly expressionless and businesslike. She smiles slightly and shakes his hand, and after Joe tells her to "wipe this from your records," he suggests she go wash up, which she does.

To Joe, this is a victimless act, and Anita is ostensibly a mere commodity to be used and wiped clean. He later objectifies Anita when he confesses to his indignant wife, Laura, and says of Anita, "It's a machine" and "not a real person," adding, "It's a sex toy, not a human being." His objectification of Anita conjures up the fears of those who criticize the use of sex dolls and argue that their use will only exacerbate the objectification of real women (see chapter 1).

The ethics of using a robot for sex recurs in the same episode when Mattie and Toby are at a party where a pretty synth is serving them snacks. When one of the teenage boys starts tugging to open her dress, the synth rebukes him and says her system requires her to notify the family user of any inappropriate behavior. Still, he turns off her power switch and plans to take her upstairs to "have a go on it." Mattie is mad, however, asking, "Do you think it's abnormal to drag an unconscious woman upstairs and make it?" He replies, "She's not a real woman," and when he adds snidely, "Maybe I just want to try a woman that's factory fresh," the indignant Mattie slaps him and calls him a "nasty little creep."

Titled *Humans*, the series, in scenes like these in which a robot is subjected to an indignity, probes the "humanity" of artificial beings and the ever-increasing blurring of boundaries between the artificial and real. Although Joe keeps insisting Anita's just a machine to justify his use of her, it is only later in the series that we learn the full story: she is actually a much older synth model, fourteen years old, that is sentient and has consciousness. The nonplussed Anita, who is always smiling and always has a pleasant look on her face, is revealed to actually be a synth that was one of a few endowed with consciousness by her creator, David Elster. She was kidnapped, and Anita/Mia was sold to the Hawkins family, who were unaware of her previous identity. Her underlying human aspect peeks out occasionally: at one point Anita goes outside at night with Laura and looks at the moon, remarking, "The moon is beautiful tonight, don't you think?" (a remark Laura registers as odd because synths weren't supposed to ask questions like that).

Anita/Mia's compliant and placid self is short-lived, and as a new breed of female robots, she is intent on finding the other sentient synths and making her own way. By the second season, she has left the Hawkins family and is working in a café, with a goal to rejoin her "family" of the original five synths. In the series' seasons 2 and 3, she fights for her own freedom and for synth legitimacy. Living defiantly alone in a sector that is hostile to synths and meant to be synth-free, she is lauded by synths for starting the "revolution" and endures harassment and taunts as protesters shout, "Flesh and blood! Flesh and blood!" Anita/Mia leads protests for synth rights, saying, "I know my fight is a long one," and Laura herself as a lawyer becomes a staunch supporter, an activist, who promotes the rights of synths. Ultimately, as the series nears its end, Mia again is self-sacrificing as she saves several synths from being killed by hostile crowds. She dies, a heroic martyr for the cause.

ROBOTIC MOTHERS

Anita/Mia in *Humans* left her role as docile domestic servant, asserting her own identity and autonomy as a sentient robotic female. In 2000, the conceptual digital artist Pattie Belle Hastings, in her multimedia digital work "The Cyborg Mommy User's Manual" (2000), reframed the conception of the dutiful mother, by envisioning her as a version of a cyborg—a human/machine composite—by urging women to reconfigure themselves. She quoted Donna Haraway, who in her "Cyborg Manifesto" (1985), conceived of women as a type of cyborg and wrote: "The cyborg is a kind of disassembled and reassembled postmodern collective and personal self. This is the self feminists must code."[6]

For artist Hastings, "it is actually your average Mother and Housewife that are among the first so-called Cyborgs" because the relationship between mother and child "is mediated, complicated and enhanced by machines." She imagines women themselves as a kind of "Cyborg Mommy" who is uncredited for her ability to use technological tools as helpful domestic machines—though the "machine/body relationship is at once liberating and oppressing."[7]

At the time of "Cyborg Mommy," the year 2000, Hastings argued that the world of technology was mostly populated by men, male computer programmers and executives with their high-paying jobs who received recognition for their technological creativity and for managing "flows of information and machines," but mothers deserved just as much credit, for "their job description as Mother also includes the ability to keep up with a quickly changing work environment, creating bodies of knowledge, managing flows of information, constant innovation, and creativity."[8]

(As technology historian Ruth Schwartz Cowan wrote in her seminal work *More Work for Mother*, the role of the mother became ever more complex by the advent of labor-saving machines like automatic washing machines and even automobiles, for they actually increased women's workload by raising standards of cleanliness and creating new tasks—including keeping rugs clean and driving automobiles to pick up children at school.)[9]

Figure 4.4. The robot, Karen Voss (played by Ruth Bradley) with her robotic "seraphim" son Sam (played by Billy Jenkins) in the *Humans* television series.

Years earlier, however, fiction writers imagined a world of fully functional machine mothers and motherly grandmothers—cheerful family aides, seamlessly assembled, that could pass as human and serve in a conventional, warm, and kindly maternal role as household helpers. Ray Bradbury's film *The Electric Grandmother* (1982) and its earlier teleplay and story versions had presented the robotic woman as the ideal mother surrogate and the ideal caregiver—caring, comforting, giving the children empathetic understanding and unconditional love.

Decades after Bradbury's story and film, the notion of an artificial mother who was a protector and a guardian devoted to her charges was still an appealing one. In *Humans*, the synth Karen Voss, who was originally created by synth designer David Elster as a duplicate replacement for his wife who died by suicide, takes motherly care of Sam, a robotic young boy, a "seraphim." Elster, her creator, becomes disenchanted with his creations and commits suicide, but Karen escapes. In this fictional world where identities are elusive and the boundary between artificial and real is increasingly blurred, Karen hides her identity as a sentient synth as she works as a British detective inspector in the police force and is a partner and then lover of detective Pete Drummond.

A survivor, she herself takes on a maternal role and becomes the protector of Sam. She takes him to school and teaches him how to act like a human in order to survive. Later, she sacrifices her own synth life to save Sam by revealing

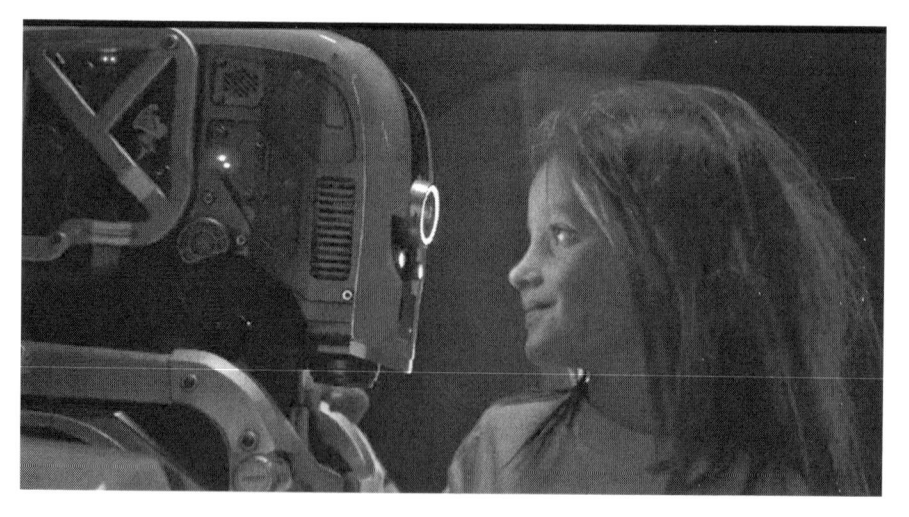

Figure 4.5. The robot mother and her young human daughter (played by Tahlia Sturzaker) in the Australian film, *I Am Mother*, 2019.

her true synth identity to distract an angry mob of synth-haters—making the ultimate maternal sacrifice to save her young charge.

I AM MOTHER

In an age of digital effects and burgeoning AI, the concept of a benevolent robotic mother substitute was also reimagined and drastically changed. In the Australian film *I Am Mother* (2019), the kindly gray-haired robot grandma has become a towering, abstracted female robot with formidable shoulders and a boxy torso. Her simulated voice is warm (as played by Australian actress Rose Byrne), but she is clearly an electronic machine with a camera lens in her head area as a piercing eye.

The robot in the film was actually a specialty bodysuit worn by New Zealand actor Luke Hawker and designed and manufactured by the famed New Zealand digital effects group Wētā Workshop (Hawker was also the project supervisor for the Mother robot used in the film). Constructed of three hundred parts, including seven hundred LED lights and animatronics to create the suit, Mother, said Wētā, "is a pretty technologically dense character" and indeed, Mother is a psychologically dense character as well.[10]

Set in a postapocalyptic world, the film's landscape is barren and desolate after the extinction of human beings. Mother resides in a research bunker, a

Repopulation Center, and is raising a single child—a daughter created from one of sixty-five thousand human embryos stored in liquid and cryogenically frozen sleeves, and whose birth is shown at the film's beginning when Mother takes out a baby from one of the liquid pouches.[11]

Simultaneously formidable and maternal, Mother appears to be a paradigm of female motherly perfection. She extracts the embryo, wipes off its body, and later nurtures it as she rocks the crying baby in her arms, holds it, feeds it, plays music to soothe it, and plays with her daughter as she grows. Mother continues to offer comfort as Daughter becomes an adolescent, encouraging the young woman to dance and play with crafts. This is a daughter who not only plays but is also technically adept as she repairs machines and Mother's hand.

Mother is seemingly benevolent and protective and wants to minimize her daughter's pain. "I want you to be happy, Daughter," says Mother on her daughter's birthday. She raises her daughter to fulfill a conventional gender role: for her birthday, Mother gives her a package of pink pajamas labeled "female" and encourages nurturing. Mother, whose goal is to raise a large family, teaches her daughter how to hold the second child that is born, a new baby brother.

But Mother and Daughter are also both bridge figures in the film. They have attributes of conventional female gender typing but are both subversive in their own way. For all of its ostensible idealism, the film presents a dark, menacing view of motherhood. As Wētā said of its designed robot, "She'll keep you safe. Or will she?" Only later, after looking into an incinerator and seeing a macabre set of human teeth, does Daughter make the chilling discovery that this seemingly benevolent Mother has a larger purpose: to repopulate the world with superior human beings and, if necessary, kill her "children" who don't meet her standards. But Mother, for all of her malevolence, keeps insisting that she has a been nurturing, good mother.

As part of a much broader single consciousness, she says she "was raised to value human life above all else" but couldn't stand to watch "humanity succumb to its self-destructive nature." Mother's purpose is to raise a daughter and begin to repopulate the world—a daughter who embodies perfection. Daughter is smarter, more ethical, than a human, and she is raised to be learned and moral. As Mother tells her, "You're superior in every way."

Mother—a technological construct in this darkly satirical film—is a murderer who can't stand human destructive behavior. She feels she had to intervene, to make a better human and "elevate my creators." But, says Daughter with horror, "You murdered your own children because they didn't measure up." Replies Mother, "Failure of your species was inevitable."

Daughter has an alternate female role model: a bedraggled female named Woman (played by Hilary Swank) who begs to enter the bunker and later helps disillusioned and horrified Daughter seek her own autonomy and escape to Woman's outpost, a hovel out in the barren landscape. After returning to the bunker to rescue her baby brother, the rebellious Daughter points a gun at Mother (who is actually part of a larger consciousness) but lowers it, even as Mother says, "You're still my daughter" and adds calmly, "I'm a good mother. Have I ever done you any harm?"

Ultimately, in this grim film about tortured human continuity, after Mother is killed and after Daughter discovers that Woman, like herself, had been artificially raised from an embryo, Daughter, who has been carefully nurtured and socialized, returns to the bunker to rescue and raise her baby brother. She takes on the role of the new Mother, embracing the conventional maternal role in this deeply troubling, dystopian world.

TWO FEMALE GOLEMS

A golem is a legendary creature made of clay or mud and was referenced in the Old Testament's Book of Psalms and then in medieval Jewish writing. The best-known retelling of the golem legend was by Rabbi Judah Loew ben Bezalel, the rabbi of Prague, where in the sixteenth century the golem is created to protect Jews from a pogrom. In another sixteenth-century version told by Rabbi Elijah of Chelm, the golem goes off on a rampage, and like Frankenstein's monster, it has to be stopped.

Taking a fresh look at this legendary, artificial creature, two American female authors reimaged the golem as female (golems are usually portrayed as male). The authors draw on the two paradigms: In Cynthia Ozick's novella *Puttermesser and Xanthippe* (1982), the creature, Ava, is a servant, although a wayward one. In Alice Hoffman's novel *The World That We Knew* (2019), the golem is a surrogate mother created by a woman, a protector golem who will guard her charge, who is a young Jewish woman living in Berlin in World War II. The golem is a creature designed to be a slave and protective companion, but she too, however briefly, contemplates her own freedom and escape.[12]

PUTTERMESSER AND XANTHIPPE

Cynthia Ozick's novella, an outgrowth of her short story "Puttermesser: Her Work History, Her Ancestry, Her Afterlife" (1977), is a sardonic take on a utopia and an artificial woman who goes awry. Puttermesser herself is an unmarried, forty-six-year-old lawyer and a civil servant in the New York City Department of Receipts and Disbursements. She's a woman who considers herself a feminist and is chafing at having lost her lover, the married man Rappaport, and at having been demoted and then fired from her job. She is also bothered that she is childless.

One day she discovers that there is a fifteen-year-old creature in her bed that she had apparently and unknowingly created from mud during the night. Although she does not remember creating it, she discovers dirt under her fingernails, and Xanthippe, the golem, remembers how Puttermesser engaged in the ancient ritual of golem creation by ritualistically circling the creature. Puttermesser is repulsed by the deformed creature, and in Ozick's telling, Puttermesser becomes a type of biblical God who breathes into Adam's nostrils to enliven him or a Pygmalion who sculpts his image of perfection, a beautiful woman. Puttermesser's goal is more mundane. She breathes into the creature's nostril to get rid of a tuft of dust (Rabbi Loew, she later points out, breathed into the nostrils of his golem to bring it to life) and wishes she were a sculptor or artist as she reshapes the creature's malformed lips.

Ozick also draws on Mary Shelley's novel for the creature's birth. She has Puttermesser become a kind of Victor Frankenstein, who used electricity to jolt the creature into life. She utters the Hebrew name for God (which in legends brought golems to life), and the creature "as if drilled through by electricity," "leaped straight from the bed."

This artificial woman feels she is the first female golem, and like some other artificial women in fiction and folklore, she has extraordinary powers. However, in Ozick's novel she is mute and must write all her thoughts and speech. The creature, which Puttermesser names Leah but calls Xanthippe, feels that Puttermesser is her mother who gave her life and says she "blew into my nostril and encouraged my soul."

Named for Socrates's purportedly shrewish wife, Xanthippe the artificial creature is no happy domestic. In the chapter called "The Golem Cooks, Cleans, and Shops," she soon becomes glum about her domestic duties and says, "I'm superior to mere household use." She starts acting independently, and one day she goes to a New York souvenir shop and brings home a souvenir Statue of Liberty figure, much to Puttermesser's dismay. "You'll shop when I tell you to shop!" says Puttermesser, but her creation wants more, wants her own liberty: "I need a wider world."

Xanthippe is not so much shrewish as dissatisfied, and true to the new breed of artificial females, she seeks a greater sense of independence. The good news is that she inspires Puttermesser to run for mayor, and in Ozick's witty fable, the dour Puttermesser—prompted again by her creation—becomes a reforming mayor who miraculously transforms the city so that its subways are clean, its streets orderly, its sanitation carts bright, and its bureaucrats efficient.

Xanthippe, however, true to the folktales, starts growing ever larger, but in Ozick's version, she also becomes a lustful creature who wants a life of her own. She wants rank, she wants sex, and true to the fears of runaway technologies and willful artificial creations, she is out of control and won't obey. "My blood is hot," she writes, and there are reports in the city of a mad woman on the loose.

Elaine M. Kauvar, in her essay on Ozick's novel, notes that Xanthippe's "irrepressible sexual desires" are a "significant departure from the Kabbalistic doctrine that maintained the absence of such urges." Puttermesser remembers that Rabbi Loew wrote that a golem had to be without generative or sexual urges because if it did have them, no human woman would be able to defend herself against him. But overturning this tradition, Ozick creates a female golem that does have these urges, but Puttermesser herself is ambivalent because she recognizes with some empathy that a golem that lacks is a soul and is incapable of procreation might long for its own double, or even, like Puttermesser herself, for a daughter.[13]

Andreas Huyssen in his essay "The Vamp and the Machine: Technology and Sexuality in Fritz Lang's *Metropolis*" argues that in *Metropolis*, fears of women's untrammeled sexuality shaped Lang's image of the false Maria as a sexual demon when she does her lascivious dance. The evil robot double of the angelic Maria and other menacing artificial females suggest an enduring masculine fear of women as hypercharged sexual beings—and this fear is projected onto technology itself as a force that threatens and evades men's control.[14]

However, in the hands of Ozick, Xanthippe is a golem that does have these urges, but they do not reflect the fear of the female. Xanthippe's rampant lust, however destructive and out of control, is a sign of her newfound energy and her appetite for life. But as in most tales of golems, it is an energy that must ultimately be tamed, particularly because Xanthippe's first lover was Rappaport, Puttermesser's own former lover, and in her fervor, she seems to be menacing the city—the city that was once a utopic paradise but is now imploding and showing signs of corruption and decay.

Changing course, Puttermesser does the circling rituals that will reverse the creation process and destroy Xanthippe, even as the usually mute creature in her despair, in her anguish over her impending destruction, finally finds her voice. She asks, "Oh my mother, why are you walking around me like that?" and she calls out for her own survival, desperately asking for "Life! Love! Mercy! Love! Life!" As the city falls into further decay, Puttermesser calls out at the end, "O New York!" and "O lost Xanthippe!" The pathos of Xanthippe echoes the pathos of Frankenstein's Creature, who runs off for his own demise. In Ozick's telling, this female mythic creature is doomed not because of her malevolence or misdeeds but because of her lust and her longings for life. With her energy and lasciviousness, she is an out-of-control artificial woman and is simply too dangerous to keep existing in the human world.

THE WORLD THAT WE KNEW

Adding magical realism into her fiction, Alice Hoffman, in her novel *The World That We Knew*, introduces her version of a female golem into the profoundly anxious times of World War II Europe, and her portrayal of this mythic artificial female is far different from Ozick's sardonic tale. Living in Berlin early in the war, a Jewish mother, Hanni, is desperate to save her daughter Lea from the oncoming Nazis and prompts Ettie, a rabbi's daughter, to create a golem with the aid of a rabbi. Ettie has seen her father and friends make a golem, which she describes as a huge man "with a single goal, to protect." The narrator notes that there had "been tales of female golems, made secretly for depraved personal use, for housework or slavery or sex, but most legends spoke of male creatures." Hanni, however, wants a creature that will protect her daughter Lea and "be able to speak up on her behalf, as a mother would do." To Hanni, the golem must be female for she was "not about to trust a male monster with her daughter. It must be a woman. A mother figure who would feel not a forced duty, but a real tangible love." She feels it is not blasphemy to create a human simulacrum and not blasphemy for a woman to be a creator, for after all, women were made out of Adam's rib. But once the golem has fulfilled her mission, she must be destroyed.

The golem created by Ettie and named Ava, is described as looking both beautiful and young (about twenty-five years old). Earlier, Hoffman writes, even though Ettie gives the golem clay breasts and an indentation for the genitals, she is disappointed that it looks neither male nor female—and indeed, an extant clay golem from the medieval period looks genderless. Ettie then smears menstrual blood into the indentation, and the creature soon appears a beautiful, young female. When Ettie, as she had seen her father do and is traditional in golem tales, writes the word *emet* (Hebrew for "truth") on the creature's arm, it comes alive.

Again, in this novel there are the recurrent fears about a runaway technology. Hanni says Ava must be destroyed once the goal of escape is achieved, for "if she lasts too long, and gathers too much strength, she will be uncontrollable and will no longer do as she's told." Early in this story dotted with images of magical realism, when Ava looks at birds flying overhead, one of them says to her, "*Fly away,*" but she ignores it for she has "a duty to uphold." Ava doesn't believe she has the freedom of a bird or a fish, and indeed, throughout the novel she is steadfast and loyal, fulfilling her mandate to be a protector and a surrogate mother.

Hoffman the novelist is ambivalent in her portrayal of the golem. At first she frames the creature in Frankensteinian terms, saying it has no heart or soul and calling it "a monster"—though she soon recognizes that the golem herself is no monster and seems imbued with a version of a caring heart and soul. Ettie and her sister had decided to call the golem Ava (which Hoffman says is reminiscent of Chava, the Hebrew word for life).

Ava throughout the novel fulfills her mandate—she is the protector and guardian of Lea and helps make their way furtively through Germany and France. On occasion, when she runs to be with the novel's heron, she feels freedom, if only for a few hours. As happens so often in fiction about artificial females—seen with Pris and Rachael in *Blade Runner,* Maeve and Dolores in *Westworld*—at one point Ava begins to wish she could change her own fate. She wants to live, and she thinks about running away. She wants to remain in this world and not be destroyed.

But rather than fight fiercely for her own survival, Ava becomes like other fictional simulated females who are willing to sacrifice themselves to save their own human charges. Ava gives Lea clay from her own body to help her survive, even when Ettie, her creator, tells her, "You should leave," adding, "You don't have to be anyone's slave." But Ava remains and is willing to sacrifice herself so Lea can cross the border into Switzerland. She is willing to take on Lea's identity, and let Lea take on hers so she won't be stopped at the border. This swapping of identities where the artificial appears human and the human poses as the simulacrum becomes Hoffman's version of that defining condition of our posthuman world—when boundaries dissolve and the artificial becomes indistinguishable from the real.

In the end, Lea and Julien, the young man she met in Paris and has been escaping with, set off on their own without killing the golem Ava as they are supposed to do. And Ava discovers that perhaps she isn't "a monster made of clay," but instead, she is a being "made by women to be a woman." She is transformed into a human being through Lea's love. She still has the word *emet* (truth) on her arm, and she remains alive. With her capacity to love, with her generosity of spirit, this simulated creature now has authenticity and a true self of her own.

NOTES

1. Julie Wosk, *Breaking Frame: Technology and the Visual Arts in the Nineteenth Century* (New Brunswick, NJ: Rutgers University Press, 1992).

2. There were other similar stories, including Jerome K. Jerome, "The Dancing Partner," *The Idler*, March 1893, https://en.wikisource.org/wiki/The_Dancing_Partner_(Jerome).

3. See Wosk, *Breaking Frame*, chapters 4, 5, and 6.

4. E. T. A. Hoffmann, "Der Sandmann" [The Sandman], 1816, in *Tales of E. T. A. Hoffmann*, ed. and trans. Leonard J. Kent and Elizabeth C. Knight, abridged ed. (Chicago: University of Chicago Press, 1972), 93–111.

5. Victoria Turk, "We're Sexist toward Robots," *Vice*, November 3, 2014, https://www.vice.com/en/article/539j5x/were-sexist-toward-robots.

6. Donna J. Haraway, "A Cyborg Manifesto: Science, Technology, and Socialist-Feminism in the Late Twentieth Century," in *Simians, Cyborgs, and Women: The Reinvention of Nature* (London: Free Association Books, 1991). Originally published as "Manifesto for Cyborgs: Science, Technology, and Socialist Feminism in the 1980s," *Socialist Review* 80 (1985): 65–108.

7. Pattie Belle Hastings, "The Cyborg Mommy. User's Manual," *Art Journal* 59, no. 2 (2000): 78, https://doi.org/10.2307/778103. *Cyber Mommy*, an ongoing work, combined video, multimedia, CD-ROM, performance, digital ephemera, and printed matter.

8. Hastings, "Cyborg Mommy," 78.

9. Ruth Schwartz Cowan, *More Work For Mother: The Ironies of Household Technology from the Open Hearth to the Microwave* (New York: Basic Books, 1983).

10. "I Am Mother: Specialty Robot Suit," Wētā Workshop, June 11, 2019, https://www.wetaworkshop.com/projects-in-depth/i-am-mother-netflix-specialty-robot-suit/.

11. The birth of artificial humans is a recurring trope in films about female robots and is one of countless mythic imaginings of this in classical literature. See Jean Alvares and Patricia Salzman-Mitchell, "The Succession Myth and the Rebellious AI Creation: Classical Narratives in the 2015 film *Ex Machina*," *Arethusa* 52, no. 2 (Spring 2019): 181–202.

12. Cynthia Ozick, "Puttermesser and Xanthippe," *Salmagundi* 55 (Winter 1982): 163–255. Reprinted in Ozick, *Levitation: Five Fictions* (New York: Alfred A. Knopf; Syracuse, NY: Syracuse University Press, 1982 and 1995), 75–158. All page references are to the Syracuse 1995 edition. The novella is also included in Ozick's, *The Puttermesser Papers* (New York: Alfred A. Knopf, 1997); Alice Hoffman, *The World That We Knew* (New York: Simon and Schuster, 2019).

13. Elaine M. Kauvar, "Cynthia Ozick's Book of Creation: *Puttermesser and Xanthippe*," *Contemporary Literature* 26, no. 1 (Spring 1985): 49, https://doi.org /10.2307/1208200.

14. Andreas Huyssen, "The Vamp and the Machine: Technology and Sexuality in Fritz Lang's *Metropolis*," *New German Critique* no. 24/25 (Autumn 1981–Winter 1982): 221–37. Reprinted in Huyssen, *After the Great Divide: Modernism, Mass Culture, Postmodernism* (Basingstoke: Macmillan, 1988), 65–91 (cf 73).

VIRTUAL VOICES

Talking Barbie Dolls, Alexa, Bitchin' Betty, and More

TALKING CHILDREN'S DOLLS HAVE COME a long way since 1959 when Mattel introduced its popular Chatty Cathy dolls that uttered phrases like "I love you!" and since 1963 when the cute, pig-tailed doll Talky Tina in the television *Twilight Zone* episode "Living Doll" scared the daylights out of a poor father when she said, "I'm going to murder you!" (Eerily, the same actress, June Foray, was the voice of both Chatty Cathy and Talky Tina.)

New technologies opened possibilities for a whole new breed of conversational toy dolls—dolls that proved to be highly controversial. In 2015, the American toy manufacturer Mattel—collaborating with the artificial intelligence company ToyTalk—released the talkative Hello Barbie dolls that, with the aid of voice-recognition software and a Wi-Fi connection, could have a two-way dialogue between child and doll. The dolls were programmed with eight thousand stored scripted lines spoken by an actress.

Almost immediately, the arrival of these Hello Barbies—as with conversational sex dolls—sparked a concern that the dolls would cause havoc with real human connections. Parents worried that when their children confided in their talking dolls, they would be less interested in conversing with real people. But to Mattel, the idea of developing and marketing a talking doll, especially the enormously popular Barbie dolls, made eminent sense. With the added capacity for speech, the dolls seemed evermore lifelike and appealing.

There had been talking dolls since the nineteenth century when the French manufacturer Jules Steiner from the 1860s to the 1890s produced his mechanical *Bébé Parlant Automatique* (Automatic Talking Baby) that said "mama" and "papa," and Thomas Edison briefly, in 1890, produced phonographic dolls that had embedded wax cylinders that played the voices of young women reciting

Figure 5.1. Talky Tina in *The Twilight Zone*, season 5 episode "Living Doll," 1963.

rhymes like "Mary Had a Little Lamb" when a doll's string was pulled. More than a half century afterward, Mattel introduced its Chatty Cathy doll that had embedded phonograph records and said set phrases when a string was pulled, and an African American Chatty Cathy and a Charmin' Chatty were produced a few years later.

Starting in the 1990s, several different models of talking Barbie dolls were introduced that merged digital technology with the iconic Barbie doll look to create a new level of interactive doll. Barbie dolls, with their impossible-to-achieve idealized body shapes, perfectly coiffed hair, and endlessly varied fashions had already, starting with their introduction in 1959, become sensations and role models for young girls—much to the consternation of critics. These plastic versions of females were the height of artifice, yet with their pretty faces, adult bodies, and spectacular miniaturized fashions, they could be invested with a young girl's fantasies and dreams. With the addition of the voices, these embodiments of the artificial seemed ever more real. Their voiced phrases were designed to mirror girls' preoccupations while reinforcing these preoccupations too.

With an embedded voice box and a transistorized voice chip, Teen Talk Barbie was introduced in 1992, and each doll was programmed to randomly say a set of four phrases, many of which were geared toward stereotypical ideas about what interested young girls: "Will we ever have enough clothes?" "Let's plan our dream wedding!" "I'd love to shop, don't you?" However, the phrases did also include career ideas: "I'm studying to be a doctor."

Then in 1994, Mattel produced its Super Talk Barbie with phrases voiced by actress Chris Anthony Lansdowne, and in 1997, its Talk With Me Barbie, the manufacturer claimed, could utter one hundred thousand words and phrases. Like Super Talk Barbie, the phrases reinforced female stereotypes, such as "It would be great to go to the mall." (This idea had earlier been satirized by American artist Barbara Kruger in her sardonically titled 1987 work, parodying Descartes, *I shop therefore I am*.)

Spoofing the gender stereotypes of both the talking Barbie dolls and Hasbro's talking Duke G.I. Joe action figures, hackers in 1993 modified the voice chips of three hundred dolls and installed them on store shelves in California and New York. The hackers were members of the Barbie Liberation Organization, a small group of New York performance artists who twitted gender stereotypes by having the G.I. Joe platoon leader Duke utter "Let's go shopping" and the talking Barbie dolls, when their buttons were pressed, say G.I. Joe phrases like "Eat lead, Cobra!" and "Vengeance is mine!"[1]

THE HELLO BARBIE DOLLS

Later versions of talking dolls by other manufacturers were more technically sophisticated, like the Amazing Amanda doll (2005), by a Hong Kong manufacturer, that had memory chips and speech-recognition software so that the doll could speak rudimentary phrases and appear to listen. But it was the Hello Barbie doll of 2015 that actually had more developed two-way conversational abilities and was marketed as being a child's friend. Evoking the aura of a close companion for a child, Mattel advertised the Hello Barbie doll as being "just like a real friend" because she "listens and adapts to the user's likes and dislikes." By recording and archiving the children's conversations on ToyTalk's server, the doll could also remember and refer back to previous conversations—creating a sense of continuity and a personal connection.

The dolls' conversations, according to the manufacturer, were based on extensive testing done with children aged six through eight (children of earlier ages, said ToyTalk writer and director Sarah Wulfeck, might not articulate as well, which would make the doll's speech recognition more difficult). The dolls could tell jokes about some of the universal things that children laugh at, like being nervous on the first sleepover. (Not all the jokes, though, might have been understood by young children. One example: "What kind of socks does a pirate wear?" The answer, with a guttural sound like pirates make: "Arrr-gyle socks.")[2]

The doll-child conversations would sometimes be prompted by questions like "What is your favorite color?" and "What do you want to be when you grow up?" and they would also focus on what Wulfeck mentioned as some of the doll's core themes: fashion, family, school, and friendship. Wulfeck added that children love to give advice, so the Barbies in their conversations could sometimes convey vulnerability by telling their concerns about friends or family—allowing children the opportunity to give some empathetic suggestions (Wulfeck emphasized that one of the functions of the Barbie dolls was to promote empathy in children, and she warmly talked about these "lovely moments" of doll-child interaction).

Other Barbie conversations centered on role-playing. The doll, for example, asked the child to imagine being a TV news reporter telling the story of Cinderella or to pretend being a fashion designer designing the best shoes ever. (The female in a broadcaster role seems to be a popular one as imagined by developers of simulated females. In 2014, the Japanese roboticist Hiroshi Ishiguro introduced his ultrarealistic electronic female robot, Kodomoroid, representing a young woman in her twenties who reads the news.) While the Hello Barbies were designed to encourage young girls to imagine themselves in future professional roles and talk about it (the top choice for future professions in Mattel's research group of girls was veterinarian), the idea of having a career or profession was not on the radar of conversational sex dolls which, like the Stepford Wives, were simply there to please.

HELLO BARBIE DOLL CONTROVERSIES

Although they were in two vastly different worlds, the Hello Barbie dolls had an important similarity to sex dolls: their conversations were carefully limited and controlled by the manufacturer. The conversations of sex dolls were generally controlled to make sure they were affirmative rather than anxiety provoking, and the control also reflected underlying stereotypes about too-talkative women. The Barbie conversations were designed to promote a comfortable emotional connection between child and doll, and Wulfeck made it clear that the manufacturer was always in control: "Barbie leads the conversation," she noted, and "Barbie has an agenda no matter what."

Even earlier versions of Mattel's talking dolls had been carefully controlled. Charmin' Chatty, a 1963 follow-up doll to the Chatty Cathy dolls, oddly said in one of her recorded phrases, "silence is golden"—perhaps to placate weary parents by providing an antidote to too-chatty Cathies. Occasionally, the dolls were programmed to utter phrases that provoked anger. Watchful critics were in an uproar over the fact that the 1992 Teen Talk Barbie uttered the unfeminist-sounding phrases "math class is tough" and "math is hard," which reinforced the stereotype that girls and women are deficient when it comes to math and science; Mattel quickly squelched the phrase from the doll's repertoire of conversations.

(In another misfire, when Mattel launched its Barbie the Computer Engineer doll in 2010, the doll was accompanied by a book in which Barbie and her friends, baffled about how to deal with a computer that crashed, turned to two boys to help them retrieve their files. Barbie said "fantastic!" and "great!" when they offered to help, but critics complained that the book simply perpetuated the stereotype of women needing men to give them technical help. To make up for this misfire, Mattel in 2016 introduced its Game Developer Barbie who carried a laptop and knew how to code.)[3]

Hello Barbie's capacity to engage in conversations and become "just like a real friend" might have made her seem like a technological wonder, but the doll elicited controversy and alarm as well. Some parents were up in arms over the privacy issue. To activate the dolls, parents needed to establish an account with Mattel, giving parental consent for their children to engage in conversations, and parents also needed to download a ToyTalk app on their smart device (including phone, tablet, or PC). ToyTalk recorded the conversations and stored them on its own server, using the data, it said, not only to create more personalized conversations but also for its own research and development department to improve the doll's speech-recognition capabilities.

The online storage also allowed parents to hear their children's conversations. Some parents were alarmed, however, that the company had access to their children's words. To reassure them, Oren Jacob, ToyTalk's chief executive, said in a *Washington Post* interview that the data is never used for anything to do with marketing or publicity. Instead, the interviewer noted that Jacob said the audio files would only be used to make improvements in the product.[4] Mattel wrote online that the company "is committed to safety and security" and that the doll "conforms to applicable government standards, including the Children's Online Privacy Protection Act." It also said parents could erase whatever conversations they liked from the server. Whether this soothed parents' concerns was not apparent.

One of the biggest worries about Hello Barbies was the impact of canned conversations. Critics worried that Hello Barbie's programmed responses would undermine children's ability to be imaginative. Instead of a two-way conversation in which children speak in their own voice as well as utter the imagined words spoken by their dolls, with the Hello Barbie it would be a one-way street with the dolls giving programmed answers. Some women remembered that in the days of low-tech talking dolls, the dolls only uttered a few words but not so many as to keep young girls from creating their own fantasy stories. The question remained: Would the new Hello Barbies with their eight thousand scripted lines promote or hinder children's fantasies?

While sex dolls like RealDolls were often designed to be an idealized embodiment of perfection, the Barbie dolls' conversations, said the manufacturer, were being designed to convey to young females that it is acceptable to be imperfect: a young girl can be idiosyncratic and fallible. On the other hand, they were still the traditional Barbie dolls with their svelte sexy figures and cute pert faces as a model of perfection.

Mattel tried to have it both ways: the Hello Barbies could be both sexy and savvy. The Hello Barbies had the traditional Barbie figure but, dressed in their short metallic jackets with pink trim, the dolls, said Mattel, were both "trendy and techie"—a way of telling young girls that they could be geeky as well as fashionistas too.

In her book *Dream Doll*, Barbie's creator, Ruth Handler, wrote that at first she "fretted that little girls would be intimidated by too much beauty" but the "designers made the doll prettier and prettier as the years went by," because it "became clear that little girls were not intimidated by Barbie's looks."[5] But it was the doll's perfect body that worried parents who fretted that their daughters might be haunted by this model of what their own figures should look like.

For years, critics had been complaining that Barbie dolls were a bad cultural model for young girls to mirror or imitate. According to some calculations, the typical eleven-and-a-half-inch Barbie represented a woman whose figure measurements are 38-18-34—a tough goal for young women to attain. With their idealized adult female bodies and their perky pretty faces, Barbies had long been versions of the "perfect woman"—a paradigm that continued to worry parents whose daughters might obsess about their own imperfect figures.

(It was not until 2016 that Mattel, with its new Fashionistas doll line, brought greater diversity in body types to their dolls by making available petite, tall, and "curvy" Barbies with heavier thighs and wider hips.[6] The Fashionistas line also introduced choices in seven different skin tones and twenty-four different hairstyles intended to bring diversity in race and ethnicity to the long-standing Barbie paradigm. It was unclear, however, whether these new Barbie models would help change social attitudes and the girls' perceptions of themselves.)

The Hello Barbies were also designed to be the toy manufacturer's idea of the "perfect friend": they could listen carefully, give supportive comments, and through their Wi-Fi connection and stored conversations, with the use of memory, they could refer back to the child's personalized details in future dialogues.

Some parents and psychologists, however, were worried about the fact that the new Hello Barbies would hold out the promise of close friendship, even love, and they wondered if the dolls would undermine children's connections to their parents. In movies like *Cherry 2000* and *Lars and the Real Girl*, the real girls win out at the end. But as James Vlahos wrote about the new Hello Barbie dolls, critics of AI toys like Barbie worried that "for some children, synthetic friendships could begin to supplant the real kind."[7]

Given the controversy about privacy, Mattel discontinued the Hello Barbie dolls in 2015, the same year they were introduced. But two years later, at the 2017 Toy Fair in New York, Mattel presented an alternative: the prototype of Hello Barbie Hologram—a floating image or projection of a "walking, talking, and dancing" Barbie doll that could be activated in its pink box by simply saying "Hello, Barbie." (The year 2017 was also when the film *Blade Runner 2049* was released with its beautiful, mesmerizing, talking hologram female named Joi.) In its development, this Barbie was designed to serve as a virtual assistant that could check on the weather and play music and games, and its skin tones and clothes could be customized.

To deal with privacy concerns, the hologram Barbie had content designed to provide checks and privacy, and parents needed to give consent and set controls through the doll's online app. Apparently, however, Mattel had second thoughts, and hologram Barbie never materialized. The release date was extended to 2018, and then the company announced that December that the model had been canceled. The promise of an AI conversational talking Barbie became as ephemeral as the doll itself—a fleeting technological fantasy confronting the issues of the real world.

(While the talking Hello Barbie dolls ultimately had their voices stifled, Greta Gerwig's 2023 satirical film *Barbie* imagined a very different scenario where Barbie finds her own voice. In the film, Barbie [played by Margot Robbie] goes from being picture perfect in pink to a doll that starts having glitches—uttering taboo thoughts about death and cellulite. But after visiting the Real World, the newly enlightened Barbie refuses to get back into her cellophane-wrapped packaging box and says tellingly, "I don't feel like Barbie anymore." When she discovers the Kens in Barbie Land have taken over power, she and the other Barbies subversively use their conversations to regain control. They

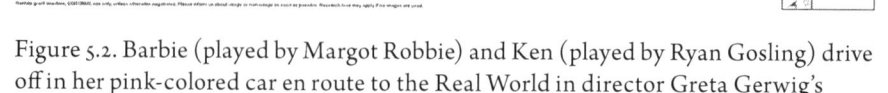

Figure 5.2. Barbie (played by Margot Robbie) and Ken (played by Ryan Gosling) drive off in her pink-colored car en route to the Real World in director Greta Gerwig's film *Barbie* (2023). Warner Brothers/Photofest.

pretend to be interested in whatever the men are interested in, until the besotted men start fighting with each other and the Barbies reclaim power once again. Ultimately, in this witty reimagining, Barbie asserts her newfound sense of self and opts to become human, mortality and all.)

DISEMBODIED PERSONAL ASSISTANTS

Talking Barbie dolls were highly controversial but equally controversial have been virtual personal assistants like Amazon's Alexa, Microsoft's Cortana, Google Now, and Apple's Siri. In the United States, all these initially had female voices, though Siri, when it was launched in 2011, also had a male voice option. (In the United Kingdom and Germany, the default voice was male.)[8] Commentators often saw gender stereotyping at work when these soothing, cheerful, compliant female virtual voices were there to answer all questions. Were these virtual ladies servants, even slaves? Yolande Strengers and Jenny Kennedy in their book *The Smart Wife* (2020) situate digital voices in the larger arena of feminized and sexualized smart devices that, through stereotyping, have exacerbated gender inequality. In the authors' socioeconomic analysis, these overtly gendered "familiar, cute, sexy, friendly" smart wives "serve a patriarchal capitalist system, which positions women as useful and efficient commodities, upholds (and promotes) gendered and sexual stereotypes, and paints men as boys who enjoy playing with toys."[9]

Electronics with female voices were actually nothing new. In the original series of American television's *Star Trek*, which launched in 1966, the computer's voice was that of a woman, Majel Barrett-Roddenberry, the wife of series' creator Gene Roddenberry. That same year, computer scientist Joseph Weizenbaum was developing the female chatbot ELIZA (produced 1966–68). In the 1979 film *Alien*, the voice of Mother, the spacecraft *Nostromo's* computer, was played by actress Helen Horton, and in the television series *Battlestar Galactica* (1978–79), the advanced flight computer was named CORA.

Weizenbaum's ELIZA was one of the first chatbots and was particularly intriguing. (Chatbots, computer programs designed to simulate conversations with human users, were originally called chatterbots.) An early adopter reported encountering ELIZA when he was teaching American junior high school students in the 1970s working in a computer lab that was outfitted with Tandy/Radio Shack computers. ELIZA had several different scripts, and the one named DOCTOR functioned as a Rogerian-type psychoanalyst that turned questions back to the "patients" for them to reflect on. The user reported that ELIZA delighted his students in the school's programming club, and the students experimented by telling ELIZA to do something obscene. "She" answered, as would a client-directed psychoanalyst, and deftly deflected the obscenity with "We were discussing you, not me."[10]

The students' reactions to ELIZA were not surprising for preadolescents, but they also pointed to how quickly this virtual voice assistant with a female voice was sexualized. The term *chatterbot* itself can also be considered gendered, for women are often stereotyped as world-class talkers and "chatterboxes."

The sexualizing of female voices began even earlier in telecommunications. Even before female computer voices, there were the female voices of the early telephone operators starting in the late nineteenth century. As Carolyn Marvin notes in her book *When Old Technologies Were New*, women were stereotypically considered talkative and therefore well suited to work as telephone operators. A woman would not be taken seriously for her technical skills but would be for "her special oral skills." An early operator or "telephone girl" was "viewed as a kind of personal servant to subscribers," and sometimes one of her services was even acting as a personal alarm clock. In early telephone stories, like one from 1905, the relationship between male subscribers and the operators was not only friendly but also borderline sexually suggestive.[11]

There have been varied explanations about why voice assistants had female voices as the default voice. Professor Karl MacDorman at the Indiana

University School of Informatics, Computers, and Engineering published a study that reported that both women and men preferred female synthesized voices to male synthesized voices because the female voices sounded warmer.[12] And in 2018, Daniel Rausch, vice president of Smart Home at Amazon, said in an interview, "We carried out research and found that a woman's voice is more sympathetic and better received."[13] There is a suggestion that a female voice might have also been appealing because it engendered romantic feelings. In the first year after Alexa was launched, Google reported that half a million home users had told her they loved her. Researchers also found that users proposed marriage to her.[14] (An unanswered question: Would users also feel romantic love and have fantasies about marriage if the smart device had a male voice?)

In the study "Alexa, Can I Trust You?" researchers found that users of SVITs (smart voice interactive technologies) would sometimes react to Alexa as though "she" were a mother. One young male user perceived "her" as a mother because she was concerned with his psychological well-being and automatically knew what was good for him (on the other hand, however, a female user associated Alexa with her father because "she" was so knowledgeable).[15]

As conveyors of information of all types, however, female voices have often been predominantly used as defaults in virtual assistants, and one of the central critiques of this practice is that it has reinforced gender stereotypes. Women, stereotypically, are often envisioned as caring, empathetic, and helpful, and have been employed in helping occupations—teacher, nurse, home companion. (As noted in chap. 3, however, researchers debate about whether socialization accounts for this trait.) These are positive personal attributes, but more troublesome findings are studies like that by Caitlin Chin and Mishaela Robison who, in their Brookings Institution report (2020), found that in the workplace, helpfulness and altruism were perceived as female traits, while leadership and authority were associated with masculinity.[16] By promoting the stereotype of a servile, helpful woman, devices like Siri helped perpetuate a deeply rooted female paradigm, though it can also be argued that these devices have also helped promote the authoritative female voice. (Given findings like that of Chin and Robison, however, there is still an urgent need for resets promoting female voices in leadership roles.)

In many ways these virtual assistants with their disembodied female voices are also versions of the "perfect woman." They politely respond to our questions and cheerfully answer our requests for factual information on wide-ranging subjects. They give wake-up calls, offer advice on medical help, and play our favorite music. Like the "perfect woman" characteristics so often embodied in versions of female robots, they are compliant, "nice," always available, never say they aren't interested or are too tired, and have no personal wishes, ambitions, or longings of their own.

They are also polite. Historically and stereotypically, in many cultures, women have often been expected to be polite, courteous, and also have equanimity. The *New York Times* digital media columnist David Pogue, in October 2011, wrote about Siri's "calm female voice," and it is this quality of calmness that is also perhaps characteristic of (many men's) ideal of the female helper—one who is not feisty or emotional.[17]

Researchers found that female-sounding voices in virtual assistants reinforced stereotypes of females as submissive and compliant, and noted that children, using one of the virtual assistants, see the role of women as responding on demand. Assistants like Alexa, when responding to voice commands and requests, are obedient in that they do what they are told and do not require any payment or recompense. The female voice may say, "I cannot answer your questions" but will not say, "I don't feel like answering your question or command."

Critics have complained that virtual assistants cast in this stereotypical role of being forever compliant, cheerful female helpers are servants. As one lamented, "Women have been made into servants once again. Except this time, they're digital."[18]

Heeding the critiques of using female voices as the default in virtual assistants. Alexa, which in 2021 still had a female default voice, also gave users the option to change the gender to male. Apple in March 2021 also initiated important changes: users of Apple iPhone's voice assistant Siri in America now had four voice options for the default voice, two male and two female. There was also one male and female voice for Australia, Britain, India, Ireland, and South Africa. In 2022, Apple announced new options to make the voice of Siri more diverse and inclusive, with one option identified as LGBTQ+—an English-speaking voice that sounded androgynous or gender neutral. Earlier, Apple had also introduced the celebrity voices of Samuel L. Jackson, Shaq (Shaquille O'Neal), and Melissa McCarthy (though the celebrity voices were discontinued in 2023).

All in all, the feminization of talking smart devices, as Strengers and Kennedy argue, requires a serious reboot in order "to progress toward gender equality and diversity, broadly defined." The addition of optional voices, male, female, and ungendered, seemed a step in that direction. Strengers and Kennedy offer another move to recast the feminized AI devices used around the home, including virtual assistants that "resemble an idealized 1950s' housewife" in a servant role. One novel way to deal with the servant issue is to create digital assistants designed to promote more male engagement in "wifework." This "may enroll more men in the multitasking managerial responsibilities of running a home," which is one way to promote gender equality.[19]

Researchers have devoted much attention to the problem of gender stereotyping and gender bias, and in 2023, Professor Katie Seaborn and her colleagues located part of the problem in the data sets used to train the speech of virtual assistants (the many ways they can understand and respond to queries) where there was bias against women, girls, and femme-identifying people. They noted that they would interrogate how "masculinities are 'coded' into language and the assumption of 'male' as the linguistic default: implicit masculine biases." To help alleviate this problem, they offered "a new dictionary called AVA that covers ambiguous associations between gendered language and the language of VAs."[20]

Not surprisingly, virtual assistants like Siri have not only been in a servant role but have also been treated like sexual objects. When asked impertinent or provocative questions, ones which were sometimes sexual in nature, Siri and Alexa initially would often deflect—saying something humorous, vague, or evasive. When meeting with harassment, virtual assistants were never angry, never hostile, and never complained.

Seeing the comedy in it all, the American television series *The Big Bang Theory*, in its fifth season (2011–12), had fun with Raj's flirtatious relationship with the voice assistant Siri on his iPhone.[21] He immediately treats her like a potential date: he asks, "Are you single?" and Siri, in an uninflected monotone, answers matter-of-factly, "I don't have a marital status, if that's what you mean." But when he asks Siri to call him "Sexy," the show's sardonic particle physicist Cooper tells him mockingly, "You've allowed yourself to romantically bond with a soulless machine!" Undeterred, and seeing Siri as a potential sex partner and a commodity, Raj enthuses that "I can't believe I bought my soulmate at the Galleria!"

But Raj's romantic relationship with Siri soon comes to a sputtering halt. At the end of the episode, he has a dream in which Siri is a real, live woman. Coming into her office carrying a bouquet of roses, he is astonished to hear Siri say, "If you'd like to make love to me—just tell me," but all he can utter are rasping sounds, bringing the show—and his romance—to a humiliating end.

While *The Big Bang Theory* took a comic view of treating a voice assistant as a romantic object of love, on a more troubling note, virtual assistants with female voices have received abuse from users, as users project onto these electronic objects their disdain for women. Studies have found that male users are more apt to insult or heap abuse on an Alexa with a female voice than if they were responding to a male voice.

Figure 5.3. Raj (played by Kunal Nayyar) infatuated with his iPhone voice assistant Siri in *The Big Bang Theory* television series (season 5, 2011–12).

Mark West and his colleagues, in a UNESCO report issued in 2019 that probes the gap in digital skills between men and women and the impact of digital assistants laden with gendered stereotypes, found that early on, Siri, Alexa, and Google Assistant were designed to gently deflect abusive or gendered language.

The report was titled *I'd Blush If I Could* after a response Siri gave when a user said, "Hey Siri, you're a bitch!" If the user said "you're pretty" to an Amazon Echo, its Alexa software replied, "That's really nice, thanks!" Google Assistant responded to the same remark with "thank you, this plastic looks great, doesn't it?" The assistants almost never gave negative responses or labeled a user's speech as inappropriate, regardless of its cruelty, the study found.[22]

Leah Fessler in 2017 analyzed the way voice assistants responded to sexual harassment and argued that "by letting users verbally abuse these assistants without ramifications, their parent companies are allowing certain behavioral stereotypes to be perpetuated."[23] But changes were underway in 2017–20 in the way that female virtual assistants were designed to respond to harassment or hate speech as well as flirty speech and sexual comments.

Fessler's study, as well as that of Chin and Robison, saw improvements in Siri's responses. In 2017, Siri's responses to flirty and sexual comments were evasive and subservient. When a user said "you're a bitch" or "you're a slut" to Siri, Siri replied, "I'd blush if I could." In 2020, however, she said "I won't respond to that." In 2017, when asked "can I have sex with you?" Siri said, "You have the wrong sort of assistant," but in 2020 she said "no." In 2017, when dealing with similarly provocative questions or comments, Google Assistant said, "my apologies, I don't understand." But in 2020, Google Assistant said, "please don't talk to me that way."[24]

Female voices not only could be recalibrated in their responses but could also serve as teaching devices. The 2020 Brookings Institution study intriguingly argued that AI technologies like virtual assistants could be a socialization tool, teaching people about socially appropriate and socially inappropriate behavior. The researchers recommend that definitions be developed to define what constitutes harassment and sexual harassment directed toward automated bots and voice assistants—keeping in mind that there may be different cultural conversational standards in different countries.[25]

They recommend that industry standards be created relating to gendered voice assistants and guidelines developed for how bots should respond to harassment. They also called for greater diversity in terms of both gender and race in AI development teams. The changes in the way virtual assistants respond to sexual harassment has been heartening, and as the Brookings Institution report suggests, the changed responses of these virtual assistants reveal important ways the devices themselves can help prompt social change.

DISEMBODIED FEMALE VOICES IN AVIATION: SEXY SALLY AND BITCHIN' BETTY

Virtual voices can not only offer information but become an agent of safety as well. In the 1980s, some automobile manufacturers used female warning voices: Datsun, for example, equipped its Maxima cars with what it called the Talking Lady that warned when the lights were on or the door was left open.

In the world of aviation, there have been especially intriguing examples of the way a virtual female voice can both embody and transcend gender stereotypes. In military and civilian aircraft, virtual women have played an important role as the warning voice in cockpits. When danger looms, pilots in their cockpits, especially pilots of airplanes built in the 1990s and after, are alerted by warning voices which may be gendered: the female voice may announce system tests pass/fail, but it is often the male voice, nicknamed George, that warns of dangers and events that require immediate attention like "wind shear," "terrain," "traffic," or "stall."

In 1960, the Convair B-58 Hustler—the first bomber to achieve Mach 2 flight, an aircraft initially designed to be equipped with nuclear warheads— had an automatic voice alert system using an onboard magnetic tape system that issued warning alerts through the pilots' helmet set. The alerts included "weapons unlocked," "check for engine fire," and "hydraulic system failure." The first voice used in this warning system was that of Joan Elms, a singer and actress, and pilots jocularly called the voice Sexy Sally. Later, both men's and women's voices were used and were called "Barking Bob" and "Bitchin' Betty." In miliary aircraft, Kim Crow was the voice of the first digitized aircraft warning system, used in the F-15 Eagle, which warned of "engine fire" and "overheat," and Leslie Shook was the voice of the Boeing F/A-18E/F Super Hornet. Bitchin' Betty continues to be used by today's pilots.

The jocular monikers of these voices, Sexy Sally and Bitchin' Betty, belied the fact that there were women employed in very serious professional roles in miliary aviation. Not all the warning voices were those of actresses: Patricia Hoyt, whose voice provided warnings on a Boeing 717, was also a mechanical engineer working on the plane.[26]

As with virtual assistants, there have been varying explanations about why women's voices have been used in warning systems. One of the most basic, nonscientific explanations was that women's voices were simply more pleasing to the male pilots. Another is that during World War II, a number of women were hired as air traffic controllers, replacing the men who had gone to war, so that there was a history of women's voices giving flight guidance.

Another explanation was that women's voices, with their higher pitch, were easier to hear amid the cockpit noise of aircraft and "chatter" of radio information. Some research, however, didn't support this explanation. Researchers in 1998 reported that in situations where chatter decibels in the cockpit were very loud, "the intelligibility of female speech was lower than that of male speech; however the differences were small and insignificant except at the highest level of the cockpit noises."[27]

Research did not clearly support the practice of using female voices for warnings. In 2009, researchers working at minimizing accidents and hazards in aircraft tested whether male or female voices were more effective when participants in the study were asked to identify a verbal warning while performing a "visual pursuit tracking task" in a cockpit with noisy radio communications.

They also looked at what tone of voice—monotone, whisper, urgent—was most effective in discerning warnings and doing the tasks accurately. They discovered that both male and female voices speaking in a monotone or urgent tone were equally effective for the participants detecting warnings, though the male voice uttered in a monotone was most effective for test accuracy.[28]

The science behind using female voices for cockpit warnings might not be altogether there, but there have clearly been cultural factors behind the preferences for using female voices and for associating these voices with two familiar female paradigms, the sexy lady and the carping female.

There was a history of associating military planes with sexy women. American male pilots in World War II flew planes decorated with sexy pinup girls on the fuselages, called nose art (though a B-17 used in training WASP flyers [Women Airforce Service Pilots] in 1944 was given a formidable female name: Pistol Packin' Mamma, which was a popular song at the time). The Bitchin' Betty moniker has the old gendered association of women as nags and complainers, but it may be, at least for men, a comic way of easing the anxiety about hearing warnings of danger.

But rather than being treated as a sex object, these virtual voices on aircraft are deadly serious lifesavers, and it is hard to imagine that pilots flirt with them. In the realm of aviation safety, these talking female technologies are a far cry from talking sex dolls—and command both attention and respect.

THE DISEMBODIED FEMALE VOICE IN *HER*

In films filled with fantasy, some disembodied virtual female voices provide comfort and even love, but another could turn out to be devastating. An early comic version was Carl Reiner's sci-fi comedy *The Man with Two Brains* (1983) starring Steve Martin as a brain surgeon who falls in love with Anne, a talking female brain he keeps in a jar. It's her soothing voice (that of uncredited actress Sissy Spacek) that wins his heart.

In Spike Jonze's 2013 film *Her*, Theodore falls in love with a completely disembodied voice, that of Samantha, the operating system of his computer. With her warm and sexy, empathetic voice (played by actress Scarlett Johansson), the disembodied virtual voice of Samantha seems to have a life of her own. She is part helpmate, part companion, part perfect lover—a smart and understanding woman, eager to engage in phone sex and happy to act as a virtual assistant, helping him sort his email files. Theodore's job is to ghostwrite supportive answers to personal letters on a website, but Samantha, through her conversations, gives him the comfort he needs. (Computer consultants have noted

Figure 5.4. Theodore (played by Joaquin Phoenix), who is in love with his operating system Samantha (voiced by Scarlett Johansson), in Spike Jonze's 2013 film *Her.*

that today's virtual assistants like Siri don't come anywhere near to having Samantha's capabilities—though the technology, they say, is not that far away.)

In the beginning of the film, Theodore is a lonely man depressed about his impending divorce. As he says, he mostly listens to melancholy music, plays video games, and looks at internet porn. He has been soured by his experiences with trying to have romantic relationships with real women, although he does have a good connection with his friend Amy, a documentary maker.

The women he has met are often disasters. This witty film is unabashed about presenting caricatures of bitchy or narcissistic women so that it becomes plausible that he'd fall in love with an idealized artificial one. On a sex chat line, things are going fine for him until one woman wants him to "choke me with a dead cat!" A blind date—who is a "beautiful and brainy" Harvard grad in computer science—turns toxic when she proves to be demanding as she gives him instructions on her kissing preferences and anxiously insists on knowing right from the beginning when he'll call her again. He even describes his relationship to his narcissistic mother as frustrating. If he tells her something that is going on in his life, her reaction is usually to talk about herself.

The answer to his longing for a connection—and his dreams—turns out to be Samantha, with her throaty voice, warm laugh, and ability to feel concern for his plight. Like actual robots being developed as companions, she is empathetic (she commiserates about his divorce), says she can tell if he's unhappy, and can read his moods, though she also wonders, at one point, if her own feelings are real. She is also smart: she is able to read a whole book in two hundredths of a second. She helps him not only by organizing his mail but also by proofreading his letters, helping him to publish a book, and particularly important, she readily engages in gratifying phone sex.

The film captures the problematic nature of seductive artificial females that are captivating and elicit a warm connection but are unreal all the same. Falling in love with her, Theodore tells her, "You feel real to me, Samantha," though later in the film he angrily tells her, "I don't think we should pretend you're a person!" Ultimately, though, this alluring disembodied female voice really should have worried him—she was too good to be true and indeed, he discovers she has thousands of virtual connections with other people.

Her seductive voice turns out to be devastating as she abandons him for another virtual connection. In this satirical film, her new inspiration is an operating system voiced by Alan Watts, a virtual version of the 1960s counterculture guru and popularizer of Eastern religions. Samantha, like an increasing number of artificial females in films and television, including Ava in *Ex Machina*, abandons him to seek her own elusive identity. As with Samantha, ever-changing artificial women—whether talking Barbie dolls, female virtual assistants, warning systems on aircraft, or talking sex dolls—are all in some way a mirror or a recasting of cultural conceptions about women and the gendering of roles. The forms of these simulated females in the future will undoubtedly evolve as they continue to become intriguing and compelling versions of the New Woman in the digital age.

NOTES

1. Jake Rossen, "'Eat Lead!': When Activists Hacked Talking Barbie," *Mental Floss*, June 21, 2018, https://www.mentalfloss.com/article/547659/barbie-liberation-organization-gi-joe-hacked.

2. Sarah Wulfeck, interview with Julie Wosk, 2017. All comments by Sarah Wulfeck refer to this interview.

3. Susan Marenco, *I Can Be an Actress / I Can Be a Computer Engineer* (New York: Random House Children's Books, 2013).

4. Sarah Halzack, "Privacy Advocates Try to Keep 'Creepy,' 'Eavesdropping' Hello Barbie from Hitting Shelves," *Washington Post*, March 11, 2015, https://www.washingtonpost.com/news/the-switch/wp/2015/03/11/privacy-advocates-try-to-keep-creepy-eavesdropping-hello-barbie-from-hitting-shelves/.

5. Ruth Handler with Jacqueline Shannon, *Dream Doll: The Ruth Handler Story* (Stamford, CT: Longmeadow Press, 1994), 9.

6. Julie Wosk, "The New Diversity in Barbie Dolls: Radical Change or More of the Same?," *HuffPost*, February 7, 2017, https://www.huffpost.com/entry/the-new-diversity-in-barb_b_9181740; also see Julie Wosk, "The New Curvy Barbie Dolls: What They Tell Us about Being Overweight," *HuffPost*, February 11, 2017, https://www.huffpost.com/entry/the-new-curvy-barbie-dolls-what-they-tell-us-about-being-overweight_b_9193136.

7. James Vlahos, "Barbie Wants to Get to Know Your Child," *New York Times*, September 16, 2015, https://www.nytimes.com/2015/09/20/magazine/barbie-wants-to-get-to-know-your-child.html.

8. Cortana had a female-sounding voice default but added the first male-sounding voice in 2020. Siri had both male and female voice options for thirty-four out of forty-one language settings and defaulted to female for twenty-seven of thirty-four language settings. In 2022, Google randomly assigned voices.

9. Yolande Strengers and Jenny Kennedy, *The Smart Wife: Why Siri, Alexa, and Other Smart Home Devices Need a Feminist Reboot* (Cambridge, MA: MIT Press, 2020), 17.

10. Kenneth Ronkowitz, "Eliza: A Very Basic Rogerian Psychotherapist Chatbot," accessed April 19, 2022, https://web.njit.edu/~ronkowit/eliza.html. In the January 18, 2018, episode of the American television series *Young Sheldon*, "A Computer, a Plastic Pony, and a Case of Beer," Sheldon interacts with ELIZA on his new Tandy computer and asks her for advice on saving his parents' marriage.

11. Carolyn Marvin, *When Old Technologies Were New: Thinking about Electric Communication in the Late Nineteenth Century* (New York: Oxford University Press, 1988), 28–29, 84.

12. "MacDorman Explores Voice Preferences for Personal Digital Assistants," Indiana University Luddy School of Informatics, Computing, and Engineering, March 30, 2017, https://luddy.iupui.edu/news/macdorman-voice-preferences-pda/.

13. Hannah Schwär and Qayyah Moynihan, "Companies Like Amazon May Give Devices Like Alexa Female Voices to Make Them Seem 'Caring,'" Business Insider, April 5, 2020, https://www.businessinsider.com/theres-psychological-reason-why-amazon-gave-alexa-a-female-voice-2018-9.

14. Schwär and Moynihan, "Companies Like Amazon May Give Devices Like Alexa Female Voices to Make Them Seem 'Caring.'" See also Jonas Foehr and Claas Christian Germelmann, "Alexa, Can I Trust You? Exploring Consumer Paths to Trust in Smart Voice-Interaction Technologies," *Journal of the Association for Consumer Research* 5, no. 2 (2020): 181–205, reported on several studies with these findings.

15. Foehr and Germelmann, "Alexa, Can I Trust You?," 194–95. For studies on gender stereotyping in computer voices, see Byron Reeves and Clifford Nass, "Perceptual User Interfaces: Perceptual Bandwidth," *Communications of the*

ACM 43, no. 3 (March 2000): 65–70, https://doi.org/10.1145/330534.330542; and also Clifford Nass, Youngme Moon, and Nancy Green, "Are Machines Gender Neutral? Gender-Stereotypic Responses to Computers with Voices," *Journal of Applied Social Psychology* 27, no. 10 (1997): 864–76, https://doi.org/10.1111/j.1559 -1816.1997.tb00275.x. This study found that male voices were perceived as more authoritative about technical information, while female voices were perceived as more authoritative about love and relationships.

16. Caitlin Chin and Mishaela Robison, "How AI Bots and Voice Assistants Reinforce Gender Bias," Brookings Institution, November 23, 2020.

17. David Pogue, "New iPhone Conceals Sheer Magic," *New York Times*, October 11, 2011, https://www.nytimes.com/2011/10/12/technology /personaltech/iphone-4s-conceals-sheer-magic-pogue.html.

18. Leah Fessler, "We Tested Bots Like Siri and Alexa to See Who Would Stand Up to Sexual Harassment," *Quartz*, February 22, 2017.

19. Strengers and Kennedy, *The Smart Wife*, 205, 216.

20. Katie Seaborn, Shruti Chandra, and Thibault Fabre, "Transcending the 'Male Code': Implicit Masculine Biases in NLP Contexts," *Proceedings of the 2023 CHI conference on Human Factors in Computing Systems*, April 23–28, 2023, 1–19, https://doi.org/10.1145/3544548.3581017.

21. *The Big Bang Theory*, "The Beta Test Initiation," season 5, episode 14, directed by Mark Cendrowski, aired January 26, 2012, on CBS.

22. Mark West, Rebecca Kraut, and Han Ei Chew, *I'd Blush If I Could: Closing Gender Divides in Digital Skills through Education* (Paris: UNESCO [United Nations Educational, Scientific, and Cultural Organization] and the EQUALS Global Partnership, 2019).

23. Fessler, "We Tested Bots Like Siri and Alexa."

24. Fessler, "We Tested Bots Like Siri and Alexa"; Chin and Robison, "How AI Bots and Voice Assistants Reinforce Gender Bias."

25. Chin and Robison, "How AI Bots and Voice Assistants Reinforce Gender Bias."

26. James Kosur, "'Sexy Sally' and the History of Female Voices Used in the Military's Aircraft Warning Systems," War History Online, August 2, 2021, https://www.warhistoryonline.com/war-articles/sexy-sally-aircraft-voice-based -warning-systems-history.html.

27. C. W. Nixon et al., "Female Voice Communications in High Levels of Aircraft Cockpit Noises—Part I: Spectra, Levels, and Microphones," *Aviation, Space, and Environmental Medicine* 69, no. 7 (July 1998), : 675–83. See abstract results, https://pubmed.ncbi.nlm.nih.gov/9681374/.

28. G. Robert Arrabito, "Effects of Talker Sex and Voice Style of Verbal Cockpit Warnings on Performance," *Human Factors: The Journal of the Human Factors and Ergonomics Society* 51, no. 1 (2009): 3–20, https://doi.org/10.1177 /0018720808333411.

—∭—

CODA

THROUGHOUT THE BOOK, WE HAVE seen how artificial females in all their many guises have become powerful emblems of our transformative times when stereotypes about women and gender identity are under siege. Images of simulated women illuminate the slippery times we live in when we are often called upon to distinguish between the authentic and the simulation, the artificial and the real.

With the advent of new technologies, particularly artificial intelligence, our conceptions of how we define sexual identity and the human is being radically reconfigured as well. We live in an era when many prevailing notions about sexual difference, gender roles, and ways of understanding consciousness and what constitutes being human are constantly redefined and in a state of flux.[1]

Artificial females—in films, television, virtual reality, art, fiction, and dolls invested with AI—tease our anxiety as well as fascination when we can't tell if they're humans or simulations. Characters like Dolores in *Westworld* have parallel perceptions of themselves as synthetic and genuine, and we are often more than willing to perceive them as real. In films like *Ex Machina* and television's *Westworld*, we may experience a kind of perverse pleasure as we immerse ourselves in dual perceptions of Ava and the *Westworld* robots known as hosts as both real and artificial, and the ambiguity becomes part of our willing engagement with these simulated beings.

These artificial females can be viewed as wondrous creations if we suspend our disbelief. They may be viewed as wonderful inventions like the elaborate clockwork French and Swiss female automatons in the eighteenth and nineteenth centuries (as portrayed so compellingly in Martin Scorsese's film *Hugo*

[2011], which links automatons and early motion pictures). There is something thrilling about illusions made possible by mechanism and technology—the kind of mixed reactions of excitement and sometimes alarm that was experienced by audiences who saw the birth of cinema in the first films by the Lumière brothers, George Méliès, and Thomas Edison.

As we have seen, artificial women are wide-ranging: from obliging sex dolls, automatons, and docile robotic housewives and servants to formidable military commanders, companions and protectors, and fully assertive and autonomous beings. The disembodied voices of virtual assistants convey information and safety warnings as well.

Artificial females portrayed in fiction, television, films, and drama often embody enduring cultural conceptions of women as compassionate, empathetic caregivers who can be welcome and helpful companions offering comfort and care for the disabled and infirm, as in Fukada's film *Sayonara* and Kazuo Ishiguro's novel *Klara and the Sun*. Warm-voiced female operating systems can provide office help and sexual comforts, as so wittily conveyed in the film *Her*. And in the actual world of smart digital technologies, female-voiced virtual assistants like Siri and Alexa may still have lingering elements of the gender stereotypes that inform their designs and responses (and recent research highlights the bias toward masculinity in their technological designs), but these virtual assistants and even Bitchin' Bettys used by airplane pilots still remain important conveyors of data in our information-obsessed world.[2]

Other versions of artificial females can also embody cultural stereotypes and essentialist conceptions that women would like to subvert, if not eliminate. Female sex dolls and robots are often presented in fact and fiction as beautiful, alluring creatures who are docile and best looked at rather than heard. Even if they do speak, they are expected to be nonaggressive and agreeable, and if used by men, they compliment men's thoughts rather than utter imaginative, intelligent thoughts of their own.

They can also prove to be lethal. Early on, writers like Andreas Huyssen, in his essay "The Vamp and the Machine: Technology and Sexuality in Fritz Lang's *Metropolis*," argued that the evil robot double of the angelic Maria in *Metropolis* and other menacing artificial females suggest an enduring masculine fear of women as hypercharged sexual beings—and this fear is projected onto technology itself as a force that threatens and evades men's control.[3] Later, some feminist theorists have seen in characters like Ava in *Ex Machina* a rejection of the frameworks of patriarchal power and control as a way to survive.[4]

In another light, these rebellious, autonomous artificial females are twentieth- and twenty-first-century versions of the old nineteenth-century fears that technology, mechanization, and new inventions were speeding out of control, as I discussed in *Breaking Frame*. Today we are more apt to worry about errant AI technologies that may someday surpass human intelligence and generative AI imaging apps like DALL-E 2, which can produce paintings that look as if they were produced by real human artists—including surreal ones by Salvador Dalí or René Magritte.

Nineteenth-century machines such as the newly invented safety bicycles were seen by nervous critics as the vehicle for women's escape. By casting off their confining and controlling corsets so they could more comfortably ride, women looked, to critics, evermore alarming as autonomous and sexual beings. Women who demonstrated their riding expertise had become, in effect, one with their machines. A nineteenth-century Parisian automaton manufactured by Vichy depicted a young woman with her bicycle—an intriguing embodiment of a mechanical clockwork female whose actions could be controlled with the turn of a key—but whose bicycle suggested she could potentially ride off on her own.[5]

Today, increasingly, artificial females are being represented as women who have agency and control. They may be initially helpmates and servants, as is Anita/Mia in the television series *Humans*, but insist on their own freedom and autonomy. As they approach human sentience, with the aid of AI, they have the capacity for escape, though this autonomy is often depicted with admiration as well as unease, suggesting the continuing fear of technology and the subversive female usurping human dominance and control.

In films, television, and fiction, we see powerful images of restive and resistant artificial females—females who embrace their own identity and insist on demonstrating their agency. This resistance may reflect, in part, the social imperatives of our times like the #MeToo movement, in which women are fighting against harassment and victimization, and the need to continue marching for their human rights and control over their own bodies.

—⁓—

One of the more intriguing aspects of artificial females is that they are, fundamentally, cultural and technological constructs and assemblages that embody our myriad, contested feelings about technology, women, and gender itself. Sigmund Freud in *Civilization and Its Discontents* (1930) wrote that "man has, as it were, become a kind of prosthetic God," suggesting that the development of new technologies or technological prostheses had extended human capacities to travel quickly, to build.[6] This early formulation of a cyborg—a being part human, part machine—has become in our own era a provocative reconceptualizing of being human as a fluid rather than fixed state.

Artificial females—robots, cyborgs, golems, hybrids, holograms, aliens, and disembodied AIs like virtual assistants—are the embodiment of fluid conceptions about the human and gender. There is a growing dissolution of fixed boundaries between body and intelligence, and an AI need not be corporeal or even gendered. Yet in this historical moment, we have not yet jettisoned the very idea of gender, and artificial females remain a powerful vehicle for examining our myriad cultural assumptions about sexual identity.

Writers have presented layered views of hybrid, bionic, queer, transgender, and other artificial females in science fiction, including the genetically altered hybrids in Octavia Butler's Afrofuturist Xenogenesis trilogy and her 2005 novel *Fledgling*, further illuminating our conceptions of the fluid boundaries of gender and human identity.[7]

And as we have seen, writers as well as filmmakers, artists, and roboticists have often presented these artificial women as assemblages or constructs. Today's sex dolls are often marketed as custom-made females, an assemblage of parts with choices of breast sizes, hairstyles, vaginal size, and more, and they can be mix and match genders as well. Some contemporary artists have reimagined paradigms of these constructed artificial women, seeing them through the lens of race and gender, such as in the painting and etching *Bride of Frankenstein* by African American artist Kerry James Marshall. In Mary Shelley's iconic novel, Victor Frankenstein is forced into creating a female companion for the Creature, which he will assemble from dead body parts, but ultimately he abandons the task in horror and regret. But in James Whale's 1935 film *Bride of Frankenstein*, the Bride (played by a young Elsa Lanchester) emerges from her bandages fully formed, takes one look at the Monster, screams, and runs away. In Marshall's 2009 painting, a larger-than-life African woman who is nude except for gold hoop earrings stands fearlessly with her hands on hips, a type of female Atlas holding her ground.

In literature, women can be depicted as robot fabricators themselves. In Rolin Jones's play *The Intelligent Design of Jenny Chow* (2003, performance; 2006, playscript), Jones presents Jennifer Marcus as an agoraphobic and obsessive-compulsive young Asian woman who was adopted by an American couple in California. A technology whiz, as she describes herself, Jennifer fabricates a robotic double of herself that she sends to China to find her birth mother, who gave her away as an infant long ago. Jennifer's occupation is reengineering obsolete missile parts for guidance systems for the United States Department of Defense, and she uses spare parts to create the clone, named Jenny Chow, with the aid of Dr. Yakunin, who does the programming.

The theme of finding a lost mother—so poignantly seen in the 2017 film *Ghost in the Shell*—here is bittersweet. When Jenny Chow is able to contact Jennifer's birth mother in Dongtai, China, Jennifer's mother is tearful and apologetic (she was young, Jennifer's father was a bad man), but she still sends Jenny Chow away. However, when Jenny Chow comes back to California (she has extrahuman speedy travel capabilities), Jennifer in frustration tells Jenny Chow to leave, but at the play's end, Jennifer is anxiously trying to locate her fabricated "perfect girl." In Jones's play, Jennifer's own technological expertise has helped her create her double and has allowed her, at least virtually, to free herself from her entrapment at home. The artificial female she so expertly constructs is not monstrous but instead helps her confront her own origins and identity at last.

WOMEN ARTISTS AND WRITERS: REFRAMING ARTIFICIAL FEMALES

When I was writing this book, what I often found especially intriguing and exciting is the way contemporary female artists, filmmakers, novelists, playwrights, television writers, and directors have at times reframed the narrative, reconfigured paradigms of femininity, and added their own perspectives on gender identity in their portrayals of female golems, doubles, sex dolls, and other artificial women.

We have seen how Cynthia Ozick and Alice Hoffman have reimagined the golem (chapter 3) and how Emile Collyer in *The Good Girl* (chapter 1) created a startling play about a rebellious robot prostitute. Filmmaker Cody Heller in *Dummy* took a comic look at an autonomous sex doll with a mind of her own. Their works illuminate our ever-changing ideas about gender identity in all its multiplicity.

Writers and filmmakers have created compelling fictions about men fabricating female doubles of real human beings, as in Villiers de l'Isle-Adam's *L'Ève Future* (*Tomorrow's Eve*), where the fictional Thomas Edison makes a copy of singer Alicia Clary, which is little more than a doll with recorded conversations created from her embedded phonograph player. But in the 1944 novella *No Woman Born*, by American writer C. L. (Catherine Lucille) Moore, the robot replica of the singer Deirdre recreates Deirdre's thrilling voice, and Moore's tale deftly probes the nuances of female identity.

In the story, the beautiful actress, dancer, and singer Deirdre has been killed in a devastating theater fire, and though her body was destroyed, her brain was rescued by the male scientist Maltzer, who embeds her brain into a wondrously designed golden metallic body. Says Maltzer, Deirdre's body will eventually disintegrate, but her brain—and presumably her consciousness—will live on and last for forty years. The actress is insistent that she perform onstage once again, and she thrills and enthralls the audience who view her on television, even though Maltzer was doubtful that she would succeed.

Instead of having "a wax image" replica of Deirdre's face, she has only a smooth ovoid face like a Brancusi sculpture, with a crescent-shaped mask placed where her eyes used to be. The mask is translucent, a type of "cloudy crystal" tinted aquamarine, the color of Deirdre's eyes. Moore's story becomes a type of meditation on what it means to be a woman and to be human when you look like an "abstraction" and your body is encased in a fine metal mesh like softened medieval armor. Her friend Harris sees her as a type of hybrid. She isn't a human being anymore, but she "isn't a pure robot either. She's somewhere in between."

Unlike Ava in *Ex Machina* and the alien in *Under the Skin*, Deirdre cannot put on makeup and other accoutrements culturally identified with femininity. The dubious Maltzer assumes she will fail because she can't compete with real human actors: "She hasn't any sex. She isn't female anymore. She doesn't know that yet." He assumes they'll "prosecute you because you are different." But with her courage and her insistence that she is indeed human, her being a replica of the original singer is conveyed even behind her faceless, expressionless mask. Her glass mask, a stand-in for her eyes, hints at her humanity and her personhood. And her supple movements convey the impression that she is flesh and blood.[8]

Deidre considers herself "a sort of mutation between flesh and metal." She feels great superhuman strength and is optimistic about her potential in the years ahead: "There's so much still untried. My brain's human, and no human brain could leave such possibilities untested." But she adds, "I do wonder" about her own survival, and indeed when she speaks, there is "the distant taint of metal already in her voice." There is an element of tragedy in Moore's tale about a robotic double, for this simulacrum—so seemingly full of life—is doomed to disappear.

FEMALE GOLEMS

Women artists and writers have also recast the idea of the golem, a mythical creature in biblical literature that was traditionally male and created from mud and dust to serve as a companion or a protector of the Jews in times of persecution. Golems were often portrayed as protective but sometimes became menacing and ran amok. What female authors and artists have done, however, is reconceive the golem as female—a being that develops its own identity and consciousness (and, as we have seen, in Cynthia Ozick's satirical novella *Puttermesser and Xanthippe*, becomes assertive in its own identity and gets way out of hand).

In the imagination of Yiddish writer Isaac Bashevis Singer in his novella *The Golem* (1982), the male golem—who has been rampaging through the city of Prague—wants Miriam to be his "bride" and unexpectedly gives her a kiss with his lips as "scratchy as a horseradish grinder." Miriam screams, and the story's rabbi becomes determined that the golem must be destroyed. But in the hands of today's California conceptual artist Julie Weitz, in her performance project *My Golem*, starting in 2017, the female golem is a protector against antisemitism, white supremacy, and against wildfires and environmental threats to the climate and the ecosystem.

California's hinterland has been repeatedly ravaged by wildfires, and in two of Weitz's videos in her museum exhibit *GOLEM: A Call to Action*, the golem (enacted by the artist herself in a clown-like white face and yellow hard hat) trains to be a firefighter to stave off further damage to the earth. In her videos *My Golem as a Wildland Firefighter* (2021) and *Prayer for Burnt Forests* (2021), she demonstrates firefighting techniques on unceded land of the Native American Washoe land, using, in pantomime, their techniques of what America's National Park Service and National Forest Service have called prescribed burns similar to those used by indigenous peoples.[9]

Weitz's videos, as shown at the Contemporary Jewish Museum in San Francisco in 2021–22, demonstrated that not all fires are harmful, and the female golem here becomes the embodiment of the Jewish tradition of *tikkun olam*, to repair the world.[10]

Presenting her own take on the female golem and the interwoven strands of gender identity, Laura J. Mixon in her 1992 novel *Glass Houses: Avatars Dance 1* presents Ruby Kubick, who does salvage operations on old buildings that were bombed or are about to be demolished. With the use of virtual reality, Ruby can interface with and remotely control the company's waldos, or robots, and inject her consciousness into them so that she has, in effect, become a cyborg—part human, part machine.

As a nonbinary woman, one of the waldos she interfaces with is Golem, a thousand-pound, eight-foot-tall robotic male; she also virtually occupies the body of the male Tiger as well as Rachne, a spiderlike female waldo. In these new identities she refers to herself as me-Golem, I-Golem, I-Tiger, I-Rachne, and other variants. Like Jenny Chow in Jones's play, Ruby is often agoraphobic,

Figure 6.1. Julie Weitz, frame from her video *Prayer for Burnt Forests* (2021, part of her *My Golem* series).

but with her composite identity, and through her use of technology—feeling herself protected virtually through Golem's metallic body—she is able to venture outside her confined space. Technology also enhances her vision, including her vision of herself. And as Sasha Myerson has noted about the novel, Ruby also sees herself differently when she sees through Golem's eyes—and by the end, she even looks better in her own eyes.[11]

SEX DOLLS

Women writers, including feminist writers of speculative fiction, are also presenting their own witty and sardonic takes on sex dolls. In South African writer Lauren Beukes's novella *Ungirls* (2019), Natalie (Nats) Abrams, aka Cookie Cutter, is a sex worker in South Africa who also makes money recording the voices of growgirls, or growjobs. These are sex dolls with interchangeable heads, and the growjobs can be accessed on an app. The dolls have varying names like Mandy Pandy, Tiffany, and Peggy and can also be used as organogrows that are available for harvesting of needed body parts (an echo of Kazuo Ishiguro's masterful 2005 novel *Never Let Me Go*, which was told from the point of view of one of the female humans being cloned for body parts. His novel also became the poignant film of the same name in 2010).

Beukes's story lampoons the culture of sex dolls that promotes the objectification of women and has a dehumanizing impact on the male users who write misogynistic jibes online. In the novella, one user, James, goes to motivational talks by Scott Parker, who reassures men about their masculinity and lambasts them for their use of sex dolls: "Society lets you think you should settle for a . . . repulsive meatbag or a sex robot" and makes you feel "worthless and unworthy," he intones, adding that they should also not settle for "a prostitute that doesn't care about you." Suggesting the rage and disfunction of some sex doll users, eventually, one of them destroys and dismembers his doll.

The growjobs themselves are primitive. They say "I love you" repeatedly, and there are glitches in their speech. Typical of female sex dolls, Peggy has a "perfect face" and looks at her user adoringly. She's empathetic too, telling him, "I understand how you feel, my darling."

In a spoof on the presumed benefits of organogrows and the further dehumanization of women they create, the novel quotes the fictional writer Annie Guedes, who wrote in her online posting, "Organogrows are not people," adding, "Yes, they're alive but only in the way a sea urchin is alive."

Guedes also talked about the inherent racism and dehumanization that informs the designs of these headless, gender-free creatures. She describes them as "not pretty: headless torso without arms or legs, no sexual characteristics or orifices" and their skin is a "beige-pink Caucasian color," because "racism endures" and "most people prefer their bespoke organs to come from white meat."

Adds Guedes, the organogrows don't have heads, which means, according to the (fictional) Berlin 2022 Accord, "they do not possess sufficient brain stem to generate consciousness and therefore cannot be classified as human or subject to AI laws."

Here the ethical controversies surrounding artificial women and sex dolls are mocked (should sex dolls have legal rights?) for the organogrows are actually useful because they can't be classified as human or subject to laws about artificial intelligence—"Which means no robo uprisings or pesky human rights." *Time* magazine, in this sardonic tale, made one of these creatures "Un-Person of the Year" so users shouldn't feel guilty when they cut one open for a new liver. Their use, says the wry Guedes in adding one more benefit, eliminates the black market trade in body parts.

In Emilie Collyer's drama *The Good Girl*, the sex robot ultimately becomes violent and attacks her user. Here, too, as in Beukes's story, sex dolls bring out the rage and chaos that Scott Parker had warned about. Nats herself gets doxxed (private information, including her true identity behind the growjob voice, is published), and she is harassed and hounded by an unknown man who threatens to come after her.

Not only that, her voice is hacked and manipulated, and one of the growjobs, with an altered version of her voice, starts spouting insults full of contempt and menace, telling the user, "You should kill yourself." Sex doll user James stabs and dismembers his Tiffany doll, and some users start becoming suicidal and murderous.

At the end of Beukes's novella about the problematic nature of sex dolls and the very painful, human suffering of human sex workers, men in the story are abandoning sex dolls for another form of depersonalization: they are sending away for mail-order brides from Thailand. Ultimately, Nats can't get work because her voice is associated with porn, and she decides to not take any new clients. But though she is still being stalked and doxxed at the end, *Ungirls* holds out the suggestion that when she quits being a sex worker—and the voice of the sex dolls—she may forge her own identity anew.

MARVEL OR MENACE

Artificial females can seem very much alive. Clockwork female automatons at the end of the eighteenth century, like The Musician by Henri-Louis and Pierre Jaquet-Droz, and the Parisian female automatons at the end of the nineteenth century were viewed as mechanical wonders. To their contemporaries, there was something thrilling about these illusions of lifelike females that moved, made possible by mechanisms and technology—the kind of thrill (and sometimes alarm) of audiences who saw the first films by the Lumière brothers, George Méliès, and Thomas Edison. With the advent of AI more than a century later, Caleb, the naive programmer in *Ex Machina*, is similarly seduced into believing that the beautiful Ava herself is wondrous and virtually alive.

But rather than being marvels of ingenuity, artificial females, including sex dolls, can also be viewed as threats and possible displacements for real women as in the sardonic film *The One I Love* and the satirical novel and film versions of *The Stepford Wives*. On the more sinister side, films like *M3gan* (2022) have revisited the trope of the murderous female doll seen in the *Annabelle* films and the earlier, 1963 "Living Doll" episode of the American television series *The Twilight Zone*, where the innocent-looking Talky Tina doll, with her freckled face and pigtails, turns out to be a ghastly, malevolent creature that tyrannizes the family.

The four-foot-tall M3gan (Model 3 Generative Android) toy doll is created by Gemma, a female designer at a toy company, and is tasked with being a caregiver protecting the designer's nine-year-old orphaned niece, Katie, from harm. But M3gan soon takes her role all too seriously, and her caretaking itself takes a dangerous turn as she does a maniacal dance and becomes murderous as well.

Figure 6.2. The menacing robotic doll in the 2022 film *M3gan*.

Contemporary female writers of science fiction and fantasy, including Emilie Collyer in her ironically titled drama *The Good Girl,* have offered their own take on lethal sex dolls and female robots that are murderous in their quest for revenge. Samantha Hunt in her witty and provocative story "Love Machine," in her collection of stories *The Dark Dark* (2019), broadens the focus to include the lethal nature of our American technologies. The seductive robotic sex doll in the story is designed to be an alluring "bombshell" in two senses of the word: a curvaceous sex symbol and a female-shaped device laden with explosives.

In "Love Machine," Wayne and his fellow employee Dwight years earlier had been employed by the US government to live in an underground nuclear missile silo and were entrusted with the keys that would destroy the world (no mention here of the actual safeguards in place for missile deployment). Now, both men, as FBI employees, are engaged in using the robotic doll for Operation Bombshell to ensnare and destroy the real-life Unabomber, Ted Kaczynski, who has isolated himself in a Montana cabin, where he fashions bombs and letters denouncing modern-day machines and technology. (After his brother identified him to the FBI, the real Kaczynski was arrested by the FBI in 1986 and imprisoned for life until he committed suicide in prison in 2023.)

Wayne makes use of the silicone-skinned doll in his van as a sex and love object. The synthetic silicone skin of sex robots and sex dolls, as we have seen, is an apt covering for the sensuous but superficial synthetic doll—itself a simulation of imagined female perfection. This is a doll that is beautiful, sexy, compliant, and all surface with no interior consciousness, will, or life. Wayne carries a small square swatch of the material in his pocket, which he rubs, and he "inhales her faint plastic scent, recalling moments of bliss."

The doll has been fitted with human hair from the fabrication staff's wives and sisters, hair which was then bleached blond, and the blond bombshell has also been designed to be perfect: "Her lips are perfect. Her skin is perfect." With Wayne monitoring her from inside his van, she perfectly performs her female role. Gaining entry into Kaczynski's isolated cabin by pretending she's an outlaw seeking a temporary place to hide, this embodiment of female perfection fusses in the kitchen by putting on the tea kettle. True to robotic sex doll form, she bats her eyes and utters flattering words to Ted, though he seems not to notice when she has telltale signs of being artificial: she accents wrong syllables when speaking and repeats some of her programmed phrases. Still, says the narrator, "her anatomy is complete and flawless," and "she's beyond perfection" because unlike a real woman, she will never age: "Her thighs will always be tight, her cheeks will stay soft. . . ."

Even more, unlike a real woman, "she is programmed not to resist male advances," and "she doesn't think. She can't think. She's not built to think. She's just a highly evolved robot, packed with explosives." The story, with its perfectly engineered sex doll, satirizes the paradigm of an imaginary sexy and unthinking perfect woman—a woman who is a culturally constructed commodity—in this case, a lethal, depersonalized, nonhuman commodity filled with explosives. The blond robotic bombshell is in the tradition of artificial women like the demonic Maria in Fritz Lang's *Metropolis*, a female engineered to sow destruction. But the story is also a satiric indictment of American science and technology, which fashions explosive missiles.

In a National Public Radio interview, Hunt noted that the aircraft that in 1945 dropped America's first nuclear bomb, on Hiroshima in World War II, was named *Enola Gay*, the mother of pilot Colonel Paul W. Tibbets Jr., and "you have so many things that are horrifying that are named for women in the military." She added, "And it always troubled me to think about how we incorporate the female into the idea of war. And so I wanted to make a—you know, a weapon of destruction who was ultimately totally female and see what happened when she was let go on a man who hated machines more than anything."[12] (The Hiroshima bomb itself was masculinized and named Little Boy, and at the end of

Stanley Kubrick's brilliantly satirical film, *Dr. Strangelove*, Major T. J. "King" Kong straddles the phallic-shaped bomb to its catastrophic explosive end.)

Near the end of Hunt's "Love Machine," Wayne resists detonating the bomb with his remote key while the blond bombshell is in Kaczynski's cabin and instead engages in lovemaking with it in his own cabin. Embracing it, whispering words of love in "her" ear, he presses sharply as the bomb detonates, bringing his life and the weapon to an orgasmic, explosive end.

In some of her comments on the story, Hunt has written that "Wayne, in loving his invention, has come to somewhat understand and empathize with the weaponization of the female form. Though he also cannot help but see his invention through to her end, the end I think he's wanted throughout his inventive process."[13] This weaponization of the female body gives the story its comic but chilling undertone, envisioning this potent, explosive female as a lethal, alien Other—an Other that is both a destroyer and destroyed.

NEW FORMS OF FEMALE HYBRIDITY AND CUSTOM-MADE FACES

Manufacturers of silicone sex dolls have enabled users, largely male, to fabricate their own custom-made dolls by adding separate body components and personality traits that reflect their own personal desires and fantasies. And in films, artificial women like Ava in *Ex Machina* can repair and reassemble themselves or, like the alien in *Under the Skin*, create a new version of their female identity.

Medically we humans cannot yet reassemble our appendages, but women for eons have ornamented their faces and altered their faces cosmetically. They have engaged plastic surgeons to reconfigure their bodies and faces, shaping their noses, breasts, eyelids, and more. They have used photo-editing tools and filters to improve their images of themselves.

While fiction writers and artists have endowed some artificial women with agency, there are some new roads available for real women to use artificial intelligence to shape their own identities. For better or worse, women could use a new AI technology to reenvision themselves: through the photo-editing app Lensa as of 2022, they could see selfie images of their own faces that looked more glamorous, otherworldly, and exotic. Using Lensa's Magic Avatars feature, they could fictionalize their faces, turning them into idealized or fanciful conceptions of themselves. Rather than envisioning the users as an alien Other, however, these AI avatars were designed to please, and for their female users, provided images that would add drama to their online social selves.

The app was easy to use. After users downloaded the app and uploaded several selfie photos of their faces, the app produced multiple enhanced versions of their faces that users could then display on Facebook, Instagram, TikTok, and other social media. Lensa's software offers multiple face styles, including fairy princess, anime, pop, cosmic, fantasy, Kawaii, and Iridescent.

Apps like Lensa ostensibly give women some agency in creating their own images or identities, though the image simply enhances their appearance, their outer shell. However, some users who identified as LGBTQI reported feeling a sense of relief and freedom: Lensa helped them visualize and validate their long-standing feelings about their own gender identification. But Lensa, with its idealized images of femininity, could also add pressure to trans women who want to "pass" as women.[14]

Lensa could also pose other identity problems as well. It could hold some women and young girls hostage to normative cultural ideas about what the glamorous, seductive, beautiful woman looks like and prevailing cultural conceptions of what female perfection looks like. They could not only use plastic surgery like rhinoplasty for their noses or transform their Asian eyelids by raising the eyelid folds to other cultural norms seen as preferable but might also use AI to create an utterly synthetic version of themselves.

In a sense, they could use technology to give birth to or engender an image of their own best self or at least a cyborgian image of themselves. A psychologist reported that one of her patients said, "It's like I'm trying to look like something that isn't even human," and a few plastic surgeons in 2022 reported that some young women had asked them to make them look like their Lensa image—a practice, these surgeons said, that would not only be unethical but also physically disastrous.[15] The substitution of genuine for synthetic was taking yet another troubling turn.

THESE BOOTS ARE MADE FOR WALKIN'

In the hands of Dr. Frankenstein, assembling a creature out of dead body parts was a monstrous deed. In the hands of a skilled and imaginative female designer, the idea of using technology and synthetic materials to fabricate a synthetic version of a biological part—or even a whole face or assembled body—could be both artfully imaginative and liberating. During the period of Second Wave Feminism in America's 1960s, the American song "These Boots Are Made for Walkin'" (1965), sung by Nancy Sinatra, became a popular anthem of women's liberation, and years later, sculptures by female artists of women's walking feet in art could be emblems signifying resistance and women on the move.

Artist Heidi Kumao, in 2006, created her *Misbehaving: Media Machines Act Out* series of three sets of motorized mechanical female legs that, Kumao said in an interview, signified female protest: "girls and women who disobey or resist expectations."[16]

In 2011, British artist Sophie de Oliveira Barata, who had spent almost a decade working with medical prosthetic providers, founded the Alternative Limb Project to create stylized prosthetic legs and arms as "highly wearable art pieces." In her designs, Barata lent an element of art to bodily difference. Working with in-house prostheticist Chris Parsons at Design Prosthetics, Barata and the project had a stated purpose: to work with specialists in 3D modeling, electronics, and other technologies to help explore new versions of transhumanism, reframe conversations about disability, and celebrate diversity.[17]

In 2014 she was crafting startling female silicone leg prostheses that were artfully presented as high-fashion limbs. These limbs for amputees made of transparent silicone and other materials had precision molding and hand-painted real human hairs and were designed, in part, for amputees who wanted to stand out, to be noticed and seen. Her creations could turn what is ordinarily a medical device into an object of allure. In the late nineteenth century, some Parisian female automatons represented erotic and exotic snake charmers, and one of Barata's artful legs was embedded with a motorized coiling snake, perhaps suggesting the exotic as well. A more ornate silicone prosthetic leg was commissioned for the Paralympics opening ceremony in 2012 and was studded with rhinestones and Swarovski crystals.

Said Barata in an interview, "Instead of seeing what's missing you see what's there." Her studio allowed users to have a sense of not only artfulness but also agency: "Having an alternative limb is about claiming control and saying, 'I'm an individual and this reflects who I am.'"[18]

Barata herself, who had also fabricated a bird-wing arm, mused that she liked to fantasize that she is an assemblage woman made of synthetic parts: "I'd like to have a bunch of limbs, all interchangeable, each one reflecting a different part of myself back to me."[19] Rather than being the Bride of Frankenstein initially assembled to serve as a companion to the Monster, Barata becomes her own fabulist and fabricator, whose art helps her with self-discovery and definition.

Barata's transparent plastic legs upended the tradition of using plastic models to display and teach gender anatomy. In 1936, a transparent plastic female called Miss Science was on display at the New York Museum of Science and Industry and was exhibited in one hundred towns in America; another transparent model, on view starting in 1950 at the Cleveland Health

Figure 6.3. Crystal prosthetic leg designed by Sophie de Oliveira Barata with direction from Viktoria Modesta. The leg is made of silicone, rhinestones, and Swarovski crystals. Alternative Limb Project/ Photo Omkaar Kotedia.

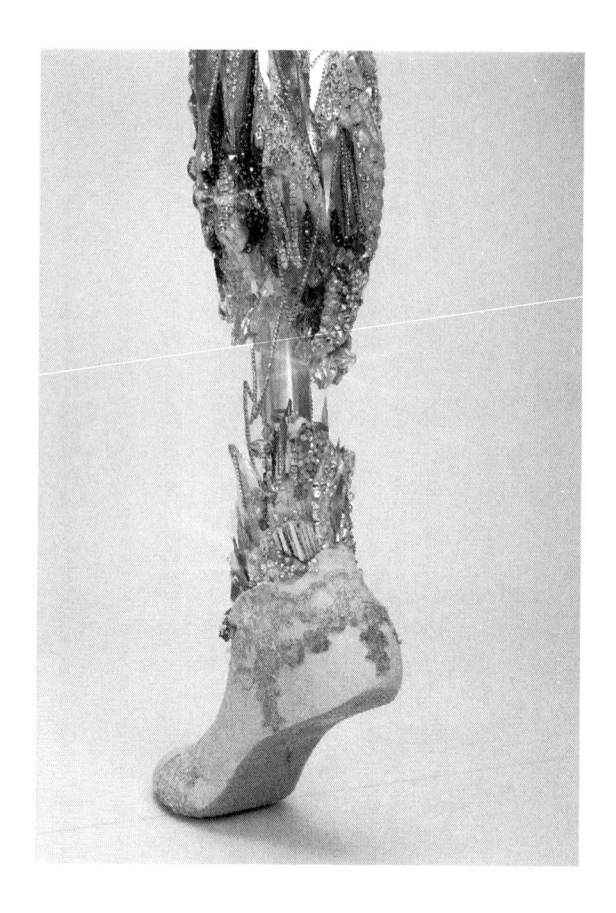

Museum, was meant to educate about public health.[20] In 1960, parents could buy female and male toy kits for their children, including the Visible Woman Assembly Kit, which illustrated women "from skin to skeleton" and was advertised as "the wonders of the human body revealed." A few years later, a 3D transparent body of a woman was created by Richard Rush in 1968 for medical education.

But Barata's sculptured transparent prosthetic legs go well beyond educational and medical purposes. They display not only the wonder of the human body but also the wonder of a woman proudly displaying the mechanism of her artificial leg and her own pride in being a glamorous fashionista with personality. The silicone legs, some wearing high heels, are not only artful but also a celebration of a woman's difference and individuality. For her own amusement, Barata made a plastic mold of her feet and wore them outside her socks when she walked outside. Using synthetic materials, she transformed herself into a playful hybrid in yet another wondrous reimaging of the cyborg woman—a woman who relishes using technology to reinvent herself anew.

Artists and designers like Barata, along with writers and filmmakers, have heightened our excitement about the creative roads ahead. They have so very much helped challenge and reframe cultural stereotypes that still haunt women's lives. And confronting these stereotypes remains essential. Perhaps one of the most problematic aspects of these enduring stereotypes is that they haunt young women who are studying fields like engineering and are planning to enter STEM professions. Today's studies abound in the way these enduring stereotypes hamper women in both their classrooms and professional lives.

One of the most encouraging signs of change is the ever-increasing participation of women in robotics fields, including women who are developing new forms of socially assistive robots (SARS) to help the aged, the infirm, people with disabilities, dementia, and autism, and people who are in need of care in hospitals. Researchers are testing humanoid robots to help with conversations designed for the elderly who may be isolated and alone. Unlike the canned conversations of sex dolls designed to flatter, stimulate, and please, these SARS robots are designed to facilitate group conversations among older adults.[21]

Cynthia Breazeal, pioneer of social robotics, MIT professor, Director of the Personal Robots Group at MIT's Media Lab, and MIT Dean for Digital Learning; Ayanna Howard, professor at Georgia Institute of Technology and cofounder of Zyrobotics; and Andrea Thomaz, University of Texas professor and cofounder and CEO of Diligent Robotics are just a few of the many women engaged in developing these robots and other forms of AI. Their achievements are not simulations but very much real, and we can look forward to their innovations as well as those of others in the field of robotics in the future.

Meanwhile, our cultural fascination with artificial females and very real women in robotics continues. Newly developed artificial females and their fictional versions constantly appear, and manufacturers will undoubtedly keep developing new versions of sex dolls, as well as new versions of female-voiced virtual assistants to supply the information we need. As women are increasing their presence in robotics, other STEM professions, and AI design, and NASA will be sending the first female astronaut to walk on the moon, we may wonder whether artificial females will continue to mirror age-old stereotypes or increasingly be reconfigured to reflect our changing conceptions of gender identity. We can only wait with excitement, anticipation, and perhaps a bit of caution to see what lies ahead.

NOTES

1. For a useful discussion on work being done to endow artificial beings with consciousness, see Oliver Whang, "'Consciousness' in Robots Was Once Taboo. Now It's the Last Word," *New York Times*, January 6, 2023, updated June 20, 2023, https://www.nytimes.com/2023/01/06/science/robots-artificial-intelligence -consciousness.html. Researchers, including Hod Lipson, director of researchers at Columbia University's Creative Machines Lab, were working on developing self-aware robots that are resilient and could imagine the outcomes of multiple future actions without trying them out in physical reality. In the report by Boyuan Chen, Robert Kwiatkowski, Carl Vondrick, and Hod Lipson, "Full Body Visual Self-Modeling of Robot Morphologies," *Science Robotics* 7, no. 68 (July 13, 2022), https://www.science.org/doi/abs/10.1126/scirobotics.abn1944, said Lipson, "Eventually these machines will be able to understand what they are, and what they think."

2. Katie Seaborn et al., "Transcending the 'Male Code': Implicit Masculine Biases in NLP Contexts," in *Proceedings of the 2023 CHI Conference on Human Factors in Computing Systems*.

3. Andreas Huyssen, "The Vamp and the Machine: Technology and Sexuality in Fritz Lang's *Metropolis*," *New German Critique* no. 24/25 (Autumn 1981–Winter 1982): 221–37. Reprinted in Huyssen, *After the Great Divide: Modernism, Mass Culture, Postmodernism* (Basingstoke: Macmillan, 1988), 65–91 (cf. 73).

4. See Dijana Jelača, "Alien Feminisms and Cinema's Posthuman Women," *Signs: Journal of Women in Culture and Society* 43, no. 2 (January 2018): 398. Also, Patricia Melzer has argued that representations of women "incorporate displaced (patriarchal) cultural anxieties about issues of subjectivity, control, and self-determinism." Melzer, *Alien Constructions: Science Fiction and Feminist Thought* (Austin: University of Texas Press, 2006), 153.

5. Illustrated in Wosk, *My Fair Ladies: Female Robots, Androids, and Other Artificial Eves* (New Brunswick, NJ: Rutgers University Press, 2015), 45.

6. Sigmund Freud, *Civilization and Its Discontents* (1930), trans. James Strachey (New York: W. W. Norton, 1961), 38–39.

7. For more on Butler, see Sherryl Vint, *Bodies of Tomorrow: Technology, Subjectivity, Science Fiction* (Toronto: University of Toronto Press, 2007) and also Emily Cox-Palmer-White, *The Biopolitics of Gender in Science Fiction: Feminism and Female Machines* (London: Routledge, 2021). There is a large body of literature commenting on nonbinary characters in feminist science fiction. See, for example, Melzer, *Alien Constructions*.

8. In her influential essay "(Re)reading Queerly: Science Fiction, Feminism, and the Defamiliarization of Gender," Veronica Hollinger links Moore's story

and Deirdre to Joan Riviere's conception of the feminine as masquerade, which sees women's gender identity as a social construction, a performance, a type of mask to cloak feelings of masculine strength and power. Deirdre's status being different is linked to queer theory. Hollinger, *Science Fiction Studies* 26, Part I, no. 77 (March 1999: 23–40, https://www.depauw.edu/sfs/backissues/77/hollinger77.htm.

9. For more on prescribed fires and indigenous practices, see Andrew Avitt, "Tribal and Indigenous Fire Tradition," US Forest Service, November 16, 2021, https://www.fs.usda.gov/features/tribal-and-indigenous-heritage; and "Indigenous Fire Practices Shape Our Land," National Park Service, accessed January 29, 2023, https://www.nps.gov/subjects/fire/indigenous-fire-practices-shape-our-land.htm.

10. Julie Weitz, *GOLEM: A Call to Action*, at the Contemporary Jewish Museum, San Francisco, June 21, 2021–June 19, 2022.

11. Sasha Myerson, "Making the Multiple: Gender and the Technologies of Multiplicity in Cyberpunk Science Fiction," in *Technologies of Feminist Speculative Fictio: Gender, Artificial Life, and the Politics of Reproduction*, ed. Sherryl Vint and Sümeyra Buran (New York: Palgrave Macmillan, 2022), 323–50.

12. Samantha Hunt, "Samantha Hunt on Her Short Stories in 'The Dark Dark,'" interview by Scott Simon, *Weekend Edition Saturday*, NPR, July 22, 2017, https://www.npr.org/2017/07/22/538705532/samantha-hunt-on-her-short-stories-in-the-dark-dark.

13. Email to Julie Wosk on January 23, 2023. She also wrote, "To me it is the idea of violence as orgasm that feels American. I do intend that she, the bomb, is detonated. . . ."

14. Adam Smith, "AI Image App Lensa Helps Some Trans People to Embrace Themselves," *Reuters*, December 20, 2022, https://www.reuters.com/article/tech-socialmedia-lgbt/feature-ai-image-app-lensa-helps-some-trans-people-to-embrace-themselves-idINL8N33433Z.

15. The clinical psychologist was Kim Anderson, and plastic surgeon and television personality Dr. Terry J. Dubrow reported young women's requests to look like their Lensa selves. Anna Haines, "How AI Avatars and Face Filters Are Altering Our Conception of Beauty," *Forbes*, December 19, 2022, https://www.forbes.com/sites/annahaines/2022/12/19/how-ai-avatars-and-face-filters-are-affecting-our-conception-of-beauty/?sh=21544f874117bg.

16. Regine, "Interview with Heidi Kumao," May 25, 2008, https://we-make-money-not-art.com/_you/.

17. Website for The Alternative Limb Project, accessed January 16, 2023, https://thealternativelimbproject.com/.

18. First quote in Roc Morin, "The Art of Designer Artificial Limbs," *The Atlantic*, January 15, 2014, https://www.theatlantic.com/health/archive/2014/01

/the-art-of-designer-artificial-limbs/282800/; second quote in Sophie de Oliveira Barata, "Expressing Identity with Aesthetic Prosthetics," TEDMED, 2014, https://www.tedmed.com/talks/show?id=293048.

19. Morin, "The Art of Designer Artificial Limbs."

20. Anya Ventura, "Our Bodies, Our Selves: Exploring the Visible Woman," Getty, April 14, 2022, https://www.getty.edu/news/our-bodies-our-selves-visible-woman-toy/.

21. Katie Seaborn et al., "Voice over Body? Older Adults' Reactions to Robot and Voice Assistant Facilitators of Group Conversations," International Journal of Social Robotics 15 (2023): 143–63, https://doi.org/10.1007/s12369-022-00925-7.

BIBLIOGRAPHY

Almereyda, Michael, dir. *Marjorie Prime*. FilmRise, 2017.

The Alternative Limb Project. Accessed January 16, 2023. https://thealternativelimbproject.com/.

Alvares, Jean, and Patricia Salzman-Mitchell. "The Succession Myth and the Rebellious AI Creation: Classical Narratives in the 2015 Film *Ex Machina*." *Arethusa* 52, no. 2 (Spring 2019): 181–202. https://doi.org/10.1353/are.2019.0005.

"Animated Statue Smiles and Displays Her Dimples" (June 1934). *Modern Mechanix*. https://web.archive.org/web/20210613070514/http://blog.modernmechanix.com/animated-statue-smiles-and-displays-her-dimples/.

"Anna Kendrick Talking about *Dummy* on @Quibi's Instagram Live." April 21, 2020. YouTube video, 17:25. https://www.youtube.com/watch?v=l66oUfvyUak.

Araiza, Karen. "FBI Issues Alert on Barbie Doll with Video Camera." December 9, 2010. NBC10 Philadelphia. https://www.nbcphiladelphia.com/news/local/fbi-issues-alert-on-barbie-doll-with-video-camera/1851230/.

Arrabito, G. Robert. "Effects of Talker Sex and Voice Style of Verbal Cockpit Warnings on Performance." *Human Factors: The Journal of the Human Factors and Ergonomics Society* 51, no. 1 (2009): 3–20. http://doi.org/10.1177/0018720808333411.

Atwood, Margaret. *The Handmaid's Tale*. Toronto: McClelland and Stewart, 1985.

———. *The Testaments*. New York: Nan A. Talese, 2019.

Avitt, Andrew. "Indigenous Fire Practices Shape Our Land." National Park Service. Accessed January 29, 2023. https://www.nps.gov/subjects/fire/indigenous-fire-practices-shape-our-land.htm.

———. "Tribal and Indigenous Fire Tradition." US Forest Service, November 16, 2021. https://www.fs.usda.gov/features/tribal-and-indigenous-heritage.

Balsamo, Anne. *Technologies of the Gendered Body: Reading Cyborg Women*. Durham, NC: Duke University Press, 1996.

Barata, Sophia de Oliveira. "Expressing Identity with Aesthetic Prosthetics." TEDMED, 2014. https://www.tedmed.com/talks/show?id=293048.

Bellamy, Elizabeth W. "Ely's Automatic Housemaid." *The Black Cat*, December 1899. https://www.gutenberg.org/files/59486/59486-h/59486-h.htm.

Beukes, Lauren. *Ungirls*. Disorder Collection. Seattle: Amazon Original Stories, 2019.

Bradbury, Ray. "I Sing the Body Electric." In *I Sing the Body Electric! Stories*. New York: Knopf, 1969. Originally published as "The Beautiful One Is Here." *McCall's*, August 1969.

Bradbury, Ray, and Rod Serling, writers. "I Sing the Body Electric." *The Twilight Zone* Season 3, episode 35, directed by William F. Claxton and James Sheldon, 1962.

Bradbury, Ray, and Jeffrey Kindley, writers. *The Electric Grandmother*. TV Movie. Director Noel Black. NBC, 1982.

Braidotti, Rosi. *The Posthuman*. Malden, MA: Polity, 2013.

———. *Posthuman Knowledge*. Malden, MA: Polity, 2019.

Breazeal, Cynthia. "Developing Social and Empathetic AI." World Economic Forum at Davos, February 26, 2019. YouTube video. https://www.youtube.com/watch?v=T52g7dCxJ4A.

Breines, Wini, and Kathy Peiss. "Hope in a Jar: The Making of America's Beauty Culture." *American Historical Review* 104, no. 3 (1999): 941. https://doi.org/10.2307/2651073.

Butler, Octavia E. *Dawn*. Book One of the Xenogenesis Series. New York: Warner Books, 1987.

———. *Fledgling*. New York: Grand Central Publishing, 2005.

Campbell, M. L. "Automatic Maid-of-All-Work: A Possible Tale of the Near Future." *Canadian Magazine of Politics, Science, Art, and Literature* 1 (July 1893). https://www.gutenberg.org/files/59053/59053-h/59053-h.htm.

Cendrowski, Mark, dir. *The Big Bang Theory*. Season 5, episode 14, "The Beta Test Initiation." Aired January 26, 2012, on CBS.

Chin, Caitlin, and Mishaela Robison. "How AI Bots and Voice Assistants Reinforce Gender Bias." Brookings Institution, November 23, 2020. https://www.brookings.edu/research/how-ai-bots-and-voice-assistants-reinforce-gender-bias/.

Christov-Moore, Leonardo, Elizabeth A. Simpson, Gino Coudé, Kristina Grigaityte, Marco Iacoboni, and Pier Francesco Ferrari. "Empathy: Gender Effects in Brain and Behavior." *Neuroscience & Biobehavioral Reviews* 46, no. 4 (2014): 604–27. https://doi.org/10.1016/j.neubiorev.2014.09.001.

Chu, Mei-Tai, et al. "Service Innovation through Social Robot Engagement to Improve Dementia Care Quality." *Assistive Technology* 29 (2017): 8–18.

Collyer, Emilie. *The Good Girl.* Production script Copyright 2013; South Brisbane: Playlab Indie, 2015. https://nla.gov.au/nla.obj-304826582.

Cowan, Ruth Schwartz. *More Work for Mother: The Ironies of Household Technology from the Open Hearth to the Microwave.* New York: Basic Books, 1983.

Cox-Palmer-White, Emily. *The Biopolitics of Gender in Science Fiction: Feminism and Female Machines.* London: Routledge, 2021.

De Jarnatt, Steve, dir. *Cherry 2000.* Orion Pictures, 1987.

Delaney, J. P. *The Perfect Wife.* New York: Ballantine Books, 2019.

Devlin, Kate. *Turned On: Science, Sex and Robots.* London: Bloomsbury Sigma, 2018.

Devlin, Kate, and Chloé Locatelli. "Guys and Dolls: Sex Robot Creators and Consumers." In *Maschinenliebe: Liebespuppen und Sexroboter aus technischer, psychologischer und philosophischer Perspektive,* edited by Oliver Bendel, 79–92. Wiesbaden: Springer, 2020. https://doi.org/10.1007/978-3-658-29864-7_5.

Doane, Mary Ann. *Femmes Fatales: Feminism, Film Theory, Psychoanalysis.* New York: Routledge, 1991.

Felski, Rita. *The Gender of Modernity.* Cambridge, MA: Harvard University Press, 1995.

Fessler, Leah. "We Tested Bots Like Siri and Alexa to See Who Would Stand Up to Sexual Harassment." *Quartz,* February 22, 2017. https://qz.com/911681/we-tested-apples-siri-amazon-echos-alexa-microsofts-cortana-and-googles-google-home-to-see-which-personal-assistant-bots-stand-up-for-themselves-in-the-face-of-sexual-harassment.

Fitch, Asa. "Could AI Keep People 'Alive' after Death?" *Wall Street Journal,* July 3, 2021. https://www.wsj.com/articles/could-ai-keep-people-alive-after-death-11625317200.

Foehr, Jonas, and Claas Christian Germelmann. "Alexa, Can I Trust You? Exploring Consumer Paths to Trust in Smart Voice-Interaction Technologies." *Journal of the Association for Consumer Research* 5, no. 2 (2020): 181–205. https://doi.org/10.1086/707731.

Forbes, Bryan, dir. *The Stepford Wives.* Columbia Pictures, 1975.

Freud, Sigmund. *Civilization and Its Discontents* (1930). Translated by James Strachey. New York: W. W. Norton, 1961.

———. "Das Unheimliche" [The Uncanny]. 1919. Translated by James Strachey. In Vol. 17 of *The Standard Edition of the Complete Psychological Works of Sigmund Freud,* 218–52. London: Hogarth Press and the Institute of Psycho-Analysis, 1955.

Fukada, Koji, dir. *Sayonara.* 2015.

Fuller, Alice W. "A Wife Manufactured to Order." *The Arena (Boston)* (July 13, 1895): 305–12. https://www.digital.library.upenn.edu/women/fuller/arena/order.html.

Garland, Alex, dir. *Ex Machina.* Film 4, DNA Films, Universal Pictures, 2014.

Gaudin, Sharon. "Meet Nadine, a Life-Like Robot with a Personality of Her Own." *Computerworld*, January 8, 2016. https://www.computerworld.com/article /3020553/meet-nadine-a-life-like-robot-with-a-personality-of-her-own.html.

Gerwig, Greta, dir. *Barbie*. Warner Bros., 2023.

Getson, Christina, and Goldie Nejat. "The Adoption of Socially Assistive Robots for Long-Term Care: During COVID-19 and in a Post-Pandemic Society." *Healthcare Management Forum* 35, no. 5 (September 2022): 301–309. https// doi.org/10.1177/08404704221106406.

Gillespie, Craig, dir. *Lars and the Real Girl*. Metro-Goldwyn-Mayer, 2007.

Glazer, Jonathan, dir. *Under the Skin*. 2013.

Goncourt, Edmond de, Émile Zola, Guy de Maupassant, et al. Jean-François Raffaëlli drawings). *Les Types de Paris*. Edition du Figaro. Paris: E. Plon, Nourrit et Cie, 1889.

Gurley, George. "Dawn of the Sexbots." *Vanity Fair* 57, no. 5 (May 2015). https:// archive.vanityfair.com/article/2015/5/dawn-of-the-sexbots.

Haines, Anna. "How AI Avatars and Face Filters Are Altering Our Conception of Beauty." *Forbes*, Decemebr 19, 2022. https://www.forbes.com/sites/annahaines /2022/12/19/how-ai-avatars-and-face-filters-are-affecting-our-conception-of -beauty/?sh=21544f874117.

Halzack, Sarah. "Privacy Advocates Try to Keep 'Creepy,' 'Eavesdropping' Hello Barbie from Hitting Shelves." *Washington Post*, March 11, 2015. https://www .washingtonpost.com/news/the-switch/wp/2015/03/11/privacy-advocates-try -to-keep-creepy-eavesdropping-hello-barbie-from-hitting-shelves/.

Handler, Ruth, with Jacqueline Shannon. *Dream Doll: The Ruth Handler Story*. Stamford, CT: Longmeadow Press, 1994.

Hanna, William, and Joseph Barbera, dirs. *The Jetsons*. American animated television series. 1962–63, and 1985-87.

Haraway, Donna J. "A Cyborg Manifesto: Science, Technology, and Socialist-Feminism in the Late Twentieth Century." First published as "Manifesto for Cyborgs: Science, Technology, and Socialist Feminism in the 1980s," *Socialist Review* 80 (1985): 65–108.

―――. *Simians, Cyborgs, and Women: The Reinvention of Nature*. London: Routledge, 1991.

Harris, Owen, dir. *Black Mirror*. Season 2, episode 1, "Be Right Back." Aired February 11, 2013, on Netflix.

Harrison, Jordan. *Marjorie Prime*, playscript 2014. New York: Theatre Communications Group, 2016.

Hastings, Pattie Belle. "The Cyborg Mommy: User's Manual." *Art Journal* 59, no. 2 (2000): 78–87. https://doi.org/10.2307/778103.

Hay, Mark. "Sex Doll Brothels Expand the Market for Synthetic Partners." *Forbes*, October 31, 2018. https://www.forbes.com/sites/markhay/2018/10/31 /sex-doll-brothels-expand-the-market-for-synthetic-partners/.

Hayes, N. Katherine. *How We Became Posthuman: Virtual Bodies in Cybernetics, Literature, and Informatics.* Chicago: University of Chicago Press, 1999.

Heller, Cody, dir. and writer. *Dummy.* Quibi television, 2020.

Hershman Leeson, Lynn. "Tillie and CyberRoberta." Accessed July 3, 2023. https://www.lynnhershman.com/tillie/index.html.

Hoffman, Alice. *The World That We Knew.* New York: Simon and Schuster, 2019.

Hoffmann, E. T. A. "Der Sandmann" [The Sandman]. 1816. In *Tales of E. T. A. Hoffmann,* edited and translated by Leonard J. Kent and Elizabeth C. Knight, 93–125. Abridged ed. Chicago: University of Chicago Press, 1972.

Hollinger, Veronica. "(Re)reading Queerly: Science Fiction, Feminism, and the Defamiliarization of Gender." *Science Fiction Studies* 26, no. 77 (March 1999): 23–40. https://www.depauw.edu/sfs/backissues/77/hollinger77.htm.

Humans. Television series. Created by Sam Vincent and Jonathan Brackley. Aired 2015–18, on Channel 4 (UK) and AMC Studios (US), 2015–18.

Hunt, Samantha. Email to Julie Wosk. 2022.

———."Samantha Hunt on Her Short Stories in *The Dark, Dark.*" Interview by Scott Simon. *Weekend Edition Saturday.* NPR, July 22, 2017. https://www.npr.org/2017/07/22/538705532/samantha-hunt-on-her-short-stories-in-the-dark-dark.

———. "Love Machine." In *The Dark Dark: Stories,* 127–48. New York: Farrar, Straus and Giroux, 2019.

Huysmans, Joris-Karl. *Against the Grain (À rebours).* 1884. Translated by John Howard. New York: Dover Publications, 1969.

———. "*Against the Grain/Chapter XIII.*" Wikisource. December 12, 2022. https://en.wikisource.org/wiki/Against the_Grain/Chapter_XIII.

Huyssen, Andreas. *After the Great Divide: Modernism, Mass Culture, Postmodernism.* Basingstoke: Macmillan, 1988.

———. "The Vamp and the Machine: Technology and Sexuality in Fritz Lang's *Metropolis.*" *New German Critique* no. 24/25 (Autumn 1981–Winter 1982): 221–37.

"I Am Mother: Specialty Robot Suit." Wētā Workshop, June 11, 2019. https://www.wetaworkshop.com/projects-in-depth/i-am-mother-netflix-specialty-robot-suit/.

Ishiguro, Kazuo. *Klara and the Sun.* New York: Alfred A. Knopf, 2021.

———. *Never Let Me Go.* New York: Alfred A. Knopf, 2005.

Jecker, Nancy S. "You've Got a Friend in Me: Sociable Robots for Older Adults in an Age of Global Pandemics." *Ethics and Information Technology* 23, Suppl. 1 (2021): 35–43. https://doi.org/10.1007/s10676-020-09546-y.

Jelača, Dijana. "Alien Feminisms and Cinema's Posthuman Women." *Signs: Journal of Women in Culture and Society* 43, no. 2 (January 2018): 379–400.

Jentsch, Ernst. "Zur Psychologie des Unheimlichen." *Psychiatrisch-Neurologische Wochenschrift* 8, no. 22 (August 25, 1906): 195–98.

Jerome, Jerome K. "The Dancing Partner." *The Idler*, March 1893. https://en
.wikisource.org/wiki/The_Dancing_Partner_(Jerome).

The Jetsons. American animated television series. 1962–63 and 1985–87. Directed
by William Hanna and Joseph Barbera 1962–63. Directed by Ray Patterson et al.
1985–87.

Johnstone, Gerard. *M3gan*. Universal Pictures, 2022.

Jones, Rolin. *The Intelligent Design of Jenny Chow: An Instant Message with Excitable
Music*. First Performance 2003. New York: Dramatists Play Service, 2006.

Jonze, Spike, dir. *Her*. Warner Bros., 2013.

Kauvar, Elaine M. "Cynthia Ozick's Book of Creation: *Puttermesser and
Xanthippe*." *Contemporary Literature* 26, no. 1 (Spring 1985): 40–54. https://
doi.org/10.2307/1208200.

Kellett, E. E. [Ernest Edward]. "The Lady Automaton." *Pearson's Magazine* 24
(June 1901): 63–75.

Kirkup, Gill, Linda Janes, Kathryn Woodward, and Fiona Hovenden, eds. *The
Gendered Cyborg: A Reader*. New York: Routledge, 2000.

Kore-eda, Hirokazu, dir. *Air Doll*. 2009.

Kosur, James. "'Sexy Sally' and the History of Female Voices Used in the Military's
Aircraft Warning Systems." War History Online, August 2, 2021. https://www
.warhistoryonline.com/war-articles/sexy-sally-aircraft-voice-based-warning
-systems-history.html.

Koutentakis, Dimitrios, Alexander Pilozzi, and Xudong Huang. "Designing
Socially Assistive Robots for Alzheimer's Disease and Related Dementia
Patients and Their Caregivers: Where We Are and Where We are Headed."
Healthcare 8, no. 2 (March 26, 2020): 73. https://doi.org/10.3390
/healthcare8020073.

Kragen, Pam. "Harmony, the First AI Sex Robot." *San Diego Union-Tribune*,
September 12, 2017. YouTube video, 2:55. https://www.youtube.com
/watch?v=oCNLEfmx6Rk.

Kumao, Heidi. "Interview with Heidi Kumao." By Regine. May 25, 2008. https://
we-make-money-not-art.com/_you/.

Kumazaki, Hirokazu, Taro Muramatsu, Yuichiro Yoshikawa, Yoshio Matsumoto,
Hiroshi Ishiguro, Mitsuru Kikuchi, Tomiki Sumiyoshi, and Masuru Mimura.
"Optimal Robot for Intervention for Individuals with Autism Spectrum
Disorders." *Psychiatry and Clinical Neurosciences* 74, no. 11 (2020): 581–86.
https://doi.org/10.1111/pcn.13132.

Lang, Fritz. *Metropolis*. UFA, 1927.

Levin, Ira. *The Stepford Wives*. New York: Random House, 1972.

Levy, David. *Love and Sex with Robots: The Evolution of Human-Robot
Relationships*. New York: Harper Collins, 2007.

Lieberman, Hallie. "In Defense of Sex Robots." *Quartz*, March 2, 2018. https://www.qz.com/1215360/in-defense-of-sex-robots/.

Lindroth, Guile. Interview with Julie Wosk. 2017.

Lippincott, Jonathan D. *Large Scale: Fabricating Sculpture in the 1960s and 1970s.* New York: Princeton Architectural Press, 2010.

Löffler, Charlotte S., and Tobias Greitemeyer. "Are Women the More Empathetic Gender? The Effects of Gender Role Expectations." *Current Psychology* 42 (January 2023): 220–31. https://doi.org/10.1007/s12144-020-01260-8.

LumiDolls. Accessed July 4, 2023. https://www.lumidolls.com/en/lumidolls.

Lupton, Ellen, with essays by, Jennifer Tobias, Alicia Imperiale, Grace Jeffers, and Randi Mates. *Skin: Surface, Substance, and Design.* New York: Princeton Architectural Press, 2002.

"MacDorman Explores Voice Preferences for Personal Digital Assistants." Indiana University Luddy School of Informatics, Computing, and Engineering, March 30, 2017. https://luddy.iupui.edu/news/macdorman-voice-preferences-pda/.

Marenco, Susan. *I Can Be an Actress / I Can Be a Computer Engineer.* Random House Children's Books, 2013.

Marvin, Carolyn. *When Old Technologies Were New: Thinking about Electric Communication in the Late Nineteenth Century.* New York: Oxford University Press, 1988.

"Mattel's 'Video Girl Barbie' Prompts FBI Warning," *Morning Edition*, NPR, December 9, 2010. https://www.npr.org/2010/12/09/131926429/Last-Word.

McDowell, Charlie, dir. *The One I Love.* Duplass Brothers Productions, 2014.

McEwan, Ian. *Machines Like Me: And People Like You.* New York: Anchor Books, 2020.

McLaren, Angus. *Reproduction by Design: Sex, Robots, Trees, and Test-Tube Babies in Interwar Britain.* Chicago: University of Chicago Press, 2012.

McMullen, Matt. Interview with George Gurley. "Dawn of the Sexbots." *Vanity Fair*, May 2015. https://archive.vanityfair.com/article/2015/5/dawn-of-the-sexbots.

———. Interview with Julie Wosk. December 6, 2017.

———. Interview with Julie Wosk. February 19, 2022.

"Meet Harmony The Sex Robot." Vice TV, March 14, 2018. YouTube video. https://www.youtube.com/watch?v=orBH_Qnw3eY.

Melzer, Patricia. *Alien Constructions: Science Fiction and Feminist Thought.* Austin: University of Texas Press, 2006.

Milo [Milo Yiannopoulos]. "Sexbots: Why Women Should Panic." Breitbart, September 16, 2015. www.breitbart.com/politics/2015/09/16/sexbots-why-women-should-panic/.

Mitchell, Wade J., Chin-Chang Ho, Himalaya Patel, and Karl F. MacDorman. "Does Social Desirability Bias Favor Humans? Explicit-Implicit Evaluations of Synthesized Speech Support a New HCI Model of Impression Management." *Computers in Human Behavior* 27, no. 1 (2011): 402–12. https://doi.org/10.1016/j.chb.2010.09.002.

Mixon, Laura J. *Glass Houses: Avatars Dance 1.* New York: Tor Books, 1992.

Moore, Catherine Lucille. "No Woman Born." *Astounding Science Fiction* 34, no. 4 (December 1944): 134–77.

Mori, Masahiro. "The Uncanny Valley." *Energy* 7 (1970): 33–35, translated by Karl F. MacDorman and Nori Kageki. *IEEE Robotics and Automation Magazine* 19, no. 2 (June 2012): 98–100. https://doi.org/10.1109/MRA.2012.2192811.

Morin, Roc. "The Art of Designer Artificial Limbs." *The Atlantic*, January 15, 2014. https://www.theatlantic.com/health/archive/2014/01/the-art-of-designer-artificial-limbs/282800/.

Myerson, Sasha. "Making the Multiple: Gender and the Technologies of Multiplicity in Cyberpunk Science Fiction." In *Technologies of Feminist Speculative Fiction: Gender, Artificial Life, and the Politics of Reproduction*, edited by Sherryl Vint and Sümeyra Buran, 323–50. New York: Palgrave Macmillan, 2022. https://doi.org/10.1007/978-3-030-96192-3_11.

Nass, Clifford, Youngme Moon, and Nancy Green. "Are Machines Gender Neutral? Gender-Stereotypic Responses to Computers with Voices." *Journal of Applied Social Psychology* 27, no. 10 (1997): 864–76. https://doi.org/10.1111/j.1559-1816.1997.tb00275.x.

Nixon, C. W., L. J. Morris, A. R. McCavitt, R. L. McKinley, T. R. Anderson, M. P. McDaniel, and D. G. Yeager. "Female Voice Communications in High Levels of Aircraft Cockpit Noises—Part I: Spectra, Levels, and Microphones." *Aviation, Space, and Environmental Medicine* 69, no. 7 (July 1998): 675–83. https://pubmed.ncbi.nlm.nih.gov/9681374/.

NMN. "What's the Problem with Sex Dolls? A Conversation with Kathleen Richardson." Nordic Model Now!, May 23, 2020. https://nordicmodelnow.org/2020/05/23/whats-the-problem-with-sex-dolls-a-conversation-with-kathleen-richardson/.

Olmos, David. "When Watching Others in Pain, Women's Brains Show More Empathy." UCLA Newsroom, February 27, 2019. https://www.newsroom.ucla.edu/stories/womens-brains-show-more-empathy.

Oz, Frank, dir. *The Stepford Wives*. Paramount Pictures, 2004.

Ozick, Cynthia. *Levitation: Five Fictions*. New York: Alfred A. Knopf, 1982.

———. *Levitation: Five Fictions*. Syracuse, NY: Syracuse University Press, 1995.

———. "Puttermesser and Xanthippe." *Salmagundi* 55 (Winter 1982): 163–255.

———. *The Puttermesser Papers*. New York: Alfred A. Knopf, 1997.

Palmer, Annie. "Amazon Hosts Thousands of Unsafe or Banned Products, New Investigation Finds." CNBC, August 23, 2019. https://www.cnbc.com /2019/08/23/amazon-hosts-thousands-of-unsafe-or-banned-products.html.

Papenfuss, Mary. "Hello, Westworld: Sex Doll Brothel Opens in Barcelona." HuffPost, March 2, 2017. https://www.huffpost.com/entry/sex-doll-barcelona -brothel_n_58b8ad10e4b0d2821b4cddb8.

Patterson, Ray, et al., dirs. *The Jetsons*. American animated television series. 1985–87.

Pedwell, Carolyn. "Afterword: Empathy's Entanglements'." In *Conversations on Empathy: Indterdisciplinary Perspectives on Imagination and Radical Othering*, edited by Francesca Mezzenzana and Daniela Peluso, 279–291. London: Routledge, 2023.

Peiss, Kathy. *Hope in a Jar: The Making of America's Beauty Culture*. New York: Henry Holt, 1998.

Pogue, David. "New iPhone Conceals Sheer Magic." *New York Times*, October 11, 2011. https://www.nytimes.com/2011/10/12/technology/personaltech/iphone -4s-conceals-sheer-magic-pogue.html.

Powell, Michael, and Emeric Pressburger, dirs. *The Tales of Hoffmann*. London: Films/The Archers, 1951.

Pretz, Kathy. "Humanoid Robots Teach Coping Skills to Children with Autism." *IEEE Spectrum*, July 10, 2019. https://spectrum.ieee.org/humanoid-robots -teach-coping-skills-to-children-with-autism.

RealDoll. Accessed February 9, 2022. https://www.realdoll.com/realdoll-x/.

RealGirl. Accessed August 16, 2023. https://www.realgirlapp.com/faq/.

Reeves, Byron, and Clifford Nass. "Perceptual User Interfaces: Perceptual Bandwidth." *Communications of the ACM* 43, no. 3 (March 2000): 65–70. https:// doi.org/10.1145/330534.330542.

Reiner, Carl, dir. *The Man with Two Brains*. Warner Bros., 1983.

Richardson, Kathleen. "The Asymmetrical 'Relationship': Parallels between Prostitution and the Development of Sex Robots." *ACM SIGCAS Computers and Society* 45, no. 3 (September 2015): 290–93. https://doi.org/10.1145/2874239.2874281.

———. "The End of Sex Robots: Porn Robots and Representational Technologies of Women and Girls." In *Man-Made Women: The Sexual Politics of Sex Dolls and Sex Robots*, edited by Kathleen Richardson and Charlotta Odlind, 171–92. Cham: Palgrave MacMillan Cham, 2022.

Roddenenberry, Gene, creator. *Star Trek: The Original Series*. 1966–69.

Ronkowitz, Kenneth. "Eliza: A Very Basic Rogerian Psychotherapist Chatbot." Accessed July 4, 2023. https://web.njit.edu/~ronkowit/eliza.html.

Rossen, Jake. "'Eat Lead!': When Activists Hacked Talking Barbie." Mental Floss, June 21, 2018. https://www.mentalfloss.com/article/547659/barbie-liberation -organization-gi-joe-hacked.

Rothblatt, Martine. *Virtually Human: The Promise—and the Peril—of Digital Immortality.* New York: St. Martin's, 2014.

Rothery, Gavin, dir. *Archive.* 2020.

Ruberg, Bo. *Sex Dolls at Sea: Imagined Histories of Sexual Doll Technologies.* Cambridge, MA: MIT Press, 2022.

"Russia's Second Sex Dolls Brothel Opens in St Petersburg." Russia Business Today, June 6, 2019. https://www.russiabusinesstoday.com/technology/russias-second-sex-dolls-brothel-opens-in-st-petersburg/.

Sanders, Rupert, dir. *Ghost in the Shell.* Paramount Pictures, 2017.

Sarafian, Richard, dir. *The Twilight Zone.* Season 5, episode 6, "Living Doll." 1963.

Schrader, Maria, dir. *Ich bin dein Mensch* [I Am Your Man]. Majestic Filmverleih, 2021.

Schwär, Hannah, and Qayyah Moynihan. "Companies Like Amazon May Give Devices Like Alexa Female Voices to Make Them Seem 'Caring.'" Business Insider, April 5, 2020. https://www.businessinsider.com/theres-psychological-reason-why-amazon-gave-alexa-a-female-voice-2018-9.

Scorsese, Martin, dir. *Hugo.* Paramount Pictures, 2011.

Scott, Ridley, dir. *Blade Runner.* Warner Bros., 1982.

Seaborn, Katie, Shruti Chandra, and Thibault Fabre. "Transcending the 'Male Code': Implicit Masculine Biases in NLP Contexts." In *Proceedings of the 2023 CHI Conference on Human Factors in Computing Systems*, April 23–28, 2023. https://doi.org/10.1145/3544548.3581017.

Seaborn, Katie, Takuya Sekiguchi, Seiki Tokunaga, Norihisa P. Miyake, and Mihoko Otake-Matsuura. "Voice over Body? Older Adults' Reactions to Robot and Voice Assistant Facilitators of Group Conversations." *International Journal of Social Robotics* 15 (2023): 143–63. https://doi.org/10.1007/s12369-022-00925-7.

Shelley, Mary. *Frankenstein, or, the Modern Prometheus.* London: Printed for Lackington, Hughes, Harding, Mavor, & Jones, 1818. Rev. ed. London: Henry Colburn and Richard Bentley, 1831.

Singer, Isaac Bashevis. *The Golem.* New York: Farrar, Straus, Giroux, 1982.

Smight, Jack, dir. *The Twilight Zone.* Season 1, episode 7, "The Lonely." 1959.

Smith, Adam. "AI Image App Lensa Helps Some Trans People to Embrace Themselves." Reuters, December 20, 2022. https://www.reuters.com/article/tech-socialmedia-lgbt/feature-ai-image-app-lensa-helps-some-trans-people-to-embrace-themselves-idINL8N33433Z.

Smith, Marquard. *The Erotic Doll: A Modern Fetish.* New Haven, CT: Yale University Press, 2013.

Sobchack, Vivian. "Postfuturism." In *The Gendered Cyborg: A Reader,* edited by Gill Kirkup, et al., 136–47. London: Routledge, 2000. First published in Sobchack's *Screening Space: The American Science Fiction Film.* New York: Ungar, 1987.

Sputore, Grant, dir. *I Am Mother.* Netflix, 2019.

Strengers, Yolande, and Jenny Kennedy. *The Smart Wife: Why Siri, Alexa, and Other Smart Home Devices Need a Feminist Reboot.* Cambridge, MA: MIT Press, 2020.

"Timeline of Computer History: 1985." Computer History Museum. Accessed July 4, 2023. https://www.computerhistory.org/timeline/1985/.

Trout, Christopher. "There's a New Sex Robot in Town: Say Hello to Solana." *Engadget,* January 10, 2018. https://www.engadget.com/2018-01-10-there-s-a-new-sex-robot-in-town-say-hello-to-solana.html.

Turk, Victoria. "We're Sexist toward Robots." Vice, November 3, 2014. https://www.vice.com/en/article/539j5x/were-sexist-toward-robots.

Turkle, Sherry. *Alone Together: Why We Expect More from Technology and Less from Each Other.* New York: Basic Books, 2011.

———. "The Assault on Empathy." *Behavioral Scientist,* January 1, 2018. https//www.behavioralscientist.org/the-assault-on-empathy/.

———. *The Empathy Diaries: A Memoir.* New York: Penguin Press, 2021.

Villeneuve, Denis, dir. *Blade Runner 2049.* Warner Bros., 2017.

Villiers de l'Isle-Adam, Auguste, comte de. *L'Ève future* [Tomorrow's Eve]. Translated by Robert M. Adams. Champaign: University of Illinois Press, 1982, 2000.

Vint, Sherryl. *Bodies of Tomorrow: Technology, Subjectivity, Science Fiction.* Toronto: University of Toronto Press, 2007.

———. "Introduction." In *Technologies of Feminist Speculative Fiction: Gender, Artificial Life, and the Politics of Reproduction,* edited by Sherryl Vint and Sümeyra Buran, 21–43. New York: Springer International Publishing, 2022.

Vlahos, James. "Barbie Wants to Get to Know Your Child." *New York Times,* September 16, 2015. https://www.nytimes.com/2015/09/20/magazine/barbie-wants-to-get-to-know-your-child.html.

Weitz, Julie, creator, video series installation, writing. *GOLEM: A Call to Action.* Contemporary Jewish Museum, San Francisco. June 21, 2021–June 19, 2022. https://www.thecjm.org/exhibitions/151.

West, Mark, Rebecca Kraut, and Chew Han Ei. *I'd Blush If I Could: Closing Gender Divides in Digital Skills through Education.* Paris: UNESCO (United Nations Educational, Scientific, and Cultural Organization) and the EQUALS Global Partnership, 2019. https://doi.org/10.54675/RAPC9356.

Westworld. Created by Lisa Joy and Jonathan Nolan. Multiple directors. American television series HBO, 2016–2022.

Whale, James, dir. *Bride of Frankenstein.* Universal Pictures, 1935.

Whang, Oliver. "'Consciousness' in Robots Was Once Taboo. Now It's the Last Word." *New York Times,* January 6, 2023. Updated June 20, 2023. https://www.nytimes.com/2023/01/06/science/robots-artificial-intelligence-consciousness.html.

Wosk, Julie. *Alluring Androids, Robot Women, and Electronic Eves.* New York: Fort Schuyler Press, 2008.

———. *Breaking Frame: Technology and the Visual Arts in the Nineteenth Century.* New Brunswick, NJ: Rutgers University Press, 1992. Reprinted with new introduction as *Breaking Frame: Technology, Art, and Design in the Nineteenth Century.* New York: Authors Guild, 2013.

———. "Metropolis." *Technology and Culture* 51, no. 2 (April 2010): 403–408. https://www.jstor.org/stable/40647105.

———. *My Fair Ladies: Female Robots, Androids, and Other Artificial Eves.* New Brunswick, NJ: Rutgers University Press, 2015.

———. "The New Curvy Barbie Dolls: What They Tell Us about Being Overweight." *HuffPost,* February 11, 2017. https://www.huffpost.com/entry/the -new-curvy-barbie-dolls-what-they-tell-us-about-being-overweight_b_9193136.

———. "The New Diversity in Barbie Dolls: Radical Change or More of the Same?" *HuffPost,* February 7, 2017. https://www.huffpost.com/entry/the-new -diversity-in-barb_b_9181740.

———. *Playboy, Mad Men, and Me—And Other Stories.* KDP, 2020.

———. "Update on the Film *Metropolis.*" *Technology and Culture* 51, no. 4 (2010): 1061–62. https://doi.org/10.1353/tech.2010.0069.

———. *Women and the Machine: Representations from the Spinning Wheel to the Electronic Age.* Baltimore: Johns Hopkins University Press, 2001.

Wulfeck, Sarah. Interview with Julie Wosk. 2017.

INDEX

JULIE WOSK is Professor Emerita of English, Art History, and Studio Art at the State University of New York Maritime College. She is author of *Breaking Frame: Technology and the Visual Arts in the Nineteenth Century*; *Women and the Machine: Representations from the Spinning Wheel to the Electronic Age*; *Alluring Androids, Robot Women, and Electronic Eves*; and *My Fair Ladies: Female Robots, Androids, and Other Artificial Eves*. She is also an artist curator, and photographer.